Join the Dream Team of Modern Organic Gardening

"We have visited all of the master gardeners profiled in this book, walked their gardens and farms, and seen for ourselves how and why their systems work. Our book offers a synthesis of the philosophies and practices of this 'Dream Team.' "

BILL MOLLISON on how to "read" your landscape and design a bountiful garden that virtually sustains itself—even in areas with low rainfall

JOHN JEAVONS on growing your most important crop—your garden soil!—and how you can raise more vegetables in less space than you ever thought possible

ALAN YORK on pruning and other biodynamic techniques to promote maximum yield of beautiful fruits

CAROL DEPPE on seed saving and do-it-yourself plant breeding—including easy instructions for creating unique flowers and vegetables in your own garden

ALAN KAPULER on planning a garden of diversity with families of your favorite plants—that actually helps preserve endangered species

WES JACKSON & MASANOBU FUKUOKA
on the principles of "polyculture" that can help us grow abundant food without chemical pesticides or fertilizers

All of these pioneers believe that we can create our own versions of paradise in our backyard gardens and neighborhoods—and that together we can preserve the bounty of our planet. This book shows you how.

Gardening for the Future of the Earth

Howard-Yana Shapiro, Ph.D.
and John Harrisson

Bantam Books

New York ~ Toronto ~ London

Sydney ~ Auckland

GARDENING FOR THE FUTURE OF THE EARTH
A Bantam Book/January 2000

Library of Congress Cataloging-in-Publication Data

Shapiro, Howard-Yana.
Gardening for the future of the earth/Howard-Yana Shapiro and John Harrisson
p. cm.
Includes bibliographical references (p.).
ISBN 0-553-37533-4
1. Organic gardening. I. Title. II. Harrisson, John 1952-
SB453.5 .S558 2000   99-41605
635'.0484 21--dc21
Published simultaneously in the United States and Canada

Bantam Books are published by Bantam Books, a division of Random
House, Inc. Its trademark, consisting of the works "Bantam Books"
and the portrayal of a rooster, is Registered in U.S. Patent and
Trademark Office and in other countries. Marca Registrada. Bantam
Books, 1540 Broadway, New York, New York 10036

PRINTED IN THE UNITED STATES OF AMERICA ON ACID-FREE PAPER
FFG/ 10 9 8 7 6 5 4 3 2 1

contents

Gardening for the Future of the Earth

introduction:

A Call to Action

The key to the future of the world lies in gardening. In countries such as the United States and Britain, among many others, gardening is the leading leisure-time activity. There are few, if any, other pursuits in which you can say that you learn something new every day. To witness change and growth and evolution and the cycle of nature in our gardens or even on our windowsills is truly miraculous, and one of the greatest joys in life. Gardening is a primary activity that connects us to the earth, upon which we depend for our survival. It is incumbent upon us to garden, and to do it to the best of our ability. To that end, this book presents a synthesis of the methods and systems of the worldwide leaders in sustainable gardening and growing practices. We invite you to take away those ideas, concepts, and techniques that appeal to you and apply to your garden, and to hold other parts in your personal bank of useful information.

In the pages that follow, we touch on the critical environmental and spiritual problems facing us and describe how individual actions rooted in the garden and around the home can make a positive difference. We show how easily change can be achieved with plants, soil, and water— whether you are a skilled gardener or not—by adopting sustainable gardening solutions.

Each of us can make a positive difference by doing something as easy as composting to build soil, or as challenging as changing the way we view our relationship with the world. Gardening is both a means and an end. Sustainability is about producing the food and resources we need without depleting the environment qualitatively or quantitatively. Our true wealth lies in the source of what we consume— especially the quality of our soil and water —and not in the product itself. Sustainable systems are those that provide through the generations. If we want to bequeath a viable and healthy planet to our children and grandchildren, then we must all adopt a mind-set of sustainability.

In this book, you will learn from master gardeners who are pioneering sustainable techniques that you can employ to create a garden of change and take a step forward toward reclaiming paradise on earth. From its considerable experience as a certified organic seed and food company, Seeds of Change, a leader in the field of ecosane gardening, constructs and presents a coherent gardening system based on the strengths of the foremost schools of sustainable practices. Never before has the best of permaculture, biointensive, biodynamic, and kinship systems, among others, been synthesized into a program that can be easily replicated by gardeners and that empowers them to work in harmony with nature.

Gardening for the Future of the Earth integrates techniques for creating gardens of the future based on the preservation of biodiversity, establishing perennial sources of food, and strengthening the healing bond between humans and the earth. This information, drawing on the depth and breadth of the pioneering systems and techniques of cultivation presented here, will enable you to apply this knowledge toward understanding how to practice sustainable gardening at home, and how that act can have measurable impact beyond your own front door.

In order to fully appreciate how the individual and cumulative actions of millions of gardeners can transform backyards, neighborhoods, watersheds, ecosystems, regions, and nations, it is important to understand the destructive influence that traditional agriculture has had upon the earth for thirty thousand years. Historically, agriculture has been a process of consuming the earth and moving on without replenishing it. As this process speeds up mind-numbingly in the modern age of mechanized, chemical agriculture, pollution and loss of habitat are resulting in the eradication of large populations of small mammals, reptiles, birds, insects, and plants upon which our own survival as a species depends.

Sanity and survival demand that we change the way in which we interact with our environment. Each year two million

It's More Than Just Vegetables

Paul Mueller, an organic grower from Guinda, California, points out that gardening is not just about having tomatoes and peppers and flowers. "Growing a garden is so empowering, just through the process of planting a seed and watching it grow and seeing the fruits of that process," he says. "No matter who you are, it makes you richer and deeper and more understanding of all the cycles of the universe, and of your relationship to them. We need to grow gardens, and each of us needs to help others to grow them."

What Can One Individual Do?

I have gardened and farmed sustainably for nearly thirty years, ending up in the arid high transition zone of northern New Mexico, where the land has been farmed continuously for thousands of years. I live in an amazingly diverse ecosystem that extends to the Rio Grande. When I first moved to El Guique over eight years ago, I counted only 28 species of birds. Since then, I have made a conscious effort to preserve and create biodiversity and to use sustainable practices to maintain and improve the health of the soil and the purity of our water. It is no coincidence that today I can count 140 different bird species, and as the great migration occurs every year from the northern Rockies and the Great Plains, I am amazed at what a simple act of habitat preservation and construction has accomplished.

In other ways, too, planting a garden of diversity, protecting natural resources, and understanding the local ecosystem has been revelatory. The conservation of life and diversity is one of the greatest joys I can share. Each one of us has the ability to spread sustainable gardening practices throughout our neighborhoods, communities, states, and ultimately whole regions. If each of us, in permitting destructive agriculture to run roughshod, has been part of the problem up to now, henceforth each one of us is part of the solution.

I have observed with great pride and satisfaction the spread of organic gardening and farming in my region—northern New Mexico—in the last decade, and all it took were some committed individuals and growers who began on their own, in isolation, but who educated their peers and found a willing audience and market for their produce because their methods made sense and the food they produced tasted good and was nutritious. —*H.S.*

Although I grew up on the outskirts of London, some of my earliest memories from almost forty years ago are of golden wheat fields growing just a block away. These, of course, have long since been built on and paved over. The local farm to which the whole family would bicycle every Saturday afternoon for fresh free-range eggs is now a housing development.

My father made the most of his suburban

garden, which occupied about a quarter of an acre, and he grew much of the vegetables and fruit that we ate—from carrots, cabbages, spinach, beans, and peas to berries, apples, pears, and plums. He also took great pride in his flower beds, and especially his extensive collection of climbing, rambling, and bush roses. My older brother and I, as well as my mother, were pressed into regular weekend gardening service, and little did I know then that my father was an enthusiastic practitioner of sustainable gardening techniques. I doubt he even looked at it that way, but he did have a strong belief that the way he gardened was efficient and cost-effective, and resulted in prodigious and never-failing yields; most of all, it *felt right*. He composted everything he could, he saved rainwater in big wooden barrels to use on the garden, and he used organic fertilizer and soil amendments.

My father told me that he had learned most of his gardening techniques from Lady Astor's head gardener, Mr. Glasheen. The Astors were an aristocratic English family who owned a large estate—Cliveden—about ten miles farther out from London, as well as a home in London's famous Eaton Square (Lady Nancy Astor was American by birth and became the first woman member of the British Parliament). Mr. Glasheen, who lived nearby, oversaw the Astors' large traditional English garden and the kitchen garden that fed the entire household, and that also supplied the London house when they were in residence there. It was Mr. Glasheen who advocated the method of double digging and persuaded my father to prepare the soil this way for his vegetables. I never heard my father refer to this as the French intensive method of soil preparation, but as John Jeavons explains in Chapter 3, France is where this crucial sustainable technique originated.

My brother and I were actually the ones who double-dug the beds in the spring and mixed the compost into the soil (this was just one of our innumerable gardening responsibilities). We enjoyed the physical exertion and we appreciated the results come harvest time; of course, the extra allowance my father dispensed as incentive didn't hurt! My father would cover the seedlings when they poked through the ground with glass cloches to protect them from a late frost or hungry birds, and then we enjoyed watching the cycle of nature unfold, helping it along its way with our family weekend gardening schedule. These are among my happiest memories, and my gardening "apprenticeship" and early experiences taught me many invaluable lessons about nature and the value of life.

—J.H.

acres of arable land in the United States are lost to soil erosion, most of it entirely preventable. Worldwide, about 30 percent of cropland has been lost to soil erosion in the last forty years of the twentieth century. Collectively, the human race lives on one-twelfth of the planet's area, but we have already discarded three-quarters of all productive soil. The restoration of lost soil is not nearly as easy as its loss has been: The replacement of just 1 inch of topsoil takes five hundred years by natural processes. Millions of acres of arable land are rendered unusable because of urbanization and road building.

Wide use of insecticides, herbicides, and inorganic fertilizer has polluted our soil and water and stripped the soil of nutrients, compromising our health and the nutritional value of the food that we eat. Despite a tenfold increase in insecticide use in the United States since 1945, crop loss due to insects has doubled. Further, it is estimated that less than 0.1 percent of insecticides applied actually reaches the target pests. Meanwhile, they indiscriminately wipe out beneficial insects that are essential for pollination and pest control.

Crop loss due to pests, diseases, and weeds in the modern system of mecha-nized, commercial, chemical agriculture is hardly any less than in organic agriculture. And yet billions of pounds of chemicals are dumped on the land every year in the name of agricultural productivity. It is no wonder that the incidence of cancer, immune disorders, and many types of syndromes and illness is on the rise; modern agriculture, ironically, is killing us. In addition to twenty thousand human deaths worldwide every year due to pesticide poisonings, it is estimated that as many as thirty million domesticated animals are lost. Clearly, most meat, eggs, milk, and other animal products—let alone food plants that are sprayed—are seriously affected to some degree by these man-made agents.

With the world's population rising, the pollution problem growing ever more acute, and the planet's nonrenewable natural resources progressively being depleted, something has to give. Many experts, in fact, believe we are on the cusp of a shake-down in the current scheme of things. A general consensus places the time scale at fifteen to twenty-five years, at most, before the fragile house of cards that is the modern commercial agricultural system comes crashing down. The world could then face

When I Rule the World...

Bill Mollison, the originator of the permaculture system, once asked me what I would do if I was appointed emperor of the United States for one day. My answer was simple: I would issue a decree stating that if you don't garden, you pay a huge tax. ✒️ **I find it socially and historically interesting that in times of grave crisis, such as wartime or during the Depression, we turn to gardening.**

Socioeconomic commentators have even noted that during the optimistic days of bull markets, home gardening goes way down, but during bear markets, when the economy is in a downturn, people rush out, buy seeds, and get down to work in the garden. It is when we feel threatened or vulnerable that we turn to our gardens to guarantee our food supply, with good reason. What we need to do is to act on this mentality all the time, and we each need to adopt some of the techniques described in this book so that we can garden sustainably and organically for all our futures.

When I read of yet another case of golf courses closed or gardeners unable to venture out on their lawns because of the risk of toxic shock, I can only think: "Have we lost our minds?" —*H.S.*

an unimaginable crisis in food supply, which is why the message of this book is so timely: We can change the way we garden and make our preferences known *now*, while there is time to make a difference. If enough of us plow a sustainable furrow and create change, the course of the agricultural juggernaut can be changed to avert disaster.

We do not believe that gardeners or farmers are consciously making destructive choices. However, we also strongly believe that it is wrong and foolhardy for people to do harm to others, to themselves, or to the earth, individually or collectively. It is clear that modern gardening and agriculture cannot be "business as usual," and the systems that we examine and draw upon in this book—permaculture, biointensive and biodynamic gardening, kinship gardening, and perennial polycultures, to name some of them—offer a wealth of potential for providing positive and constructive models for the future.

Gardening for the Future of the Earth describes a wide range of actions you can choose to take in your garden, or even on your windowsill, to effect positive change. These actions are not a pipe dream—at Seeds of Change, we practice aspects of all these

systems and methods at our research sites, and we have a network of like-minded gardeners and farmers worldwide who do the same. We have visited all of the master gardeners profiled in this book, walked their gardens and farms, and seen for ourselves how and why their systems work. Theirs are not academic theories—they are practical, working systems that can be applied universally. This book offers a synthesis of the philosophies and practices of this "Dream Team" of sustainable agriculture.

In this book, we begin by taking a virtual-reality tour of what the garden of change looks like, sounds like, and smells like, and in so doing, we lay the foundation for sustainability. First, we examine what can be learned through simple observation and the interpretation of natural patterns that occur on every scale. Familiarity with your environment and an accurate reading of natural events and cycles is the foundation for turning your ecosystem into a positive resource, and for working advantageously with nature to garden more efficiently and sustainably. Based on this information, we proceed to review how sustainable systems such as permaculture, biointensive gardening, and minifarming can turn observation and natural patterns to best advantage while preserving and creating beneficial diversity. Garden design—the appropriate placement of component elements of a garden—is the key to efficiency and sustainability, especially when you can make small changes that have a large impact. Ultimately, garden design is ecology in action.

Next, we examine how we can each take action to reverse the damage that has been (and is continuing to be) done to our most important gardening resources: our soil and water. Soil is the medium in which our food plants grow, and by understanding how it is depleted, we can take the positive and all-important step of building soil and restoring its health. This is the prerequisite for growing healthy, nutritious crops in a sustainable manner. Likewise, the demand on the supply of water worldwide is at critical levels, imperiling our health, our well-being, and ultimately our survival. There are strategies, however, that each of us can employ in our homes and gardens to protect and conserve our supply of water. We can maximize "harvesting" and retention of the water that falls on our houses and gardens, we can recycle it as many times as possible, and we can clean it by means of biological meth-

ods. There are many simple ways of conserving water around the house and in the garden, and in addition, we need to effect change on a macro level by educating our families, friends, and neighbors about the issues and by demanding honest and open public debate. As communities and as a society as a whole, we need to demand of our elected representatives and government that we be provided with clean water as a basic right.

In the second half of the book, we examine practical steps that the individual can take and concrete methods of gardening for the future that both are sustainable and support biodiversity. The first model we describe—kinship gardening—is a system that encourages gardeners to leave the realm of the familiar and explore evolution-based planting arrangements that support the conservation of plant diversity. Species worldwide are disappearing at an alarming rate. In the United States alone, between 10 and 20 percent of the twenty-five thousand plants native to this country are endangered, and we are confronting an unprecedented ecocrisis. Each of us can take steps to counter this loss of biodiversity. If you are passionate about gladioli, for example, you can choose to grow other relatives from the same family, such as wild iris and saffron crocus. From there, you can add kin from related families, such as sego lily and Indian cucumber root. Soon an interest in one species can result in a garden of coevolved species and a gardener who has become a guardian of diversity.

Next, we discuss the importance of seed saving and plant breeding, which allow all gardeners true independence. By describing these practices, and especially the work of Carol Deppe, a Harvard-trained geneticist and science writer, we encourage you to grow what you like to eat and what pleases your eye, to follow your passions, and to go beyond what the major seed companies offer. Seed saving and plant breeding lead to increased biodiversity, lessened reliance on monocultures, and greater resistance to blight and disease. We describe the importance of conducting garden and variety trials, and how to go about them.

Finally, we conclude our virtual-reality tour by way of describing Wes Jackson's model of perennial polycultures. There are numerous advantages to such a system: food crops can be grown more productively compared to monoculture while at the same time protecting the soil, promoting biodiversity, improving soil quality, and greatly reducing the amount of water needed and the use of chemical fertilizers, herbicides, and insecticides.

In addition to the actions described in this book that the individual can take in the immediate context of the home and garden, there are external actions that you can pursue, many of which are touched upon in the chapters that follow. You can use your wallet to influence the way food is produced, and you can ask your supermarket to carry organic produce and environmentally friendly products. As the civil rights and gender equality movements have proved over the last generation, demands for change become particularly effective and forceful when individuals band together to form groups whose voices cannot be ignored.

One individual with a digging fork and a small garden *can* make a difference. Currently, two-thirds of all home gardeners consider themselves already practicing, or open to, organic techniques. Gardening is one of the few places in our culture where we are all on the same footing, from rich to poor and everyone in between. This book is a blueprint for action. We hope to inspire you by showing that sustainable techniques are all around you and being practiced more than you might imagine.

Most of us can recall how our lives changed for the better forever the first time we tasted food or cut a flower that we had grown. If you have never enjoyed a similar experience, it is well worth remedying the situation! Likewise, this book will provide information and, we hope, the inspiration to plant medicinal herbs, a kinship garden, or site-appropriate plants based on observation and conscious garden design, for example. Most important of all, to effect the garden of change, we need to *act*. Each of us needs to select from the valuable information gathered in this book those elements that make the most sense or seem the most appropriate to our garden or backyard, and just go out and act on them. Do it now, for the future of all of us.

voices of hope and change

> Our ideas are only intellectual instruments which we use to break into phenomena;
> we must change them when they have served their purpose,
> as we change a blunt lancet that we have used long enough.
> —Claude Bernard

All of the visionaries whose work is profiled in this book are motivated by their personal observations that the problems caused by unsustainable farming and gardening practices are getting worse with every passing year. In response to this situation, each of these individuals has devised a solution that has worldwide application for gardening in every ecozone.

The members of this eminent group of sustainable-system advocates have practiced their theories all over the world, and they average over twenty-five years each of hands-on experience. The ideas presented here have all been rigorously proven. While the particular system each works within may not in itself be totally sustainable, it is how we interpret these systems and how careful we are in gardening and growing our food that lead to sustainability on a broad scale.

All of these pioneers also believe that application of aspects of their practices can make it possible for us all to enjoy our own version of paradise (interestingly, the word is derived from the Persian *pairi daeza*, the name given to the lush, cultivated orchards and walled gardens where everything needed for sustenance could be grown). Miniature versions of paradise exist, after all, in places as diverse as the Brooklyn Botanic Garden, Kew Gardens, and innumerable other botanical gardens around the globe, as well as desert oases, Andean mountainsides, and tropical jungles. Paradise can be created in our own backyard gardens and in urban settings. That we all have the ability to construct practical, site-appropriate, efficient ecosystems—both small and large—based on paying attention to our landscape is a

common theme sounded by these pioneers. It is also the message of this book.

BILL MOLLISON is a remarkable Australian who was born and raised in Tasmania. A self-described biogeographer, he began developing the permaculture system during the *1970*s after realizing that key elements of the ecosystem in which he grew up were disappearing. Permaculture (the name is derived from "*perma*nent agri*culture*") is about working with, rather than counter to, nature. Mollison defines permaculture as "the conscious design and maintenance of agriculturally productive ecosystems that have the diversity, stability, and resilience of natural ecosystems. It is the harmonious integration of landscape and people providing their food, energy, shelter, and other material and nonmaterial needs in a sustainable way." At the center of Mollison's system is the strategic placement of plants, trees, crops, and livestock in conjunction with carefully designed water catchment and irrigation techniques to produce a permanent and sustainable system of gardening or farming. There are currently over seven hundred teachers and centers of permaculture in *180* countries worldwide.

JOHN JEAVONS is the master practitioner of "growing" soil. Described by former Congresswoman Claudine Schneider as "our hope for the future," Jeavons has dedicated his life to researching the smallest practical area for growing enough food for one person, or, as he puts it, "the smallest area in which I could grow all of my food, clothing, income, building materials, so that, if everyone were growing their food in a similar way, there would be enough resources for everyone to have plenty." Jeavons' work began in the early 1970s, and his search for the answer to the question he set himself led him to study many diverse systems, including the miniaturization of agriculture that the Chinese developed thousands of years ago and the French intensive technique popular in the last century and promoted in the United States by Alan Chadwick. While U.S. commercial agriculture and chemical, nonorganic gardening are *depleting* the soil eighteen to eighty times faster than it builds in nature, Jeavons' "Grow Biointensive" system of gardening and minifarming, if used properly, has the capacity to *build* the soil up sixty times faster than occurs naturally. Using raised beds of approximately 100 square feet each that take just eight hours to prepare initially and then ten to fifteen minutes per day to maintain, Jeavons has found that his methods can yield from two to six times (and as high as thirty times) the U.S. agricultural average while using 67 percent to 88 percent less water, more than 50 percent less purchased organic fertilizer (if any), and 99 percent less energy per pound of food produced. Jeavons' philosophy of getting more from less can ultimately turn scarcity into abundance.

MASANOBU FUKUOKA, a plant pathologist, developed the system that he calls "natural farming" in the south of Japan following his realization that the chemical agricultural methods introduced in his country by Americans after World War II were rapidly weakening and depleting the soil, making crops progressively more dependent on synthetic fertilizers and pesticides. Fukuoka realized that it was only a matter of time until the land would become unproductive. He saw that sustainability and diversity were the keys to our own health and ability to feed ourselves in the future.

Fukuoka develops the soil by growing

leguminous crops that enrich it and keep it permanently mulched. The roots aerate the soil and obviate the need to cultivate it. Natural farming involves not following certain traditional agricultural practices such as plowing, fertilizing, and composting, thereby reversing the land's dependence on man's intervention. Fukuoka believes that this intervention has badly upset the natural balance; by cooperating with nature rather than trying to improve on it, we all benefit. Gardening becomes considerably easier, and yields markedly improve. Fukuoka was long thought of as an eccentric, but no longer. His impressive results speak for themselves, as does his profound understanding of the ecosystem. In addition, the studies he has completed on annuals, biennials, and perennials have wide application in many different regions of the world.

ALAN YORK, a viniculturist, orchard farmer, and former president of the Biodynamic Farming and Gardening Association, is a leading practitioner of biodynamic techniques. These are based on the work of Rudolf Steiner, the Austrian educator and philosopher, who observed during the 1920s that declining crop yields and a drop in their nutritional values were due to the growth of modern chemical agriculture and the disruption of natural forces and processes. The biodynamic system Steiner developed is based on a holistic approach, involving the conservation of all resources and especially the recycling of all organic matter to improve soil fertility, and the use of balanced organic fertilizers and soil amendments. These biodynamic preparations, in conjunction with composting and the interaction of cosmic influences, are the main regenerating forces of any garden or farm, replenishing the minerals and nutrients in the soil.

Biointensive gardening methods were introduced to the United States by Alan Chadwick, who developed a legendary student garden at the University of California campus at Santa Cruz. Chadwick used biointensive organic techniques to convert four acres of poor clay soil into a miniature paradise that achieved four times the yield of commercial agriculture. York was a student of Chadwick's and became his garden supervisor, and his extraordinary fruit orchard and vineyard work in northern California bears witness to the efficacy of biodynamic methods. As York says, "Building soil is the foundation to sustainable gardening, as opposed to gardening nutrients from the soil that are never replaced. Building soil also means developing sustainable nutrition in terms of our own life forces, and imbuing us with a sense of personal responsibility in all of our actions so that we don't look to the government or the next person to do things." Sustainable gardening must regenerate and nurture the soil, and healthy bodies, minds, and spirits depend on healthy soils for sustenance and well-being. York's view is that we as individuals must take it upon ourselves to achieve this balance.

ALAN KAPULER, biologist, botanist, and research director for Seeds of Change, has used the work of Danish botanist Rolf Dahlgren to develop a kinship gardening system, which illustrates and conserves diversity while simultaneously educating practitioners about the interrelationships of plant species and their family groupings. Based on a working model of the world's plant gene pool, Kapuler has effectively created a mapping system and a strategic plan for preserving plant diversity that also provides a guide for choosing plants for our gardens. Kapuler urges us to grasp the reality that sustainable cultivation involves more than improving soil fertility or macro garden design, and kinship gardening is an exciting example of how our homes and gardens can and must play a crucial role in preserving plant diversity for future generations.

Biological Literacy

"We need to learn everything we can about gardening—we need to become biologically literate. We can all do it, and it doesn't take much time. It's more relevant even than computer literacy."

—JOHN JEAVONS

Kapuler, whose seed collection was the foundation for Seeds of Change, provides a broader perspective for his methods: "Diversity is unknown to almost all of us because the creation is so profoundly immense. How do we empower ourselves to become more involved in the actual conservation, preservation, continuity, and understanding of our relationship to living organisms? One of the best ways is to grow a kinship garden and to collect the seeds." Kapuler is an avid seed collector, and he views this process as vital in completing the cycle of creation, growth, and fruition; best of all, it requires no money. Instead, says Kapuler, "it requires intelligence, which allows us to build true wealth, which is a devotion to learning and caring about our planet."

WES JACKSON, president of the Land Institute in Salina, Kansas, is a native Kansan whose grandparents and parents were farmers. He grew up on a diversified farm and trained in biology, botany, and genetics before establishing a career in academic teaching. However, he could not ignore the threat posed by population growth, nor the destructive effect of agriculture on the land he loved so much. Possessing what Wendell Berry has described as an extraordinary quality of insight,

Jackson was able to make the connections between worrisome agricultural issues (soil loss, pollution, and resource depletion) and contemporary social problems that include a decline in spiritual values. Jackson realized that technological solutions alone were not the answer, and that radical problems require radical solutions.

As a result, Jackson established the Land Institute as a nonprofit educational research organization dedicated to the study of sustainable agricultural alternatives and sustainable systems of energy, waste management, and shelter. From here, Jackson has developed a radical solution to the destructive and depleting forces of modern commercial agriculture: perennial polycultures. In this innovative system, a diversity of herbaceous perennial seed-producing plants—grain crops—provides permanent ground cover while producing food.

1
pattern and observation:
The Web of Connections

> True wealth is a deep understanding of the world you live in.
> —Bill Mollison

Universal patterns occur in nature that can be observed on every scale. Step outside your door and employ the fundamental tool of gardening—observation. Notice where the prevailing winds come from. How does rainfall run off your farmland, your city rooftop, or your suburban lot? Where is there shelter and shade, how much sunlight do you receive, and how do these climatic and environmental factors affect what you can grow? When you become familiar with the natural patterns that affect your location, you can begin to work with them to your advantage and turn them into resources.

Australian Bill Mollison, who coined the term *permaculture* and pioneered this innovative system of sustainable agriculture in the late 1970s, has based his theories and their practical application on observation and pattern. Permaculture is predicated on working with nature rather than trying to subjugate it, and the key to achieving this is to observe the way in which nature works. Mollison emphasizes that protracted and thoughtful observation is the essence of permaculture, as opposed to protracted and thoughtless action. The overall integrated functions and evolutions of ecosystems must be taken into account, not just specific, limited results or yields. As Goethe said, "Nothing happens in living nature that is not in relation to the whole."

Mollison began developing the permaculture system as a direct result of personal observation: "As a child, growing up in Tasmania, I lived in a sort of dream, and I didn't really awaken until I was twenty-eight. I spent most of my early working life in the bush or on the sea. I fished and hunted for my living. It wasn't until the 1950s that I noticed large parts of the system in

which I lived were disappearing. First, fish stocks became depleted, and some types disappeared. Then I noticed the seaweed around the shorelines had gone. Large patches of forest began to die. I hadn't realized until those things were gone that I'd become very fond of them, that I was in love with my country."

An early influence on the development of Mollison's theories was P. A. Yeomans' book *Water for Every Farm*, which discussed the pattern of landscape and its influence on the collection of water. Mollison was farming at the time, and Yeomans' theories on pattern struck him as blindingly innovative and totally different from the way farmers are traditionally taught to think. Instead of seeing land in terms of fields, paddocks, and fenced areas, Yeomans viewed the land in terms of topographical contours and the consequent flow of water, putting it in a completely new and productive perspective. In his book, Yeomans also pointed out that streams and rivers follow consistent, universal patterns. Their characteristics are such that they can be classified in "orders," or progressions of magnitude, from rivulets to creeks and up to the largest type, estuarine rivers. The fauna and flora associated with each order are predictable wherever in the world they are located.

Mollison tested these theories for himself and concluded that they worked: "I found I could predict by sampling one stream, wherever it was, that there would be certain fish that belonged to that particular 'order,' which was typical of streams everywhere. The same would hold true for rivers or river estuaries. Everything started to make a lot of sense, as order—recognition of patterns—came out of jumbles, and I began to understand how things organize themselves. Later on, I applied these principles of observation to patterns of tree formation, erosion, and even to human settlements, from villages to towns to cities." Before long, Mollison came to recognize a universal principle: "What it comes down to is that it's all the same, whether it's water flow, human particles, or molecules that build a tree: The constituent parts are flowing to create a form, and the form always remains essentially the same in each case. If you understand this, you understand everything."

Mollison realized that despite the plethora of books on gardening, none dealt with the issue of energy flow through the garden as a whole. The effects and potential of such energy flows as solar gain, shade, natural water flow, and wind had not previously been thought of in terms of the whole system, but Mollison recognized that these were pivotal planning issues for gardening, and incorporated them into his theory of permaculture. Mollison emphasizes that garden design must be based on observation and an understanding of pattern, and for this reason, design cannot be done solely off-site. In Bill Mollison's permaculture system, garden design is based on pattern; observing pattern and using it in garden design creates productive interrelationships between the constituent elements—the plants, landscape, and external forces of nature.

Mollison has trodden every square inch of his land, and if he is planning to change or add a feature to the landscape, he walks and observes the site. He says: "I don't understand the need to detach from the site, whether it's a backyard, garden, or larger piece of land. Theorizing or thinking things out in your head is not the way to go. It's always the site that's telling you what to do. That's where the inevitability comes from, the site." While a good map and other secondary data can provide plenty of useful topographical or geological information about an area, they should be used in conjunction with firsthand observation and should never be a substitute for it.

Observation in the Permaculture Model

Observation is not a skill that is easily taught, and in that sense, it may appear subjective and unscientific. However, it is the only reliable method of revealing processes and dynamic interactions so that the gardener can devise a design that works with nature and saves time and energy by implementing the smallest change that will have the desired effect—another important tenet of permaculture. Establish your site in a way that helps eliminate redundant and unnecessary work.

Mollison describes a number of attitudes that facilitate accurate "reading" of a landscape or garden. First, he recommends adopting a childlike, nonselective, and nonjudgmental approach. As adults, we tend to block out simplicity; it is important to review the garden or site with fresh eyes. Scott Pittman, a practicing permaculturist and associate of Bill Mollison who lives in New Mexico, describes this process as a type of meditative state; he himself relaxes and "gets quiet," unfocusing his vision so that only peripheral images affect him.

Second, take a thematic or step-by-step approach, focusing on one aspect at a time, such as water flow, potential energy sources, soil or vegetative color, or the appropriate placement of crops and flowers. Use this basic system of analysis, and after a while, patterns of tree location, prevailing winds, or animal life should become apparent. Another tack is to take an empirical approach, where observations of wind, temperature, sunlight, and rainfall are recorded, if necessary by equipment. Using a notebook, sketchbook, camera, video recorder, or tape recorder can help document these events. Finally, you can take an experiential approach, which involves using your senses to measure the ambience and pattern of a site. Scott Pittman focuses on the information that all his senses, not just sight, relay. For example, sensing heat and cold or feeling stress from the effort of walking over steep terrain can be valuable indicators of favorable or unfavorable landscape features. Bear in mind that a one-time observation is insufficient; each of the seasons has its own characteristics and provides its own clues.

Following these methods of observation singularly or in tandem, it is always important to record what Mollison describes as "value-free and noninterpretive" notes about what you have seen or experienced, which means not making judgments or guesses too soon and thereby incorrectly interpreting observations. After collecting on-site information and analyzing your experiences, the accumulation of off-site data is equally important to building an accurate analysis of your garden or property. Off-site data include contour, land use, and soil maps; field guides and other sources of information that can help you identify trees, plants, weeds, insects, and wildlife; and the results of formal analytical tests of your soil and water.

Examples of Applying Observation

Bill Mollison provides examples of how to interpret observations: "Reading the landscape is a matter of looking for *landscape indicators*. Vegetation in particular provides information about soil fertility, availability of moisture, and microclimate. Rushes, for example, indicate boggy soils or seepages; dandelions and blueberries indicate acid soils; and docks suggest compacted or clayey soils. Large trees growing in dry regions indicate a source of deep water. An abundance of thorny or unpalatable weed species (thistle, oxalis, sodom apple) indi-

cates overgrazing or land mismanagement, and erosion gullies and compacted pathways will give you confirmation of this. A plant flowering and fruiting earlier than others of the same species indicates an advantageous microclimatic condition, and

---

You observe a lot, watching.

—YOGI BERRA

....

trees growing with most of their branches on one side indicates the direction of strong prevailing winds."

As wind speed increases, the leaves and branches of trees change their form and the exposed leaf area is reduced. Each different type of tree sways and bends with different amplitude; the trees on the edge of a wood or forest tend to be sturdier than those occupying a more sheltered location. Trees deform or "flag" permanently in strong prevailing winds and are excellent indicators of the effects of these winds. In doing so, they provide what Mollison describes as an "on-site record of wind history." For example, where trees have a symmetrical shape and show no deformities, wind is not likely to be a factor on the site in question. In moderate to strong

East Meets West in the Ozarks

The experience of Lavinia (Vinnie) McKinney provides a perfect example of how the simplest of observations can transform an individual's life. Vinnie's farm, Elixir Farm Botanicals, is set in rolling Ozark country in southern Missouri. On three acres, Vinnie is cultivating over 150 species of indigenous (that is, native to the Ozarks or the Midwest) and introduced medicinal plants such as echinacea (native), ginseng (native), goldenseal (native), Oriental garlic (introduced), Korean mint (introduced), licorice (introduced), and burdock (introduced), for the purpose of harvesting their seeds. Vinnie's farm was the first in the country to specialize in Chinese and native medicinal plant seeds. Many of the plants that are grown at Elixir Farm are rare or threatened, and what makes this garden so special is that many of the native plants are analogs of medicinal plants that have been cultivated in China (a geographically quite separate botanical region) for thousands of years.

Since the 1700s plant collectors, botanists, and herbalists have documented the remarkable similarity between certain plant species in eastern Asia and the eastern United States. It is believed that during the Tertiary Period, about fifty million years ago, a relatively uniform forest covered the Northern Hemisphere but that geological and climatic changes resulted in the isolation of similar plants in these two very different locations. Another theory suggests that flora spread across a land bridge to North America from either the east or the west.

When Vinnie purchased her Ozark farm in 1973, she continued the cattle operation that came with it—though converting it to an organic farm—until 1984. Then, while considering alternative uses for the land, she and her good friend Steven Foster, a botanical researcher and author, came to the realization by means of simple observation that over a hundred of the indigenous plants that existed in the various microecosystems on the farm were similar to those used in Chinese medicine. Recognizing that in its most natural and productive form farming is site-specific, low-impact, and self-sustaining, Vinnie decided to organically cultivate the native medicinal plants that were already there.

Since Vinnie's commercial operation began in the late 1980s, a steady inflow of new seeds and plants from friends and private collectors has broadened the inventory. There are also several areas on the farm where there is "wild cultivation": areas that the plants have selected for themselves. Specimens of these particular plants have been brought into the cultivated garden, which is visited daily, as reminders of where the wild plants are in their cycle, thus providing a continuing tool for observation. The benefits of observation work for Vinnie in other ways, too. "One time, someone sent me two types of *Xanthium*, or burrweed, used in Chinese medicine. I grew it and thought it looked familiar. When I went down to the riverbank, there it was. In this country, it's called *Xanthium strumarium*, or cocklebur. It's exciting when something like that happens."

flagging, larger branches are permanently bent away from the direction of the wind, or all branches are swept to leeward. Severe flagging, where the tree trunk is bent over in addition to the branches, indicates strong and consistent prevailing winds. Such information can be used to place windbreaks in the appropriate place to deflect damaging winds, to protect fruit orchards, and to reduce heat loss in homes.

Among the landscape features that indicate actual or potential problems are pernicious weeds, marshy areas, soil erosion, rocky ground, or compacted, poor-looking soil. Some of these conditions can be turned to your advantage; for example, marshy areas can be developed into a wetland area or a pond, and certain trees such as olives will grow adequately in poor, dry soil.

Although we live in a society that emphasizes linear thinking, gardening does not require us to execute neatly linear or geometric designs. We are invariably better off when we avoid these patterns, as nature does; nature, after all, usually displays rounded contours. Mollison observes, "In designing with nature, rather than against it, we can create landscapes that operate like natural healthy systems, where energy is conserved, wastes are recycled, and re-

sources made abundant." Likewise, a simple comparison between wild and cultivated landscapes is likely to reveal ground cover of some kind in the former. This observation should suggest that we use mulch of some kind in our gardens to mimic a natural process. Mulch retains moisture, keeps the ground cool, encourages the activity of earthworms and micro-organisms, and increases fertility.

Climatic conditions are a primary determinant of gardening strategies. Observing how general weather trends progress through the seasons and affect your microclimate allows you to design your garden or site to buffer extremes of climate. Again, working with nature's design is crucial, and it can have tremendous benefit for your plantings.

The following climatic factors are among those that can be observed to your great potential benefit:

SUNLIGHT~
In triggering the chemical process of photosynthesis, sunlight provides the essential source of energy for plants. Sunlight is also absorbed by water and soil, as well as your house's roof, walls, and other manmade structures, and it is in turn radiated

as heat energy. Some parts of the garden will receive full (unobstructed) sunlight every day and some will be in full shade, while others will receive a mixture of sun and shade, depending on the time of day or year. Noting this information will affect which plants are located in which area of the garden, and in what relationship to the structures.

Dark objects (including man-made structures, vegetation, and mulch) tend to absorb light, while light-colored ones, including water, reflect it. Therefore, using a dark mulch in winter or spring can help warm and insulate the ground, for example. Conversely, plants with light-colored leaves or light-colored mulch (such as straw) can be used to reflect sunlight toward nearby plants located in darker places. Reflecting sunlight can also be beneficial in minimizing water evaporation.

Moreover, creating sun traps in the garden can help growth, while reflected sunlight can be used for heating and as a source of indirect light. Siting a greenhouse against the wall of a house is an obvious method of transforming sunlight into solar gain because the radiating heat from the house will warm the greenhouse. At the same time, heat loss from the house

will be minimized because the greenhouse acts as an insulator.

Creating shade with trees, plants, and structures can be an important aspect of garden design, as shade protects plants from the full intensity of sunlight. You can predict the shading effect of planting certain trees or plants by holding a pole or some object of similar size in the sunlight and observing how and where the shadow falls. Remember the time of year and observe the path of the sun, and take these factors into account.

RAINFALL AND WATER~

Observing trends in rainfall and the flow-through of water in your garden or on your site enables you to design a system to retain as much water as possible, whether in the soil, in vegetation, or in a storage system (see Chapter 4). The idea is to reuse water (including household "gray water") as advantageously and as many times as possible, particularly in drier climates. In doing so, you can create new and beneficial habitats that will also minimize soil erosion.

Knowledge of annual rainfall and seasonal rainfall trends can help you determine the sustainability of your gardening practices and the type of plants appropriate for your site. Although most gardeners rely mainly on public water supplies or their own well water, the more rainfall you are able to harvest, store, and use on your site, the more sustainable your garden. All gardeners everywhere should harvest water.

WIND~

Very strong winds can be quite destructive. Therefore, observing wind patterns will provide the information you need to design your garden, house, and other structures in such a way that the effect of the wind is minimized. Plant wind-tolerant trees such as poplar, beech, sycamore, and willows as windbreaks to protect your plants and property. Hedges, shrubs, and fences can also be used to protect gardens, while glass cloches can be used for small plants or seedlings. Windbreaks should be used, if necessary, not just to protect the garden against prevailing winds but also to protect it against winds that come from other directions and may bring cold weather and windchills that can be even more damaging to vegetation. Natural windbreaks are preferable to artificial ones because although they let some wind through, the wind is slowed down, whereas rigid, impermeable barriers create potentially destructive leeside turbulence.

Information on species of local trees suitable for use as windbreaks can usually be obtained from local forestry or agricultural offices, or from the local parks department. It is important to pick species that can be easily grown in your locale, since these require minimal care. Take steps to protect them initially with simple, locally available structures, and water them efficiently until they become established. Consider especially rare species that thrive in your local ecosystem but that are being eliminated elsewhere by habitat destruction.

Observing the prevailing winds is also important in assessing pollination patterns, so that your garden can be designed to take advantage of those winds, or, conversely, to avoid unwanted downwind cross-pollination.

Accurate off-site data on wind can be obtained from local weather stations and newspapers, and on-site information can be gained from your neighbors, especially if they happen to be the observant type. If you are new to the area, they can provide helpful information about wind patterns, and comparing notes after storms can also be of mutual benefit. However, existing trees provide the most reliable evidence of wind direction and strength. The shape of

"No New Thing Under the Sun": Some Historical Antecedents of Observation

John Jeavons, who practices "Grow Biointensive" minifarming in northern California, gives a historical example of how observation of nature independently led to biointensive techniques in ancient civilizations as diverse as those of the Mayans, Chinese, Greeks, and Bolivians. "These societies followed natural patterns and didn't plant their crops in rows; instead, they used raised-bed techniques—the precursors of the French intensive gardening technique and the biointensive system. The ancient Greeks observed that plant life thrives in landslide areas where the loose soil allows air, moisture, warmth, nutrients, and roots to properly penetrate. The naturally curved surface area between the two edges of the landslide bed provides more surface area for the penetration and interaction of the natural elements than a flat surface. The Mayans built raised beds on a foundation of stone, with channels of similar width in between the beds. In the rainy season, they grew corn on the raised beds, which were above the flood level in the channels below. In the dry season, they grew corn in the channels that were no longer flooded, thus doubling the yield of the land. In Bolivia, the beds were nine feet high, and the crops they grew were protected from frosts because cold air sinks and the raised beds were unaffected.

"These methods were replicated by the University of Pennsylvania in conjunction with the Bolivian government, and when a severe frost hit, only ten percent of the potato crop was lost, compared with close to one hundred percent on nearby farms not using the raised-bed technique. When the French developed the raised-bed technique in the nineteenth century, they discovered that a differential of just a few inches meant that their crops did not freeze. The organic matter they added to the soil, with all the microbes throwing off heat, helped too. But the raised-bed design, taken from observation of nature, is similar in principle to the placement of fruit orchards on valley hillsides. Both techniques minimize frosts, because warm air rises at night and cold air falls, in the case of the orchards, to the valley floor."

the trunk and form of the whole tree indicates whether it is growing in a sheltered environment or whether it has been stressed and blown by wind (see pages 25–28). Put up a colorful windsock, some flags, and some wind chimes so you can see the air currents and listen to the wind.

MICROCLIMATIC FACTORS~

Observing and interpreting climatic differences between your particular location and your area or region in general can be pivotal in garden design. Understanding your particular microclimate can help you to modify its negative aspects or enhance its positive aspects. For example, by creating sun traps and diverting cold air with natural vegetation, trellises, or walls, you can extend the growing season and minimize frosts. Observing the first and last frost dates and collecting information from past years will help you accurately define your particular growing season.

Observing the topography of your site is particularly important and will help make certain gardening decisions simple; for example, some plants prefer a sunny southern aspect, while others thrive in a northern or eastern exposure. Likewise, if your land slopes toward the sun, solar gain and heat radiation will raise its temperature, and shadows cast by vegetation or structures will be much shorter than if the land is flat. These areas will be best for those plants that thrive in direct sunlight, but may require well-planned irrigation. On the other hand, land sloping away from the sun (north-facing slopes in the Northern Hemisphere) will be prone to longer shadows and cooler temperatures. Slope also affects ground temperature; cold air falls from uphill, while warm air will rise uphill at the end of the day. Warm thermal zones and "sinks" of cold air are formed as the ground cools. However, warm air can be trapped as it rises on a slope by windbreaks, while sinking cold air should be allowed to escape or diverted to prevent forming a particularly cold microclimate that may induce frost, for example. The gradient of slope also affects wind as well as the flow of water; both travel faster over steeper terrain. Creating windbreaks and contouring the land to control water and prevent erosion are examples of applying such observations. Slopes make natural irrigation easier provided water is stored upslope (see Chapter 4).

Natural Features

Like climate, the form of your landscape can be an important factor in determining garden design. Scott Pittman suggests that the first step in observing and assessing your garden is to look at a comparable patch of wild vegetation nearby. The natural landscape appears disorderly and random at first glance, whereas most traditional gardens are likely to have sequences of like plants growing in patches or neat rows. This monocultural pattern is the optimal setup for insect and other predation; Pittman compares this to keeping all of your valuables in one spot in your house so that a burglar's job is made all the easier. In nature, plant and animal diversity and a mixed habitat reduce the likelihood of pest infestations, and the natural scattered pattern of plants makes it more difficult for pests to become established in significant concentrations.

Mollison enjoins gardeners not to confuse order and tidiness: "Tidiness separates species and creates work (and may also invite pests), whereas order integrates, reducing work and discouraging insect attack. Creativity is seldom tidy. Perhaps we could say that tidiness is something that happens when compulsive activity replaces thoughtful creativity." Aggregate crop yields under the mixed permaculture model are greater than those in monoculture, and will be under any system that features biodiversity designed to be mutually beneficial. The gardener's role is to manage the system so that cooperative species (or "guilds") are placed together, and noncooperative ones are segregated or controlled (see page 34). For example, some crops benefit from the foraging action of chickens; others would be destroyed by chickens. Black walnut trees typically inhibit the growth of many species because of chemicals their roots release into the soil—a process called allelopathy. But in nature, species are selected that will adapt themselves to this condition and flourish.

The identification of guilds, or harmonious groupings of trees and plants, is also effected by observation. Guilds are mutually beneficial in that they can provide shelter for smaller plants, protecting them from climatic extremes, while at the same time these plants can provide nutrients (for example, in the case of nitrogen-fixing plants), reduce root competition from invasive grasses and weeds, and deter pests by discharging natural chemicals or by hosting beneficial insect predators (birds or other insects). Some plants placed appropriately, such as lamb's-quarter (*Chenopodium album*), act sacrificially, by attracting pests, which then spares neighboring plants from the worst effects of predation. Yet others attract, trap, or disable pests. We can use these observations to design gardens based on such groupings, ideally incorporating a higher proportion of food-yielding trees and plants that also will yield significant pest-control opportunities.

One example of a plant-animal guild identified by Scott Pittman is the juniper-piñon guild common in the southwestern United States, consisting of twenty to thirty species of plants and animals. The juniper is always the pioneer tree of the guild, and once established, it drops resinous needles over time that pile up over the root zone. This acts as a seed bed for plants, such as gama grasses, yucca, and mountain mahogany, that are attracted to the moist, spongy, and slightly acidic conditions. In time, squirrels attracted to the habitat will drop and bury pine nuts, which grow into piñon trees that will eventually compete with and replace the junipers. Similar patterns evolve with other guilds in every type of environment. The four prairie

species that Wes Jackson at the Land Institute in Kansas advocates for a beneficial and sustainable perennial polyculture—Illinois bundle flower (*Desmanthus illinoensis*), eastern gama grass (*Tripsacum dactyloides*), Maximilian sunflower (*Helianthus maximillianii*), and wild rye grass (*Leymus racemosus*)—provide another excellent example (see pages *196–197*). To quote the film *Field of Dreams*, "If you build it, they will come"; or perhaps in this case our motto might be, "If you build it, the sequence will occur." A realistic goal to set ourselves is to establish guilds that build upon themselves naturally and that culminate in our desired ends.

The Role of Fauna

Observing and researching the creatures that form the food chain in the garden can also prove to be of great benefit to you as a gardener. For example, if most of us think back to our youth, we realize that creatures such as frogs, lizards, birds, and butterflies are considerably scarcer now than before. This is partly due to the destruction of habitat and partly because of the huge amounts of chemical pesticides and insecticides that farmers using modern agricultural methods (and many gardeners) have applied to the land. As gardeners, we can encourage beneficial creatures not only by planting beneficial guilds of plants but also by creating habitat—for example, by planting trees strategically so that insect-eating birds can perch in them near the garden (even large daisies and sunflowers can serve the same purpose), or by installing birdbaths in our plots. Additionally, we can set up nesting boxes and bat houses for these beneficial predator species. Observation and research enter into this strategy because placement is all-important; for example, bat houses should be attached to a cool side of the house, preferably catching the morning sun. Nesting boxes should be placed in realistic locations, based on observation or information derived from reference books, and out of the reach of cats. In the Middle East, pigeon cotes are put up for the manure they provide. Bird books and field guides will also provide the necessary information to help you set up conditions and habitats in your garden for beneficial swallows or martins, or "mosquito hawks," commonly called dragonflies, for example.

In the same way, observing and learning about which beneficial insects prey on noxious bugs allows you to use natural forms of pest control that avoid poisoning the soil and water and destroying soil organisms that are so crucial in supplying plants with nutrients. Certain wasps feed on bean beetle larvae, for example; introducing umbels and daisies to your garden attracts these wasps, gives them shelter, and provides homes for other beneficial predators as well, providing a natural solution to insect control. In his own garden, Scott Pittman observed that it was only the bean plants in direct sunlight that had a larva problem, so one obvious solution was to grow bean plants in partial shade in future seasons.

By observing nature, we can also conclude that all healthy ecosystems—including gardens—need predators, even large animals such as foxes and coyotes, which eat substantial numbers of voles and moles that consume vegetables, crops, and grasses, and can cause havoc in flower beds. It is better to factor in the small percentage of plant loss from insects or rodents than it is to poison our ecosystem with pesticides. Mollison estimates that a 5 to 10 percent loss is acceptable in ideal garden conditions. Research shows that applying chemical pesticides and herbicides has negligible net effect on pests anyway, while polluting the soil and our water supply to a dangerous extent. First, only *1* percent or less of the chemicals applied reach their pest targets, according to Dr.

David Pimentel, of Cornell University. Second, insects and pathogens are constantly evolving resistance, creating a vicious cycle demanding increased chemical application and reselection through breeding. Third, Pimentel estimates that crop losses resulting from the abandonment of pesticides would increase only from the current 33 percent to approximately 42 percent, and there would be no serious food shortages as a result.

Likewise, even weeds, commonly regarded as a garden scourge, have a positive function: In the appropriate locations, they break up and condition the soil, help retain moisture, and can provide fodder for animals as well as beneficial material for composting. Even though they compete for valuable soil nutrients and may strangle the growth of productive plants, weeds can be seen as part of a pattern of use in a sustainable system. Ideally, observation should be allied with a state of mind that teaches us to look at the positive potential of aspects of natural systems that we have been conditioned to regard as negative. For example, instead of viewing water as a problem that must be diverted with culverts, ditches, and drains, we can gain from the permaculture model, which uses these constructions to create an opportunity for harvesting, storing, and using water catchment productively. By acknowledging predators and weeds as part of a pattern of increasing fertility and as something we can usefully take advantage of, we are able to clearly see our garden in a different and more productive light.

Pattern

"Pattern recognition can follow observation," says Scott Pittman. Pattern is the template into which we fit the information assembled from observation and research; it reveals how all the component elements are stitched together and interwoven. As Bill Mollison points out, pattern is also applicable to a number of other fields, and an understanding of basic patterns teaches us much about nature and natural phenomena.

Mollison observes that "in a natural landscape, each element is part of the greater whole, a sophisticated and intricate web of connections and energy flows. If we attempt to create landscapes using a strictly objective viewpoint, we will produce awkward and dysfunctional designs because all living systems are more than just the sum of their parts."

Viewing landscape in terms of pattern

rather than unconnected parts is one of the most difficult and complex aspects of observation and design. While some people are adept at recognizing and "reading" patterns, most of us are not, though we could learn by practice. In earlier times, before written language, tribal societies saw themselves as a part of the pattern of the landscape, and their knowledge was passed on in carvings, weavings, myths, stories, songs, and dances that recorded and mimicked patterns of nature—celestial progressions, the seasons, crop cycles, and weather patterns. Mollison suggests that with the advent of writing, symbols (letters of the alphabet) have replaced the former connection to reality and experience, and as a result we have become divorced from the patterns of nature. Symbolic knowledge (another kind of pattern) has replaced knowledge of pattern except in those societies that have maintained their traditions and close interaction with the landscape. The Aboriginal people of Australia, for example, are taught to see and think in terms of pattern from an early age, and they use the information they learn to their advantage; for example, in locating food. Mollison cites native groups in the South Pacific that plant certain crops,

such as tubers, only after a certain tree blooms. The results bear out the validity of this simple observation, as earlier crops frequently fail.

Day to day, we are surrounded by a complex array of shapes and forms, and many of the most basic patterns can be observed in quite distinct contexts. For example, wave patterns can be seen in water, sand dune formations, and fossils; curled "jet" shapes are common to lava flows, rivers in flood, fungi, and ferns. Cloud forms occur not only in puffy white clouds but also in tree canopies and porous calcite rocks.

Thou cunning'st pattern of excelling nature.

—WILLIAM SHAKESPEARE, *Othello*

Galaxy-type spirals can be observed in the seed head patterns of sunflowers and in whirlpools; overlapping spirals form leaf shapes that are also seen in flower petals, pinecones, and pineapples. Curved stream lines form in water, and netlike matrices occur in honeycombs, dried mud cracks, tree bark, the interior of bones, and basalt columns (such as the Giant's Causeway in

Northern Ireland). Circular "target" patterns can be seen in cross-sectional tree rings and shells, while islands and lichens are examples of scatter patterns. What most of these different patterns have in common is that they are caused by flow or growth. They can all be seen as consequences of fractal geometrics.

Another type of pattern—dendritic, or treelike branching—occurs in stream and river formations, blood vessels, and "fingers" of atmospheric lightning, as well as in trees, which branch out successively as they grow upward. A set pattern of branching and consistent ratios occur in each of these quite different contexts. For example, both rivers and trees typically branch between five and seven times, with an average of three main branches adjoining the main stem. Each branch is typically twice as long as the next smallest, with the angle between them about 36 to 38 degrees. Each branch is referred to as an "order" of branching, and most phenomena can be classified in the same way within seven orders. This applies not only to rivers and trees but also to waves, mountains, and human settlements, from hamlets and villages to cities. These same patterns occur universally, wherever in the world you choose to look, making landscape design decisions much

easier and more predictable. Mollison's theories of pattern demonstrate that all natural phenomena occur in a specifically limited number of variations, and general patterns can be observed in relation to size. For example, objects of large size move slowly because of gravity and inertia, while small things move fast, and yet smaller objects move slowly because of their size in relation to the surrounding environment and the force of friction.

All patterns have boundaries and edges (ecotones), and in nature, edges or interfaces that divide different media (water, air, land, or soil) or neighboring types of ecology or landscapes (such as forest and meadow, cropland and orchard, plain and marsh, desert and grassland, mountain and valley) are areas of the richest environment and greatest ecological diversity and productivity. (Alan Chadwick, a pioneer of biointensive gardening, called this "the area of discontinuity.") This is not only because resources from both ecologies are brought into play, maximizing diversity, but also because edges often support species unique to these margins. Edges attract debris and other materials that can be important to the microecology of the location—garden borders and fences accumulate leaves or soil blown by the wind, for example, and the jetsam found on the beach at the high-water mark can include seeds, nuts, and spores. These are all reasons why villages, towns, and great cities have historically been founded in places that border two or more such zones. In the next chapter, we examine how designing our gardens to introduce or accentuate areas of edge can be of tremendous benefit.

Another pattern that we can apply to our gardens is that of "stacking" (or "annidation," as Mollison terms it, after the Latin word for "nest," referring to the pattern of storing or "nesting" different-sized bowls or Russian dolls one within the next). Using the dimension of height can greatly enhance the yield and health of the ecosystem. In the wild, we find plant species at varying heights: an overstory or canopy of large trees, a middle level of smaller trees, and an understory or lower level of shrubs, small plants, creepers, and grasses. Each of these levels contains species that use the available light. The root zone is also likely to yield productively. This pattern, too, can be incorporated into garden design (see page *61*).

Succession is yet another natural pattern that we can observe and allow for in a garden setting. In nature, what Mollison describes as "a sequence of processes" cre-

ates new microecosystems in areas devastated by flood, fire, or avalanche, for example. In the case of the last, aspen trees are the pioneer species that follow the paths of rockslides; they thrive in the poor soil conditions, beginning the processes and conditions suitable for natural reforestation. As detailed earlier, piñon trees replace junipers, the pioneer species, and they in turn provide the conditions necessary for ponderosa pines, which represent the climax of the pine forest species in regions such as the American Southwest. On abandoned farmland in New England, aspens, poplars, alders, and small conifers are often the pioneer species, typically mixed with an understory of sweet birch, witch hazel, blueberries, and wildflowers. These then provide the platform for the dominant, climax forest species such as chestnuts, oaks, and maples.

In areas affected by fire, erosion, or overgrazing, thistles and other weeds as well as herbs are often the pioneer species that stabilize the landscape, paving the way in time for other plants, crops, or trees. Pioneer plants serve numerous purposes, including loosening and conditioning the soil, fixing nitrogen, stabilizing eroded or steep terrain, making trace minerals such as phosphate and calcium accessible for

One Expert's Application of Natural Patterns

Alan York is a biodynamic viniculturist and apple grower (and former president of the Biodynamic Farming and Gardening Association) who studied under the legendary British guru of biodynamic agriculture, Alan Chadwick. Chadwick was a former thespian who practiced Rudolf Steiner's principles of anthroposophy and

biodynamic gardening. Much of Alan York's work in his 21-acre orchard in northern California's Anderson Valley is based on observation of natural patterns, which he then applies to his apple trees. Alan's techniques are now influencing a significant sector of the wine grape production and apple-growing business in the United States.

Like Bill Mollison and Masanobu Fukuoka, York's philosophy is based on simplicity: Understand the growth habits of trees and vines and then do the minimum necessary to help them maximize production. York grasped the princi-

ples of observation only by practice. He recalls what was for him a painful learning experience when he was working with Alan Chadwick: "Talk about not seeing the forest for the trees! I'd been working with a patch of tomatoes for a whole day, planting and tying them, when Alan arrived to view my progress. After about five seconds, he asked me what I was doing about all the tomato hornworms that were infesting the plants. I was staggered—I hadn't noticed them because I was so focused on the immediate job at hand. I was truly embarrassed, but it taught me that to be able to properly observe events, or a field or landscape, you need to be detached, distanced from the immediate, and independent of what it is you need to observe."

York says, "I like to keep my methods sufficiently simple that I could take the first person off the street, explain my principles to them, and let them loose in the orchard. Even if they've never seen an apple tree before, if they can't understand my method inside an hour or two, then it's too complicated." York trains his trees as espaliers along rows of wire, and his rules are indeed few but simple. First, he prunes all "risers," any branch that grows straight up; second, he removes any branch that is more than half the size of the branch it grows off. "Some pruning manuals will tell you the ratio is one-third, but I'm trying to keep it simple," York explains. Third, York will "brunt" lateral branches, or partially snap them so they grow in the direction he wants and let more light into the center of the tree. And that, put very simply, is it.

These basic rules are based on observation of "tree architecture," natural growing patterns, and yields, and York's results are spectacular. When he started out growing apples, York explains that all he could afford to do was to observe natural patterns. "I remember visiting untouched abandoned orchards and seeing how wild apple trees grew. That's when I came up with rules that I now follow, through this type of observation." York admits he sometimes needs to get far enough away from a row of trees, or a single tree, to be able to take in the whole pattern and to arrive at a pruning or shaping strategy. His actions have become instinctive, so that the rules that his hypothetical man on the street would go by become instead an aesthetic ratio. That is the ultimate skill of applying observation. The results have universal application; as York says, "Details change from site to site; principles don't."

York acknowledges that the productivity of his orchard has much to do with ground surface management, and this too is shaped by observation of natural conditions. He keeps the soil covered with grasses and clover, which minimize extremes in climate, and he uses a small flock of sheep to graze between rows in sequence; he uses a low, portable electrified fence to keep them herded into the space he wants. The sheep's hooves help to break down the soil's crust, and their manure enhances and speeds the process of soil enrichment. As a result, York's organic fertilizer inputs are minimal and his herd of sheep makes mowing unnecessary. All his sheep require is occasional kelp to supplement their diet.

other plants, and creating shade for other species. The timeline of succession can be significantly shortened in a garden setting by introducing a polyculture of trees, crops, and vegetables (see Chapter 8).

Cooperating with Nature

Japanese master gardener Masanobu Fukuoka provides another excellent example of a brilliantly conceived and executed application of observation. The personal epiphany that led him to adopt his "do nothing" approach to gardening is described in Chapter 8, but once he returned to his father's citrus and grain farm, he quickly learned through observation and experience the difference between doing nothing and abandonment. He observed that man had disturbed the delicate balance of nature through his unthinking, clumsy intervention, and that as a result, the land had become dependent on this activity.

Fukuoka writes a vivid word picture that most of us can probably identify with: "Make your way carefully through these fields. Dragonflies and moths fly up in a hurry. Honeybees buzz from blossom to blossom. Part the leaves and you will see insects, spiders, frogs, lizards, and many

other animals bustling about in the cool shade. Moles and earthworms burrow beneath the surface. This is a balanced rice field ecosystem. Insect and plant communities maintain a stable relationship here. It is not uncommon for a plant disease to sweep through this area, leaving the crops in these fields unaffected.

"And now look over at the neighbor's field for a moment. The weeds have all been wiped out by herbicides and cultivation. The soil animals and insects have been exterminated by poison. The soil has been burned clean of organic matter and microorganisms by chemical fertilizers. In the summer you see farmers at work in the fields, wearing gas masks and long rubber gloves. These rice fields, which have been farmed continuously for over 1,500 years, have now been laid waste by the exploitive farming practices of a single generation."

A personal turning point occurred for Fukuoka when he passed a field that had been untilled and unused for several years. He saw vigorous rice seedlings growing through the undergrowth of weeds and grass, and he realized then that all he had to do was to cooperate with nature rather than to strive to improve on it. It was at this

"The industrial mind is a product of that awful combination of the Enlightenment and fossil fuels. You have Descartes' assumption that knowledge is adequate to run the world, and if the knowledge is adequate, then all you need is the materials from an extractive economy to make that happen. In that mind-set, when the raw materials and the energy supply are used up, we'll think up something else.

"The problem is that we assume we have all the knowledge we need, when we really don't. If we were to acknowledge our fundamental ignorance, then we could start trusting the natural integrities inherent within the various ecosystems—alpine, tropical, rain forest, coral reef, prairie. We don't have to know or understand everything; we can take advantage of those natural integrities. That's how we will be able to get out of the mess we're in."

point that Fukuoka decided to adopt his "natural-farming" techniques. By working with the natural environment, labor-intensive activities such as plowing, fertilizing, and flooding rice fields were unnecessary.

Fukuoka recognizes the necessity of intervening to repair damage already done and to restore the land's fertility. However, beyond that, his natural system of farming advocates taking no action if crops can grow perfectly well without it, and intervening as little as possible. Instead of tilling the soil, Fukuoka lets crop and plant roots do the work of loosening and aeration, having observed long ago that microorganisms cultivate the soil perfectly well on their own. By mulching his fields with the threshed straw from his grain crops and rotating leguminous cover crops, Fukuoka does the minimum work to enhance the soil's fertility. Having observed how grains and grasses grow naturally, Fukuoka sows his grain crops the same way: broadcasting seed by hand in fields while the current grain crop is still standing, then covering them with straw mulch from the maturing crop. The mulch protects the seed from predators such as birds, and also retains necessary moisture. It interweaves the sequences of planting, harvesting, and regrowth.

Fukuoka's system avoids chemicals and debunks the myth that it is necessary (or desirable) to leave land fallow. Just as Bill Mollison advocates vertical "stacking" of vegetation in a garden (see page 39), so Fukuoka stacks his land with multiple uses: His seed grows in the same field at the same time as his mature crop, and a permanent mulch of clovers fixes nitrogen in the soil. Other plants such as daikon radish and burdock reach deep into the soil to bring minerals into availability. Beneficial foragers such as chickens and ducks periodically scavenge the fields of harmful insects while adding manure. Fukuoka has practiced his natural farming for over fifty years, and his soil continues to improve each year.

Fukuoka's techniques mean that marginal farming land can be used for crops without harmful effects such as erosion, and that depleted soil can be rehabilitated in a relatively short time span. While he suffers some crop loss due to insects and plant disease, the vibrancy of his system and the health of the vegetation mean that only the weakest plants are affected. (Healthy soil means healthy plants, and insects and disease attack weak plants.) This observation, in turn, leads Fukuoka to insist that a healthy ecosystem is the best control against predation, whereas chemical agriculture depletes and weakens the soil and plant life, starting a vicious cycle of pests, pesticides, and yet further weakness.

In his book *The One-Straw Revolution*, Fukuoka writes that observation must be undertaken in the context of the whole ecosystem: "An object seen in isolation from the whole is not the real thing. Specialists in various fields gather together and observe a stalk of rice. The insect specialist sees only insect damage, the specialist in plant nutrition considers only the plant's vigor. This is unavoidable as things are now…. It is impossible for specialized research to grasp the role of a single predator at a certain time within the intricacy of insect interrelationships. There are seasons when the leaf-hopper population is low because there are many spiders. There are times when a lot of rain falls and frogs cause the spiders to disappear, or when little rain falls and neither leaf-hoppers nor frogs appear at all. Methods of insect control which ignore the relationships among the insects themselves are truly useless."

OBSERVATION AND RECOGNITION, THEN, take many forms and can be applied to a broad range of environmental factors affecting and relating to the garden. The common theme of the master gardeners we have profiled is that observation of nature can help us to learn about it and then to copy it. Mollison encapsulates the consensus when he says, "If we attack nature we attack and ultimately destroy ourselves…. Harmony with nature is possible only if we abandon the idea of superiority over the natural world. Claude Lévi-Strauss, the French anthropologist, said that our profound error is that we have always looked upon ourselves as 'masters of creation,' in the sense of being above it. We are not superior to other life forms; all living things are an expression of life."

Instead of trying to dominate nature, inevitably waging a losing and destructive battle, we can seek to understand it and cooperate with it to our advantage. Observation and understanding of pattern require patience and practice, and as we shall see in the next chapter, mastering them provides the basic tools that we need to design and implement gardens for the future of the planet and our own sustainability. As Mollison observes, "Good designers try to fit all their components into a pleasing and functional form, to obey the rules of flow and order, and to compact space." Next, we turn to some examples of the principles we should apply in sustainable garden design.

2
design:
Working with Nature

Keep it small, and keep it varied.
—Bill Mollison's "Golden Rule" of garden design

Sustainable systems of design provide us with the opportunity to create and maintain a garden, farm, or ecosystem that supports an enormous amount of diversity. It is possible to design a backyard that is in harmony with nature, produces food or flowers, and provides shelter and habitat. Efficient use of your space and the efficiency of food production are the keys. If pattern gives us an understanding of the big picture, design involves putting into action what we have observed.

The most comprehensive source of information on overall garden planning and design is Bill Mollison. The system of permaculture that he has pioneered, and that is now practiced extensively worldwide, is geared to small sites and hand tools, or modest fuel users such as chainsaws, small tractors, and mowers on larger sites. It eschews major machinery and high technology, but it is far from dependent on laborious drudgery. Instead, Mollison describes permaculture as focusing on designing the garden or farm "to best advantage, using a certain amount of human labor (which can include friends and neighbors), a gradual buildup of perennial plants, mulching for weed control, the use of biological resources, alternative technologies that generate and save energy, and a moderate use of machinery, as appropriate. Small-scale, intensive systems mean that much of the land can be used efficiently and thoroughly, and that the site is *under control....* If you want to know how to control your site, start at your doorstep."

Permaculture is based on some simple design principles that have universal application:

✎ **Work with nature, rather than against it.**
All of the master gardeners we include in this book agree on this point. To quote Masanobu Fukuoka, "If we throw nature out the window, she comes back in the door with a pitchfork." As modern chemical agriculture proves (and as we shall examine in the following chapters), attempting to intervene in the natural cycle and manipulate nature backfires on us, often in wholly unpredictable ways.

✎ **The problem is the solution.**
"Everything works both ways. It is only how we see things that makes them advantageous or not," says Mollison. When one expert gardener recently told him about a snail problem, Mollison replied that the land did not have a snail problem, but rather had a duck deficiency. He added that perhaps the gardener should enter the lucrative escargot market. "Everything is a positive resource; it is up to us to work out *how* we may use it as such." Using observation and pattern recognition is the precursor to designing your garden in such a way as to turn the landscape, climate, and growing conditions to your benefit.

✎ **Make the least change for the greatest possible effect.**
Take the most efficient course of action, while using the least effort. For example, Mollison counsels, "When choosing a dam

site, select the area where you get the most water for the least amount of earth moved."

✹ The yield of a system is theoretically unlimited.

"The only limit on the number of uses of a resource possible within a system is in the limit of the information and the imagination of the designer," says Mollison, pointing out that even though you may see one particular area of your garden as fully utilized, another design-conscious person might see additional possibilities.

✹ Everything gardens.

Every element in an ecosystem—whether humans, animals, microorganisms, or plants—affects its environment. "When we examine how plants and animals change ecosystems, we may find many allies in our efforts to sustain ourselves and other species." Organisms are the cellular components of ecosystems, in the same way that cells make up our bodies.

MOLLISON DEFINES PERMACULTURE DEsign as "a system of assembling conceptual, material, and strategic components in a pattern that functions to benefit life in all its forms." In a garden where nothing is connected to anything else, the result is plenty of hard work and inefficiencies. The key to designing a backyard or garden (or reenvisioning and revising an existing one) so that it functions efficiently is to place the component elements correctly, where they can support and serve each other. Elements are not placed without considering their relationship to each other, and therefore the whole garden. Establish the elements of your garden with your house in mind. Mollison estimates that the energy used in a house can be reduced by up to 70 percent if the garden on the land surrounding it is carefully and properly designed. Most people place and lay out their garden close to the house without much further thought. But, for example, if you plant evergreen trees on your west wall, in the way of the prevailing winds, they will not only shelter the house but also prevent unnecessary solar heat entry late in the day. The eastern aspect should be left more open to allow for morning sun, while seasonal deciduous trees to the south will shade the house in the summer but allow solar gain during the winter.

IDEALLY, EACH ELEMENT IN THE GARDEN serves a number of purposes. For example, plants can be used not only for food but also for mulch, compost, hedging and

Nature's Firewall

One example of the value of siting components of a garden usefully and efficiently is the placement of fire-resistant vegetation. In fact, it can mean the difference between life and death. As Bill Mollison says, "You can of course build gardens that guarantee destruction. Like some areas of California, for example, we have areas of regular fire frequency in parts of Australia, especially in the outback, where a catastrophic fire will roll through on an average of every eight years. I've seen for myself people putting in driveways lined with eucalyptus and pampas grass, species highly prone to fire; when the wildfires hit next, not only will their house become incandescent but the concrete foundations will crumble and the reinforcement will melt because they just aren't thinking and planning for the inevitability of nature. The same is true of all coniferous trees because their sap and needles are highly flammable. You can choose between setting up a blowtorch of a garden or an asthmatic's nightmare of a garden, or putting in a totally safe garden that will do you no harm and will kill fire within a few meters of your house and protect you forever.

"Plant *Agapanthus africanus* and red fassinia or fig trees close to the house, and you'll be able to watch the fire fizzle out."

Red-tipped *Photinia* hedges, willows, and mulberry trees are also efficient at quenching fire. In addition, sweet potatoes and any of the members of the Liliaceae and Agravaceae families planted in a six-foot-wide border are very effective at stopping ground fires.

Ponds situated near the house are a great asset for fire protection and provide water for fire department pumping trucks. Other measures you can take to prevent fire include clearing rain gutters of leaves and other debris that might catch fire from wind-blown embers and thus ignite the roof, and installing fire-resistant metal screens over all vents to the underfloor or roof space of the house. Designing a U-shaped curve on the downhill side of the house and placing any ponds or stonework there will also protect from fire. Mollison reports that of twenty-six houses where permaculture concepts were used to design the site and gardens, all survived recent wildfires.

windbreaks, animal feed, erosion control, and so on. Trees such as acacias can provide shelter from the wind, fix nitrogen in the soil, attract pollinating bees to the nectar in their blossoms, and provide seeds for feeding poultry. Ponds can provide wild-life habitat, a source for irrigation, a resource for aquaculture (fish farming), and even a source of reflected light. Accumulating the information necessary to maximize the purposes of each element is obtained through observation (see Chapter *1*) and through study of plants or animals using reference books. These will help you to select site-appropriate species and understand their various uses.

Likewise, one of the energy-conserving rules of permaculture design is that every primary function of the site, protection against fire and provision of water, food, and energy, is served in two or more ways. For example, water is harvested from structure roofs, and by means of dams and swales (see Chapter *4*); a wide range of different kinds of fruits and vegetables (as well as annual and perennial forage for animals) are grown; and a solar energy system is backed up by a wood-burning stove. A further key aspect of site and garden design in the permaculture system is the efficient planning of energy, emphasis on biologi-

cal energy resources rather than fossil fuel resources, and energy recycling wherever possible. In this vein, water-harvesting dams or holding tanks should be placed on the high point of the property so that gravity can be used rather than mechanical pumps to distribute the water. Mollison says, "If broad initial patterning is well analyzed, and good placements made, many more advantages than we would have designed for become obvious. If we start well, other good things naturally follow on as an unplanned result."

Specific Site-Design Considerations

Permaculture garden design is predicated on efficient placement of zones containing structures, plants, and animals. Zones are planned according to how intensively the elements they contain are visited—that is, the number of times you visit an area to maintain or harvest it, or the number of times an area needs you to visit it. By planning zones, you are able to conserve energy and resources, including your own time. This is exactly the same process involved in modern interior design—for example, in planning the layout of a kitchen. Mollison observes that "those components needing very frequent observation, constant visits, work input, or complex management tech-

Flying into the Caldera

Bill Mollison's property in Tyalgum, New South Wales, is located in an ancient volcanic caldera. We were bumping along on the back of a flatbed pickup truck just high enough off the ground that we could look down on swales (long hollows or ditches) in virtually every direction. It was hard to understand the significance of the terraformed swales from the truck; at first sight, they seemed to be random, but nothing could be further from the truth. ✍|Quickly, we sensed that in this vast drought-stricken region, the verdant swales constructed into hillsides were in some way magical. We clambered down from the truck to inspect some of them.

Regardless of size—some were large enough to drive a bulldozer through, and others were smaller and hand-cut—within their planned form was a thriving, complex ecosystem that appeared oblivious to the surrounding brownness.

The swales seemed utterly flat until we noticed that when we followed them to the end, there were ponds full of life. There must have been an incline, but it was imperceptible to the naked eye. Bill laughed and told us the swales dropped only a few inches in a mile. Each pond was designed and constructed to accommodate different types of duck; some had islands for those species that preferred an island ecology for nesting, while others were home to shore nesters. Fish and crayfish were in abundance, and the air was alive with birdsong. The swales were the creators and holders of all this teeming life, and the principle now seemed so simple. But how did it work on the larger scale? We could not jump high enough or climb up into the trees far enough to see the whole picture. This seemed like the right time to take to the air and use the gift of flight so that we could soar above the caldera and peer down onto the vast, ordered expanse below.

Once airborne in a light plane from the nearest airport, we first flew over vast fields of sugarcane, farmed intensively and unsustainably with water and chemicals. Their greenness seemed macabre, set as they were in the drought-stricken landscape. We crossed the edge of the caldera and over Bill Mollison's property. What we saw struck us more profoundly than we had expected. The lines of the swales now looked like the fine brushstrokes of an artist on a canvas—and the canvas was the earth below. There were thick lines, thin lines, circles deftly drawn into ponds, and big, bold broad strokes that were earthen dams. Rich green lines of vegetation in the swales were set against the drab wash of the brown landscape everywhere else.

It was hard to imagine designing such intricacies on a vast scale. A sense of pattern—in geology, weather, water, and vegetation—began to emerge from the air, yet Bill had designed all of this without the aid of flight. Instead, he relied on his own observation of the landscape and its interwoven natural fabric to create a luxuriant place of fecundity. He had created gardens around his house, irrigation systems, and structures that worked sustainably. From the air the loop was closed. We understood that Bill's system of permaculture worked from the focal point outward: from the house and the surrounding yard, into the garden, then to the surrounding fields, the nearby village, and then beyond. It was a profound realization: The world could be changed by stepping out of the back door first! —*H.S.*

niques must be placed very close by, or we waste a great deal of time, effort, and energy visiting them. The golden rule is to develop the nearest area first, get it under control, and then expand the edges. Too often, the beginner chooses a garden far from the

> There is no mystery nor any great problem in . . . commonsense design systems. It is a matter of bringing to consciousness the essential factors of active planning.
>
> —BILL MOLLISON

house, and neither harvests the plants efficiently, nor cares for them well enough. Any soil can be developed for a garden over time, so stay close to the home when placing the garden and orchard." Mollison stresses the importance of designing a compact system, and as we shall see a little later in this chapter, John Jeavons' biointensive techniques for growing vegetables and food crops are ideally suited to this model.

Thus, with the house as the nucleus of the site (Zone 0), the immediate surrounding zone (Zone 1) will contain elements

that are used intensively or visited daily: the vegetable and herb garden, the household compost pile, the workshop, the greenhouse, the woodpile or fuel source, the rainwater catchment tank or system, and the chicken run, for example. The only trees in this zone will be planted for shade or ornamental purposes. The next zone (Zone 2) is planned farther from the house because it is visited less frequently, although it might still be used relatively intensively. This zone might contain large shrubs, a fruit or nut orchard, a storage area or barn, hedges or natural windbreaks, small ponds, and small domestic livestock. Mollison's advice to keep the design compact means that, at least initially, it is better to grow ten trees that yield citrus or storable fruit, nuts, and oils and that can be properly manured, pruned, and watered than a greater number of trees that will be neglected. As Mollison observes, and as Fukuoka learned as a young man in his father's fruit orchard in Japan, 60 percent or more of a large orchard can be lost through poor site preparation or care. Small gardens—those in suburban areas, for example—can be designed to contain most of the Zone 1 and 2 components described here.

Farther away from the nucleus still, the

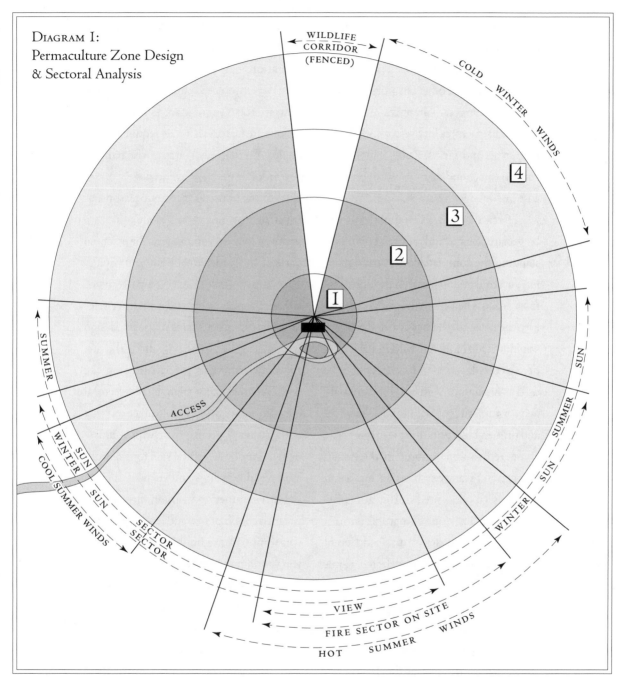

DIAGRAM I:
Permaculture Zone Design
& Sectoral Analysis

WILDLIFE
CORRIDOR
(FENCED)

COLD   WINTER   WINDS

4

3

2

1

SUMMER

SUN

WINTER   SUN

COOL SUMMER WINDS

ACCESS

SUMMER   SUN

WINTER   SUN

SECTOR
SECTOR

VIEW

FIRE SECTOR ON SITE

HOT   SUMMER   WINDS

From *Permaculture: A Designer's Manual*, by Bill Mollison.   —ILLUSTRATION BY JEFFREY L. WARD next zone (Zone 3) typically contains lower-maintenance vegetation: cover crops, larger orchard or windbreak trees. It also might contain swales and other terraformed water storage systems (see Chapter 4) and barns or shelter structures for livestock. On larger properties and farms, Zone 3 might also contain forage and cash crops, coppices, or pasture for larger livestock.

The farther two zones apply mostly to bigger sites, farms, and ranches, but understanding the complete concept and making the comparison between the outer and inner zones is helpful to the gardener whatever the scale of the backyard. Zone 4 is semimanaged land, left wild in part, bordering on wilderness or forest. It might be used as habitat for wild birds and animals, and for gathering of wild foods, firewood, and timber. It is a zone for the longer term, compared to zones closer to the house. Larger water storage systems, such as dams, are likely to be located in this zone. Beyond this radius, Zone 5 is natural, unmanaged land, where design has a different aspect, dynamic, and time scale; it is a zone where we can observe and learn.

Although this model conceptualizes zones as concentric circles moving outward from the house, the specific topography of the garden or site changes this layout. For example, plots of land are often rectangular, and houses more or less square. Other considerations may enter into the design process: For example, prevailing winds and fire danger, flood plain, road access, and soil conditions are factors that may require adjustments. Alternatively, you may wish to bring a corridor or wedge of wilderness (Zone 5) close to the house for aesthetic reasons, or construct the inner zone (Zone 1) along a pathway loop so you can visit the essential parts of the garden in one efficient trip.

Mollison takes observed patterns of climate, topography, and any other relevant factors into account in garden design by mapping a sectoral diagram of the site, superimposing this information on the conceptualized zone analysis. The sectoral diagram shows the range of direction (that is, the compass points) from which climate or topography affect the site; for example, the prevailing winds and angle of the sun in both summer and winter, direction of potential flood or fire, and landscape views you want to leave unobstructed or those you would rather screen.

The effect of this sectoral analysis is to shape the site design so that the house and other structures, trees, and plants are placed according to this information. You will want to maximize or direct some of these

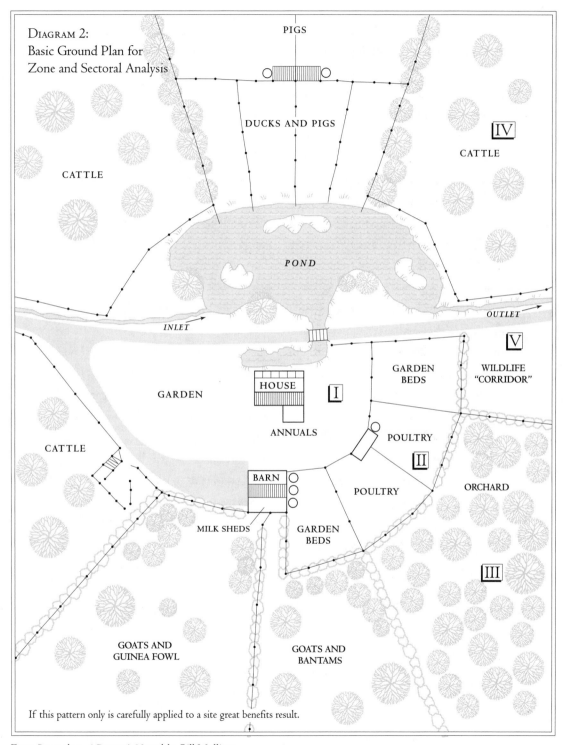

DIAGRAM 2:
Basic Ground Plan for
Zone and Sectoral Analysis

PIGS

DUCKS AND PIGS

IV

CATTLE

CATTLE

POND

IV

OUTLET

INLET

V
WILDLIFE "CORRIDOR"

GARDEN BEDS

GARDEN

HOUSE

I

ANNUALS

POULTRY

II

CATTLE

BARN

POULTRY

ORCHARD

MILK SHEDS

GARDEN BEDS

III

GOATS AND GUINEA FOWL

GOATS AND BANTAMS

If this pattern only is carefully applied to a site great benefits result.

From *Permaculture: A Designer's Manual,* by Bill Mollison.

external factors (such as sunlight and water collection), but minimize others, such as wind, flood, fire, or unsightly views. For example, you will want to design your garden and locate plants according to their preference for full sunlight, partial sunlight, or shade. Your house and greenhouse should be sited for maximum solar gain, especially in winter; placing the greenhouse next to the house or other structure will minimize that structure's heat loss. Using deciduous trees to shade the greenhouse is a very useful strategy in summer. Ponds can be placed to reflect low winter sun toward the house or shaded areas. On the other hand, shaded porches or portals on the side of the house facing the sun will keep it cool in summer.

To minimize the effects of wind, flood, and fire, you can use design elements such as windbreaks, roads, protective embankments, ponds, ditches, fences, stone walls, and clear areas to safeguard your property. Likewise, fences, hedgerows, nesting boxes, and ponds and wetland habitat can be used to deter or encourage wildlife in your garden. The ultimate key is to manage incoming energy to your advantage.

If the elements (structures, plants, and animals) you put on your site fit into the parameters set for the zone in which they are placed, and also work with the sectoral analysis, then they are well situated. By superimposing the zonal and sectoral matrices and satisfying the conditions of both, your design will work to your advantage.

Mollison provides helpful examples: "If we have a pine tree, it goes in Zone *4* (infrequent visits), *away* from the fire-danger sector (it accumulates fuel and burns like a tar barrel), *toward* the cold-wind sector (pines are hardy windbreaks), and it should also bear edible nuts as forage. Again, if we want to place a small structure such as a poultry shed, it should *border* Zone *1* (for frequent visits), be *away* from the fire sector, *border* the annual garden (for easy manure collection), *back onto* the forage system, possibly attach to a greenhouse, and form part of a windbreak system."

In addition to considering zones and sectors, a further important aspect of design to consider is the nature of the slope of your garden or property. This will help to determine the correct placement of certain elements—especially your water catchment areas, tanks, culverts, and well—and your access roads. Water catchment areas should be located at the highest point of your garden or property, with diversion channels or pipes bringing water down by gravity. Even very slight slopes with a gradient of *1:150* can be used to collect water. While the house should be sited on a less steep slope, or flat land, steep terrain above the house should be planted with suitable plants or trees to prevent erosion and to retain water. This vegetation will also protect the house from cold air at night; instead of falling down the slope to the house, the frigid air will be diverted and converted to condensation. On sloping land, road or path access to higher ground should be established for full use of the site and easy access to your water catchment system.

Application of Observation and Pattern in Garden Design

Among the patterns we observed in Chapter *1* were the beneficial conditions found in "edges," or boundaries between different types of environment; vertical "stacking," or annidation, of vegetation; and "succession," the natural sequence over time in replacement of vegetation. Introducing these patterns in our gardens is a sophisticated design skill that when done properly can yield tremendously beneficial results.

You can use the pattern of edge (page

60) in your garden by accentuating or expanding such areas or by creating them. For example, you can create small ponds and dams in open fields or yards; given

Never, no never, did Nature say one thing and Wisdom another.

—EDMUND BURKE

sufficient space, you can even create islands in the water. You can introduce water-margin plants such as rushes and water lilies, and introduce aquaculture—fish and amphibians. By planting hedgerows, orchards, or coppices of trees, you can create habitat as well as edge. Coppices, thickets of small trees and bushes, were introduced into the English landscape in the seventeenth century. In this case, fast-growing elm and beech specifically were grown for much-needed firewood. Today the ideal coppice tree is ailanthus, the "tree of heaven," which grows quickly and vigorously in city or crowded suburban environments, provides greenery and oxygen, and can also be harvested for fence posts, trellises, and firewood, providing you with additional benefits.

Furthermore, you can create edge in an upward dimension in a flat garden by mounding earth and using contours not only for planting but also as a windbreak or sun trap. Terraces, paths and garden borders, fences, and structures on the property can all be used to create edge. Bill Mollison describes a number of ingenious strategies to optimize yield and productivity by maximizing the amount of edge in a garden. Build a mound of earth and maximize its surface area by spiraling plants up and around it. This has the desirable net result of holding more plants than the same area of flat garden land. For example, all your main culinary herbs can be planted accessibly in an ascending spiral using an easily constructed mound with a base diameter of 6 feet, rising to 3 or 4 feet in height. Planting can also take into account the edge between the sun and shade preferences of plants; in the case of herbs, the sunny, dry side is suitable for rosemary, thyme, and sage, while the shadier, moister side would be best for cilantro (coriander), mint, parsley, and chives. Another technique for providing more edge area is to create borders with wavy or crenellated edges; a pond in a rounded star shape, for example, has up to double the edge area of

a perfectly circular pond occupying the same area.

This principle can be applied to beds of vegetables or flowers, increasing the area available for planting; "keyhole" beds, so called because of their shape, are a popular permaculture design that incorporates the edge effect. The "keyhole" path extends to one or both sides of the main path, and the area all around the edge of the "keyhole" is planted, offering the vegetation a variety of aspects, easy access for harvesting, and maximum edge. Similarly, a trellis designed in a zigzag pattern provides greater growing area for vine crops or climbing plants compared to a straight-line trellis or fence occupying the same space. Planting seeds or seedlings in a triangular pattern (creating a hexagonal pattern on a larger scale) allows about 30 percent more plantings compared to a square matrix because there is less space in between plants. This optimal density also reduces the amount of weeds that can grow in the gap between plants.

A further method of maximizing edge is to grow parallel strips of quite different crops ("edge cropping"), a pattern replicated from observing coastal patterns of vegetation, where forest and plants border the beach. For example, rows of fruit trees, cover crops, vegetables, and sunflowers can be planted, in a sequence allowing for shade, wind direction, and so on. Even more productive are edge-cropping rows planted in a zigzag or wavy design, as more plants can be accommodated in the same area compared to a linear design. Some farmers/gardeners, such as Howard-Yana Shapiro, at the Seeds of Change research farm, favor "rooms" of crops: a square patch of beans or cover crop, for example, surrounded by "walls" of corn, sorghum, or sunflowers. Such a patchwork or tilelike pattern (called "tessellation") is not only visually pleasing to the eye but also encourages diversity and can be used to attract bees and other pollinators in a deliberate and beneficial pattern, or to create a buffer to cross-pollination. Genetically isolated domains can be established this way to help maintain genetically pure lines. In this model, it is important to grow compatible crops or plants together, and more information on this, together with examples, can be found in the later chapter on kinship gardening.

Mollison concludes, "We need to select appropriate edge patterns for climate, landscape, size, and situation, as different kinds of systems and plant species need different approaches. Small-scale systems allow greater pattern complexity; large-scale systems must be simplified to minimize work." Diversity in all forms becomes a central tenet of sustainable permaculture systems.

INSTEAD OF JUST GROWING LOW-LYING crops that alone occupy an area of soil, you can productively use the dimension of height in creating your garden. To incorporate the pattern of annidation, or "stacking," in your garden, especially where space is limited, you can mix or intercrop low-lying plants with shrubs, climbing vines and plants, and trees. This pattern yields an added advantage: Most plants growing without shade suffer from light saturation, when the plant effectively "shuts down" because it has received sufficient light for photosynthesis; further direct sunlight will cause the plant to wilt. This can occur by midmorning in sunny climates or on sunny days in cooler areas. Most plants in natural systems prosper with some degree of shade, and using a pattern of annidation can provide this.

Mollison gives an example of how annidation can be used with a variety of species on land with adequate fertility and water: Orchard fruit or nut trees provide an overstory (or canopy) together with fast-growing leguminous pioneers such as olive and acacia that provide nitrogen, mulch, and shade. Mimosa and locust trees of the bipinnate leaf variety provide light shade as well as fixing nitrogen in the surrounding soil. An understory (or ground cover) that will keep the soil cool and moist might consist of perennial fruiting shrubs such as gooseberries and blueberries, plants such as yarrow and comfrey to provide mulch and weed control, annual vegetables such as beans and squash, and herbs. Spacing of plants will depend on light requirements and availability of water, and the vagaries of the climate.

Vertical stacking can also be achieved in the garden by using trellises set against walls, fences, and structures such as the house, toolsheds, and workshops, and by training climbing plants up trees and utility poles. This technique is particularly effective for growing plants that ordinarily take up too much space in a small garden, such as squash, cucumbers, and melons. Beans and peas can be trained up taller plants such as corn, sunflowers, and okra. You can make small terraces or raised growing areas next to walls for ferns and potted plants, and suspend hanging baskets containing plants from trees and the overhangs of structures.

Providing perches for birds in the form of small trees or a large branch stuck firmly into the ground will provide you with unparalleled insect control; the droppings provide phosphates for enriching your soil. It is also a good idea to provide water in the garden, not just for birds but also for amphibians, which have voracious appetites for insects, too.

Permaculture author Graham Bell provides a vivid example on a larger scale of the benefits of stacking by considering a traditional field of agricultural wheat, an example of monoculture growing in a single dimensional plane. In comparison, the green surface of a mature deciduous tree has a leaf area of up to 2 acres, and spaced every 12 feet (at three hundred trees to the acre), tree plantings can increase the growing area by six hundred times compared to bare soil. A combination of tree and wheat crops may yield less of each compared to monoculture plantings, but when combined, their yields are vastly superior. Other indirect advantages are improved soil, greater resistance to disease by virtue of diversity, and improved wildlife habitat.

IN A NATURAL SETTING, THE SUCCESSION of plants and trees can take years, decades, and even centuries. In the garden setting, however, we can shorten the time scale of the observed process by introducing a polyculture of trees, crops, and vegetables, coupled with foraging livestock such as chickens, ducks, or quail; chickens are particularly beneficial at speeding natural processes by scratching and digging up the ground in search of seeds and insects and manuring the soil while they cultivate. For those gardeners who prefer to encourage wildlife rather than take on the responsibility of poultry, a small pile of stones kept moist makes an ideal home for predatory beetles, frogs, and lizards that will be on constant guard for marauding insects. A swallow or martin house is a great addition to the garden, as these birds have a huge appetite for flying insects such as mosquitoes and cabbage moths. The daisy (Asteraceae) and parsley (Umbelliferae) families are effective in attracting predatory wasps.

Mollison observes that by "carefully planning the succession of plants and animals so that we receive short-, medium-, and long-term benefits . . . a forest will yield first coppice, then pole timbers, and eventually honey, fruit, nuts, bark, and plank timber as it evolves from a pioneer and young, or crowded, plantation to a well-spaced mature stand over a period of fifteen to fifty years. Unlike the processes of nature, however, we can place most of the elements of such a succession *in one planting*, so that the pioneers, ground covers, understory species, leguminous trees, herbage crop, mulch species, the long-term windbreak, and the tree crop are all set out at once."

In an area of half an acre, for example, starting from scratch, Mollison estimates that anywhere from a thousand to fifteen hundred plants would be necessary to achieve this model. While the initial plants are growing in pots and in the greenhouse, the soil can be prepared (see Chapter 3), a water retention and distribution system planned and installed (see Chapter 4), protective fences set up, mulch created, and other long-term issues planned for at the outset. A system based on succession may take up to fifteen years to become established and to begin to evolve on its own, providing its own mulch, compost crops, and fertilizers (especially if larger animals such as sheep are introduced), but a well-planned, mature system will in the long run require only management, rather than any additional input.

At the least, we can use our observation of the pattern of succession to avoid the traditional instinct to cut down vegetan or root it out entirely to expose bare il, which can be deleterious to its well-being (except for deserts, bare topsoil rarely if ever occurs in nature). We expend a lot of energy keeping our gardens "under control," but a far more efficient approach is to direct, accelerate, and thereby use the natural processes, as opposed to fighting them. In undeveloped or uncultivated areas of the garden, this means using existing weeds as mulch and compost to grow fertility (see Chapter 3). Green manure crops such as alfalfa, clovers, or buckwheat can be planted and subsequently turned into the soil and mulched. Thereafter, plants appropriate to the environment should be introduced, preferably those that will benefit the soil.

Design Considerations in Cities, Backyards, and Small Gardens

Permaculture design applies just as much to small-scale gardens as to larger areas. In terms of the zone analysis described above, space is limited to plants and animals appropriate to Zones 1 and 2 at most, but the system applied to a restricted space can be highly productive if efforts are made to maximize the usable growing area by using principles of stacking (annidation) and edge, techniques such as trellising vines and climbing plants, and methods for intensifying food production.

In small urban spaces, remarks Mollison, "it is surprising how much food can be grown on windowsills, roofs, verandas, narrow walkways, and patios. Plants can even be grown indoors in pots as long as they either get enough sun from south-facing windows or are wheeled out to sunny locations; most plants need at least six hours of sunlight a day during the growing season. Containers can be made of almost anything: plastic garden pots, waste-paper bins, old baskets, half-filled sacks, toy boxes. Poke holes in them so that water can escape, and be sure their combined weight does not bring the balcony crashing down onto the people beneath. A light soil mixture is formulated specially for container planting on balconies and roofs [to minimize weight]; it may need frequent watering." Containers with an area of only five or six square feet are sufficient to produce a good supply of salad greens and herbs for two people over the course of a summer.

As for specific plants that grow in a city environment, Mollison makes the following suggestions: "Choose plants you are certain to eat, that are particularly nutritious, and that can be picked at least twice a week, such as cherry tomatoes, parsley, chives, Swiss chard, and lettuce. If space is limited, stick to herbs that are frequently used (thyme, cilantro, marjoram, basil, oregano). Windowsill space is better used if hanging baskets or two or three shelves are added. Better still is a window-box greenhouse set out from the wall, facing the sun." For this, an alcove or boxlike structure enclosed by glass can be constructed, replacing a conventional window. In temperate areas, double-pane glass is preferable.

"On patios, plants should be in tiered plantings with taller plants closer to the wall, at the back, so as not to shade smaller species. Two or three shelves of pots or long planter boxes can be stacked vertically [to create additional space].... For apartment dwellers, a trellis is best trained around the veranda/balcony or set up against walls outside the window." Most homes have shady or dark areas, and artificial lighting can be introduced to make use of this space for plants. You can use cheap fluorescent or Gro-Lux type bulbs with red and blue light to create a balanced light spectrum. These can be bought in most nursery stores or through mail-order catalogs, and the lights can be put on timers to regulate growth and flowering. A more advanced approach is to use *400*- to *1,000*-watt halide lights with different spectrums, which are ideal for growing a wide range of plants.

Likewise in suburban areas, small yards or gardens can accommodate permacul-

The city is not a concrete jungle, it is a human zoo.

—DESMOND MORRIS

ture design elements on a small scale. Mollison describes the opportunities: "Many of these houses could accommodate a small greenhouse or shade house, trellis systems, fruit trees, a polyculture of annual and perennial plants, and some small, quiet livestock such as duck, quail, bees, and bantam chickens.... Trellises take the place of shade trees, many of which are too large for urban blocks. Always be careful to design the trellis systems so that they do not shade out ground beds of smaller plants, unless those plants benefit under shade.... Miniature fruit trees, which are grown either in the ground or in large pots, are compact (usually only *2* meters [approximately *6* feet] at maturity) and bear normal-sized fruits within a few years. Their disadvantages are initial cost, more

Crossing Swords with Our Swards

Mollison is passionate on the topic of lawns. "The American lawn uses more resources than any other agricultural industry in the world. It uses more phosphates than India, and puts on more poisons than any other form of agriculture. The American lawn could feed continents if people had more social responsibility. If we put the same amount of manpower, fuel, and energy into reforestation, we could reforest the entire continent." Incredibly, lawns use more equipment, labor, fuel, and agricultural chemicals than all large-scale farming in the United States, making it the largest single "agricultural" sector. Despite this, only some 10 percent of lawns are ever used.

Lawns are a major user of water, and in areas of scarcity such as the American Southwest, lawns constitute a serious threat to adequate water supply. The runoff from lawns that have had chemical pesticides, biocides, and fertilizer applied to them finds its way back into the riparian systems, where it contaminates and kills fish and other aquatic species. Herbicides tracked into homes from lawns have been found to be still active in carpeting after three years. Some widely used herbicides have been found to mimic estrogen in humans, bringing on early puberty in girls and genetically altering the sexual characteristics of amphibians, rendering them sterile. These chemicals do not belong in the environment and in particular should not be in the environment surrounding our homes. They are toxic to the homeowners who use them as well as to their neighbors.

Mollison traces the neatly manicured lawn ethic back to the days of the British Empire and the country estate, when "civilization" ruled and nature had to be tamed, invariably by a horde of servants. Mollison despises the nonproductive lawn as a cultural status symbol and "a forcing of nature and landscape into a salute to wealth and power, and has no other purpose or function. The only thing that such designs demonstrate is that power can force men and women to waste their energies in controlled, menial, and meaningless toil. The lawn gardener is a schizoid serf as well as the feudal lord, following his lawnmower and wielding his hedge clippers, and contorting roses and privet into fanciful and meaningless topiary."

Mollison advises lawn owners to redesign the area into a food-producing garden. A lawn of 1,000 to 1,500 square feet can be replanted with between one hundred and two hundred plant species within six months. He recommends fruit trees such as citrus, almond, persimmon, and apricot; shrubs such as gooseberries, red and black currants, blueberries, and rhubarb; salad greens and edible flowers; herbs; colorful vegetables such as green, red, yellow, and purple sweet peppers and chiles, variegated kale and cabbages, red and yellow tomatoes, yellow and green squash and orange pumpkins, and so on.

If one must have an unproductive grassy area in the garden, then a meadow mix of native grasses and flowers provides a beautiful landscape that is adapted to local rainfall and climatic conditions. These meadows, which have been successfully introduced on a wide scale in Maine and Massachusetts, for example, are also feeding grounds for seed-eating birds and other beneficial wildlife. The state of Texas has largely resown roadsides with meadow species, both improving their aesthetics and achieving great savings, and the city of Berlin, in Germany, has banned roadside lawns in favor of meadow verges. Such action eliminates the use of mowers with their noise and emissions, and the use of toxic chemicals.

To avoid withdrawal pain from the lawn culture, you can gradually convert that prized bluegrass that thrives on 40 inches of rainfall but looks tatty with 20 inches. Grass can be dug or tilled under, but the ideal lazy way to remove a lawn is to cover an area in black plastic and let this solar cooker do the work for you. If the plastic is too unsightly, then cover it with bark mulch to be used later around your new plantings. The bark will slow the process down because of the lack of heat but will eventually do the job. Alternatively, cover a section of grass with damp paper, then straw and wood chips. You can set out bulbs or scatter seed in this cover to create an attractive no-maintenance system.

care, and a shorter lifespan.... Always consider the height and spread of trees, as they may eventually shade out the garden. Almost all fruit trees can be pruned and trained against a wall or fence (espalier)."

Micro Garden Design: Preparing Vegetable Beds

When it comes to vegetable beds, whether in small suburban gardens, in city backyards, or in larger gardens, John Jeavons has the benefit of years of experience to impart. If you have at least *100* square feet of growing space, then Jeavons is your man (although his techniques can also be applied equally well to a smaller area, say, *50* square feet).

Jeavons, author of the best-selling book *How to Grow More Vegetables* (Ten Speed Press, *1995*), is a master gardener who, like Bill Mollison, possesses many valuable insights into micro garden design. Jeavons describes how he arrived at his own personal solution, the "Grow Biointensive" method of food production: "In *1963* I wanted to know what was the smallest area that you can grow all of your food—or that *I* could grow all of *my* food, clothing, income, building materials—in such a way that if everyone were growing their food in a similar way, there would be enough

resources for everyone to have plenty. Now, I didn't feel everyone should raise their food in a single way; I think that would limit diversity. But my goal was to learn how to raise food in a way that would be environmentally sound so there would be enough resources for everyone. I formally began this work about ten years later, in *1972*. I began researching information from UN statistics, and when I was fortunate enough to meet Alan Chadwick, I discovered it was going to be even easier than I thought.

"I went to the Central Valley of California and I asked farmers, 'What's the smallest area you can grow all your food in?' They told me, 'Well, if you have a thousand acres of wheat and it's a good year, you'll be able to pay the bills.' I realized they didn't have the answer I was looking for, and so I began a long quest in rediscovering the miniaturization of agriculture that the Chinese actually developed six thousand years ago."

Jeavons concludes, poignantly and pointedly, "I thought I would be able to learn everything I wanted to know in about three years. This is my twenty-eighth year, and I know about ninety-five percent of what I want to know."

At the heart of Jeavons' methods is

thorough soil preparation and maintenance—what he describes as "growing the soil," which he achieves mainly through the techniques of double digging to build soil structure and using compost to build humus (nutrient-rich, well-structured soil) and thus soil fertility. These methods are described and explained in Chapter 3. Equally important in Jeavons' methodology is garden design: creation of raised beds, spacing of plants, deliberately growing different varieties together for mutual benefit, and integrating the whole garden design synergistically. Jeavons has demonstrated that the "Grow Biointensive" method, while providing food, can also build soil up to sixty times faster than in nature, thus raising productivity at the same time. Caloric production in a given area can be increased by four to eight times or more, while income can be at least doubled. These results can be obtained while simultaneously reducing resource inputs: Water consumption can be reduced by two-thirds, and in some cases as much as seven-eighths; purchased fertilizer can be cut by half or more; and energy per unit of production can be cut by as much as 99 percent.

As we discovered in the previous chapter, several ancient civilizations adopted the technique of raised-bed gardening, either

Bill Mollison's "Food Forest"

"I live in a food forest, and as I go to sleep at night, I hear a solid thump outside—it's a papaya or avocado or some other large fruit falling. I like to live where I can hear the continuous, satisfying thump of food falling! Nothing beats a rain of food, and it avoids plowing and soil loss. The best part is, I don't have to do anything once the system is up and running.

"We all have to find ways to make the food production that's the basis of our existence work. I still don't know how to do all of it—none of us does. But if our piece of it works, then that's a start."

to copy observed natural landform patterns or to take account of climatic factors. In contrast, consider for a moment the techniques typically used by most gardeners and farmers today. Plants are grown in widely spaced rows. Cultivation involves compaction of the soil by people and machinery, greatly reducing air and moisture flow to the root zone. Heavy rainfall or irrigation floods the rows, washing soil and nutrients away and exposing upper roots. In the absence of a microclimate created by vegetation covering the ground, the soil is prone to rapid moisture loss, scorching by the sun, wind damage and erosion, and extremes in temperature. As a result, beneficial microorganisms living in the top few inches of soil (where they are mostly found) are commonly lost or destroyed.

By creating raised beds with proper soil structure that measure 3 to 6 feet wide with a convex surface, and closely planting crops so that the soil is covered by vegetation, the problems described above can be avoided while producing yields far superior to typical methods of cultivation. Jeavons recommends preparing beds with a *100*-square-foot area—say, *20* feet long by *5* feet wide, or *25* by *4* feet, which is large enough to produce as much as a year's worth of vegetables and soft fruit (over *300* pounds) for one person in a four- to six-month growing season. With a longer growing season of eight to twelve months, the same area can provide enough vegetables for two people. Once the bed has been prepared, Jeavons estimates that, on average, only fifteen minutes per day is required to maintain the bed.

The design of "Grow Biointensive" raised beds in terms of dimension yields important advantages. Jeavons observes that "the distance between the tips of your fingers and nose is about three feet when your arm is extended to the side. Thus a *3*- to *5*-foot-wide bed can be fertilized, planted, weeded, and harvested from each side with relative ease and insects can be controlled without walking on the beds. A *3*- to *5*-foot-width also allows a good miniclimate to develop under closely spaced plants. You may wish to use a narrower bed, *1½* to *2½* feet wide, for plants supported by stakes, such as tomatoes and pole peas, for easier harvesting."

As for the height of the raised bed, Jeavons recommends a curved surface *2* to *10* inches higher than the soil surrounding the bed. The high point of the bed will be in the middle, gently sloping down to each side. This helps even out the distribution of moisture. At the sides of the bed, a slope of about *30* degrees between the bed and the surrounding soil is ideal. As you are double-digging the bed (pages *100–102*), the curved form and proper height can be achieved by shaping and leveling the soil with a rake. Jeavons notes that in heavy clay soils, you may want to form a flat-topped bed in the first few years of cultivation, with a small lip on the outer edges of the bed to minimize erosion caused by watering. Orienting the length of the bed along an approximately north-south axis ensures that the sun reaches the whole bed during the day; alternatively, tall plants such as corn should be sited at the north side of the bed, working down to the shorter plants at the front, southernmost side. This is a good example of the importance of drawing upon the observations described in the previous chapter.

It is important to keep the level of the bed less than *10* inches higher than the original soil level as you dig, or you will end up with a wide, deep trench at the end of the bed and you will need to move a large amount of soil from one end of the bed to the other. This can also mean that you have to relocate a disproportionate and wasteful amount of topsoil into the subsoil area at the end of the bed. Over several growing seasons, as your soil quality improves and its texture becomes finer and looser, your bed may not be as high as it was initially. This is natural and simply indicates its superior structure. The double-digging preparation process aerates the soil—a good soil-growing medium will contain as much as *50* percent air space, which allows oxygen to reach plant roots and soil microorganisms easily. Lack of air in the soil is a common problem in most gardens. The beds should be kept evenly moist and not allowed to dry out, and they should not be compacted by being trodden on; if necessary, dig lightly with a hand fork to keep the soil aerated.

An important aspect of design in raised beds is spacing of seeds, seedlings, or plants. By planting your crops close together in the bed, a miniclimate is created close to the soil; moisture is retained by the soil far more easily, and a humidity "bubble" is created by the plants. A carbon dioxide "bubble" is also created, as the closely spaced plants shelter the metabolic processes by which the humus in the soil produces the gas, and the plants then take in the carbon dioxide that they need to thrive.

Master gardener Alan Chadwick taught his apprentices that the most important soil zone is the two inches above and below the surface. In addition, close spacing discourages weed growth and helps the soil surface remain loose by protecting it from the elements. Jeavons has found that beds that are 6 feet wide have a better miniclimate than those 5 feet or less in width, resulting in improved yields.

The same factor of miniclimate determines Jeavons' recommendations for overall bed layout. He suggests arranging the beds in a matrix that is as close to square as possible, rather than in a long, thin, rectangular pattern; again, his yields are greater using this design. As for paths between beds, Jeavons prefers a path width of as little as *1* foot, although this requires skill at maneuvering a wheelbarrow. Many people prefer paths of *15* or *18* inches, or as much as *2* feet wide, if space permits. However, the narrower the path, the more the plants benefit from the miniclimate.

Planting is another aspect of garden design to which Jeavons has dedicated much thought. He plants in a diagonally offset pattern, with each seed or plant an equal distance from all those adjacent to it.

An extensive chart in his book *How to Grow More Vegetables* lists the spacings for each major crop (see sidebar for summary). These spacings are calculated so that the leaves of mature plants just touch and create a miniclimate beneath this "living mulch" of foliage. "When transplanting or planting seeds on spacings of three inches or more," Jeavons counsels, "try using measuring sticks cut to the required length to determine where the plant should be located. Transplant or sow a seed at each point of the triangulation process. You may eventually learn to transplant with reasonable accuracy without measuring." Alternatively, measure the span of your open hand and use it as your ruler.

THE ISSUE OF GARDEN DESIGN ALSO EXtends to the interrelationship between plants and how this affects their relative placement and location. As we noted in the discussion of guild patterns, many plants enjoy mutually beneficial associations when grown together; on the other hand, some inhibit the growth of others. The study of the important associations and relationships that underlie kinship planting are detailed in Chapter 5.

Examples of Plant Spacings in John Jeavons'

"Grow Biointensive" Raised Beds

CROP	SPACING (inches)	CROP	SPACING (inches)
Alfalfa	5	Lettuce, head	12
Basil	6	Lettuce, leaf	9 ✎
Beans, lima (bush)	6	Onions	4
Beans, lima (pole)	8	Parsley	5
Beans, pinto (and red or white beans)	6	Parsnips	4
Beans, snap (bush or pole)	6	Peas, bush	3
Beets	4	Peas, pole	4
Broccoli	15	Peppers, cayenne	12
Brussels sprouts	18	Peppers, green	12
Cabbage	15	Potatoes (Irish or sweet)	9
Carrots	3	Radishes	2
Cauliflower	15	Shallots	4
Celery	6	Soybeans	6
Chard, Swiss	8	Spinach	6
Clover (red or white)	5	Squash (winter, including pumpkin)	18
Corn, sweet (nonhybrid)	15	Squash (zucchini)	18
Cucumbers	12	Sunflowers	24
Eggplant	18	Tomatoes (midget)	18
Garlic	4	Tomatoes (regular/large)	21/24
Leeks	6	Turnips	4

✎ 8 inches for winter leaf lettuce

3

soil:

The Most Important Crop

What do you think of when you hear the word *soil*? For many, it's hard to get worked up about it; it's taken for granted by most people, and all too often thought of as "dirt." But just ask an experienced gardener or farmer about soil, and the passion is unmistakable. To anyone who has run their fingers through a fine soil and felt its crumbly humus structure and smelled its fresh, sweet earthy aroma, or stopped to consider its form and potential, it is a miracle. Each handful contains millions upon millions of micro-organisms; soil is literally alive and constantly active, with its own dynamic ecosystem. In *1905* Nathaniel Southgate Shaler described in his book *Man and Earth* how soil, air, and water provide a fragile "placenta" that envelops the planet, sustaining all life. The key to survival is maintaining a healthy "placenta," and soil quality is as important an environmental factor as air and water quality. Understanding soil is the key to sustainability. It is a precious commodity; it is estimated that *1* inch of topsoil takes from fifty to two thousand years to form under natural conditions. It is most likely a new concept for many of us that soil can be actively "grown" in a far smaller time span—a matter of months or a few years. Land stewards such as John Jeavons, Bill Mollison, Masanobu Fukuoka, and Alan York, working in the fields, have developed techniques for sustainable soil improvement. These "growers of the soil," each with his own perspective, have provided through example the means of achieving abundance and verdancy.

At his farm in Willits, California, perched in an unlikely setting on a rocky hillside, John Jeavons (see page *15*) has learned to build up the soil up to sixty times faster than occurs naturally. He articulates the importance of soil health this way: "If we consume food that has been grown using methods that inadvertently deplete the soil in the growing process, then we are responsible for depleting the soil. If, instead, we raise or request food grown in ways that heal the earth, then we are healing the earth and its soils. Our daily food choices will make the difference. We can choose to support ourselves while increasing the vitality of the planet." Jeavons believes that instead of growing plants or crops, the focus should be on growing soil: "Granted, in order to grow soil, we need to grow crops. But rather than growing for the sole purpose of con-

The nation that destroys its soil destroys itself.

—FRANKLIN D. ROOSEVELT

sumption, the goal changes to one of giving and creating life—producing, in the process, an abundance of food." But he cautions, "We will not even be able to provide for our own food needs soon if we do not grow soil."

JEAVONS' CONCERN ABOUT OUR ABILITY to sustain food production is shared by a great many other practitioners as well as observers and critics of today's energy-intensive, chemical-based commercial agriculture. While it saves labor and improves yields in the short term, the hidden, ongoing legacy of chemical agriculture assumes frightening proportions. The massive input of fertilizers and pesticides destroys the natural balance and ecosystem of the soil, quickly depletes the soil of its fertility and nutrients, and, as a result, weakens crops and plants, making them further dependent on man-made chemicals that cause widespread pollution of the soil and water. In the words of Wes Jackson at the Land Institute in Kansas: "Unfortunately, commercial agriculture has proved to be one of the most destructive forces on the planet, and soil depletion and pollution are in an advanced state."

In Illinois, for example, over a twenty-year period it took a tenfold increase in chemical fertilizer application to achieve a doubling in yield. Each year up to 40 million tons of chemical fertilizers are applied to American farmland. Despite a similar massive application of herbicides, crop loss due to weeds is only slightly lower now than it was fifty years ago.

Serious soil erosion is a further by-product of modern commercial agriculture. A study conducted by Iowa State University in 1972 estimated that each year in the United States, 4 billion tons of soil were lost to water erosion due to modern methods, with up to 25 percent washing away into the Gulf of Mexico (subsequent studies show continued depletion). Ironically, this is more than the annual amount of soil loss during the 1930s, before the creation of the Soil Conservation Service. By 1981, 50 percent of the fertile topsoil of Iowa had already been lost; an average of 39 tons of soil is lost per acre of farmed land in the United States every year. Mechanized modern farming weakens and diminishes the soil up to eight times as fast as would otherwise occur; the soil is being literally strip-mined.

According to Jeavons' organization, Ecology Action, for every pound of food produced in the United States by mechanized commercial agriculture, approximately 6 pounds of soil are lost forever to erosion by wind and water. In China, approximately *18* pounds of soil are lost to erosion for every pound of food produced, and one-third of the viable topsoil base has been destroyed by chemical farming methods. Similar practices have reduced the arable topsoil in Mexico to 9 percent of the total once available.

Modern farming methods also create other devastating problems: Mechanized fence-to-fence farming has eliminated windbreaks and shelter belts; excessive irrigation has produced soil that is poisoned by salt deposits; single crops grown in row formation with exposed soil dividing the rows promotes soil erosion; and monocropping or lack of crop rotation also diminishes nutrients and weakens the soil. Other factors contribute to the problem as well, making the need to reverse the trend and "grow" soil all the more urgent. Urbanization has shrunk the acreage of land available for agriculture. Because cities have historically been established close to sources of food, their expansion has usually taken over much of the most fertile and productive soil. In fact, an average of almost 2,000 acres of prime agricultural land is developed and covered with asphalt or concrete every day, totaling 630,000 acres a year.

It is possible to turn this tide of soil depletion, erosion, and pollution and actually create and build rich, vibrant soil. There are several ways of doing this, especially in our gardens, using compost, methodical but simple bed preparation and digging techniques, and cover crops, to name a few. It turns out that gardeners know a lot more about building soil than laboratory scientists do at this point, and we examine the lessons to be learned from the practices of the most successful of these individuals, the heroes of the soil.

JEAVONS' SEARCH FOR THE ANSWER TO his question, "What is the smallest area in which I can grow all of my food and income?" is described in Chapter 2, and the resulting journey he has embarked upon since then has made a huge impact on the practice of sustainable agriculture. He advocates seeking solutions that begin on your own plot of land. "Once discovered, these personal solutions have as many varied applications as there are people, soils, climates, and cultures. My work over the last twenty-six years is a beginning point from which others can develop the new

"When we grow crops, we're growing a product. What we're not doing is growing soil, which is a living process. It's as though we're milking a cow and not feeding it. If we express this attitude in terms of a cow, it's clearly ridiculous, but when we express it in terms of soil, most people don't get it.

"It's essential that we stop growing crops and start growing soil instead. The wonderful thing is that in the process of growing soil, we'll wind up with healthy crops we can use. If we feed the soil, we feed Mother Nature, and in turn, she will feed us abundantly.

"But to go along with growing soil, we have to grow people as well—not more people, but rather people who understand the importance of growing soil. We can't just grow soil and food for ourselves—how are we going to feed other people? It's going to take every one of us, doing just a little bit, to make a difference."

combinations that will work best for them." These individual actions multiply to become the most positive big solution of all.

Understanding the Components of Soil

Each of the practitioners who offer personal solutions to the issue of healing, building, and nurturing soil agree on the starting point: First, it is necessary to understand soil's nature and components. As biodynamic gardener Alan York says, "Details change from site to site, but the principles don't." Without this understanding and a sense of connection to the soil, and without contributing to its well-being, we are literally divorcing ourselves from our roots and the land upon which, ultimately, we all depend.

Soil is derived from minuscule particles that once were rocks or minerals and have since worn down, and its characteristics reflect the nature of this original material. Over 90 percent of soil is made up from this material, and less than 10 percent or so consists of other, organic matter. Alan York best summarizes the link between soil and fertility: "Organic matter is the primary thing that we're looking at initially in fertility. A fertile soil contains between four and ten percent organic matter. When the organic matter drops below two percent, all activity in the soil and all the nutrients go to the microorganisms in the soil and the plants will basically get nothing. It's only when the organic matter rises above two percent that you are actually starting to feed plants. So the idea is to let the soil feed the plants in order to feed ourselves. What we have to do is monitor the level of

> If we insist we're going to feed humanity with the industrial mind-set, essentially we're going to unwittingly hot-wire the landscape to do it. Hot-wiring is like putting a penny in the circuit breaker and ignoring the fuse. It'll go for a while, but pretty soon, you'll smell smoke. By then, it may be too late for 911.
>
> —WES JACKSON

organic matter in the soil; it is the limiting factor to the yield one achieves.

"But it's the totality of three major components of the soil that make up a truly thriving, fertile soil: physical, biological, and chemical. The physical characteristics are the structure and texture. There are some things you can easily do, especially on a small scale, to change the texture, like adding sand, clay, or silt to the soil. Structure has to do more with the crumb and porosity of the soil. It's in the biological aspect where the organic, living matter comes in. This is what makes the nutrients available to plants. Finally, the chemical aspect deals with the minerals and actual chemical makeup of the soil."

In constructing your own personal solution to the management and growth of your soil, the first step is to know the specific type you are dealing with, which will provide the necessary information about its general characteristics; for example, whether it is sandy, claylike, or alluvial, acidic or alkaline. If you are unsure of your particular soil type, this information is usually available by consulting your local Soil Conservation Service or cooperative extension office. Thorough evaluations of your soil are also available from private pro-

fessional laboratories, while less thorough home soil test kits are also available for analyzing basic pH, nitrogen, phosphorus, and potassium levels. You can also test for

Fertility of the soil is the future of civilization.

—SIR ALBERT HOWARD, NINETEENTH-CENTURY AGRICULTURIST

levels of organic matter, calcium, and magnesium. The most important aspect of testing is to take a representative soil sample from below the surface in more than one location.

Once you have learned about your soil, it becomes progressively easier to grow and nurture it. Ideally (but not necessarily), growing soil involves ongoing observation and consistent record keeping, so that you can accurately track methods and results. By noting the effects of cultivation and aeration, weather trends, composting, and fertilizing, as well as planting and growth data, pest problems, and harvest results, you will be able to evaluate progress and make judgments about possible improvements. Even the presence of specific weeds can provide information on soil conditions; for example, dandelions can indicate heavy clay soil and acidity, and yarrow suggests low levels of potassium, while shepherd's purse favors saline soil. (For more information on this, consult Grace Gershuny's excellent book, *Start with the Soil*.) The most important thing you can do, though, is simply to spend time in your garden observing the changes, or lack of them.

John Jeavons likes to simplify his explanation of soil by making this analogy: "In baking, you take flour, sugar, and salt, and you can sift these raw ingredients through your fingers, just like soil. Likewise with soil, you have clay, sand, and silt, which form the texture. The goal is to have soil that's like a living sponge cake. Just imagine you are growing a gâteau in your backyard. What you do is to add the equivalent of the baking powder and egg or potato flour—these are the microbes, in the case of soil—and water.

"From mixing the raw ingredients, you are then ready to start on the 'baking process' (although the analogy doesn't hold up scientifically, even though the microbes do give off heat). The 'baking' part takes five to ten years or more for the soil to reach the point of a really good sponge cake. The cake is like the structure of the soil, the way it hangs together, and two of

the main elements that enable the soil to hang together are the microbial threads that the microbes exude, and the root hairs. One of the little-understood elements about roots is that they don't just sit there and drink water and consume nutrients forever; they grow out in pulses, like a heartbeat, growing and then dying, to be replaced by new ones. There are cereal rye plants that put out three miles of roots a day, but you can't go out and dig up the plant and find hundreds of miles of roots because it's a dynamic, pulsing process. When we dug one of our wheat beds in Palo Alto, the structure and richness of the soil was far greater than the sum of the materials we had put in, and its quality was greatly improved. That's the root growth, the dying back, the residues, and the microbes."

The Soil Zoo— Biology Beneath Your Feet

Soil is teeming with life, and the healthier the soil, the more diverse, complex, and interactive are its living components. It is important, therefore, that the organic components of soil are understood and nurtured so that we will be able to pursue sound soil management, which should be mainly about making conditions as favorable as possible for these soil organisms to flourish and thrive. Gardening sustainably requires management of the soil's fertility and its ability to regenerate nutrients without relying on chemical fertilizers or applying nonrenewable resources. This involves providing these organisms with ample food, air, and water for them to prosper.

By appreciating the biology beneath your feet, you can use it for the betterment of your soil, the yields of your plants, and the beauty of your garden. It becomes unnecessary to use man-made chemical fertilizers and pesticides, which poison and destroy beneficial soil life and ultimately kill the soil itself.

Bacteria, fungi, insects, earthworms, and soil organisms all perform vital fertility functions by digesting and mixing organic matter and contributing directly to humus formation (decomposed organic matter), thereby releasing nutrients in a form that plants can absorb. These organisms recycle organic waste; 60 to 80 percent of all soil metabolism is done by organisms that work to break down organic matter and enrich the soil. In other words, nature does most of the work in establishing soil fertility and "growing soil" for you! The principal aim of soil management should be to assist the activity of

these organisms by feeding them; in turn, they can better the soil.

Although we can't see them with the naked eye, soil microorganisms provide the primary link between nutrients in the soil and plant growth. The largest number and greatest diversity of microorganisms exist in the top layers of the soil and around plant roots (the rhizosphere). This is why nitrogen-fixing cover crops such as clover and vetch, which can be turned in to provide organic material and habitat for microorganisms, are particularly beneficial to soil, as opposed to crops such as corn, wheat, or tomatoes, which extract minerals from the soil. The layer of root coating on most cover crops, the mucigel, secretes a gluelike substance that interacts with the microorganisms and the soil. Once dead, the tissue discarded by roots is an excellent source of food for microorganisms, which in turn help to further fix atmospheric nitrogen, enriching the soil and providing a source of amino acids to build proteins for plant growth.

MICROFLORA~

Microflora are microscopic plant organisms that thrive on raw organic matter, ideally with a ratio of carbohydrates (carbon) to nitrogen of about 25 to 1. The more carbon in the soil, the more nitrogen microflora need to digest and process it. For this reason, it is important to control the amount of carbon you add to the soil in the form of composted material, as it may result in nitrogen deficiency in plants because the microflora will use up nitrogen first, in order to digest the carbon.

Bacteria are the most common type of microflora; an ounce of soil can contain up to eighty-five billion bacteria. Bacteria are the ancient ancestors of all living plants, animals, fungi, and algae. Bacteria are crucial in several basic soil processes, including the fixation and utilization of nitrogen into forms useful and accessible to plants, the activation of sulfur into plant metabolism, the solubilization of trace minerals useful to the plant, and the activation of important mineral cofactors such as iron, magnesium, zinc, and manganese.

Bacteria secrete enzymes to digest the food in the soil (or compost), but this process is most efficient when they have a balanced supply of micronutrients. Bacteria are most active in warm temperatures and multiply rapidly; under ideal conditions, they can double in number every hour.

There are two main groups of bacteria: *aerobic*, which need air to live, and *anaerobic*, which do not need air and may die if exposed to it. Aerobic bacteria are the most beneficial type; they are important in decomposing organic material and converting it into nitrates and sulfates. Anaerobic bacteria tend to produce foul odors through their putrefying process (they are the type of bacteria that generate byproducts such as methane and cause diseases such as botulism).

Fungi are more important than bacteria for soil activity in cool, wet climates. Fungi are nongreen organisms that lack organized plant structures such as roots, stems, and leaves. Among the hundred thousand or so species are yeasts, molds, smuts, mildews, and rusts (larger fungi include mushrooms and truffles). Fungi depend on other plants and dense organic matter, which they break down for food, creating heat and releasing carbon, nitrogen, oxygen, and phosphorus, among other elements. Like bacteria, fungi require water for survival, and like aerobic bacteria, they need air. Molds are fungi that are particularly important for humus formation; they thrive in poorly aerated or acidic soil and in low temperatures.

Mycorrhizae are fungi that have some bacterial associates living among them. They exist in a mutually beneficial relationship with plant and crop roots, especially in poor soils. They convert otherwise insoluble nutrients such as phosphorus into an absorbable form, receiving carbohydrates in return from plant roots. Plants such as orchids, citrus, and conifers depend on mycorrhizae, while others can survive without them but need them to thrive.

Actinomycetes are the most common type of soil microorganism after bacteria. Actinomycetes are threadlike bacteria (generally anaerobic) with characteristics of fungi that tend to grow in extensive colonies. They thrive in high concentrations in manure and soil with high pH and are crucial in the decomposition of organic matter and in humus formation. Many species are harmless; others are major pathogens, while some are beneficial because they are sources of antibiotics.

Algae are different kinds of simple organisms that thrive in the soil and in water. Some have a single cell, while others have many. All have chlorophyll and help purify soil, air, and water through photosynthesis; it is estimated that as much as 90 percent of all photosynthesis on the planet is due to algae. Soil algae have a high tolerance for moisture or water—as well as drought—and are able

to fix nitrogen from the air. Their growth is particularly stimulated by manure.

Soil health is also influenced by the activities of microscopic as well as large visible animal inhabitants of the soil, such as those micro- and macrofauna listed below.

MICROFAUNA~

The small, often microscopic animals that inhabit the soil are important organisms because they break down organic matter and feed on smaller microfauna and microorganisms, keeping them in check.

Nematodes are among the most common and important of all soil organisms. They are a large group of slender worms—over fifteen thousand types have been identified to date—that range in size from microscopic to several inches in length. Nematodes help break down organic matter, and by eating bacteria, algae, and soil pests, they keep the soil in balance. Common nematodes are threadworms and eelworms; some are parasitic in animals and humans, such as hookworms, lungworms, and trichina.

Protozoa are single-cell organisms with plantlike or animal-like characteristics that traditionally have been classified as animals. They are now properly regarded as neither, instead grouped in a classification of their own. Protozoa are diverse; some are simple organisms, such as amoebas, while others, such as paramecia and ciliates, are more complex. They thrive in moist soil everywhere and are an important contributor to soil fertility by consuming bacteria, regulating their populations, and keeping them in their growing phase, thereby enhancing the rate at which bacteria decompose dead organic matter in the soil. Protozoa excrete nitrogen and phosphorus, which also contribute to fertility.

MACROFAUNA~

There is a wide diversity of larger animals that live in the soil.

Insects such as beetles, mites, ants, centipedes, butterfly and moth larvae, and other small creatures such as spiders and slugs all aerate soil and break down larger organic matter. Although some insects are plant pests, they should be regarded as part of the balance that keeps the soil system in check.

Earthworms were described by Darwin as "the intestines of the soil." They are excellent recyclers of decomposing organic matter, and they improve soil fertility by means of their high-nutrient castings, which form a key element of truly rich humus. As "nature's ploughmen," earthworms aerate the soil, making them indispensable for healthy soil. Earthworms prefer good soil, and their presence in numbers is therefore a good sign. You can encourage their activity by mulching in winter to protect their habitat from climatic extremes (preferably feeding them compost or organic matter beneath the mulch) and by avoiding pesticides and weed or lawn products that will kill them; you can even "import" them. They will thrive as long as you keep them fed properly.

Small reptiles, birds, and mammals such as rats, mice, gophers, and other burrowers are usually considered pests, and some species can cause damage to your garden, but reptiles—especially small snakes and lizards—and birds play an important role in keeping smaller pests (such as grasshoppers, predator beetles, aphids, slugs, snails, and larvae) in check. Most can be beneficial to the extent that they aerate and mix the soil and add enriching manure.

Larger animals—livestock—are favored by many gardeners and small farmers because they can stimulate grass and plant

▲ Everything gardens: different plants, different heights, different flower sizes, different habitats, different plant functions. The whole is stronger than its components if designed with understanding.

◄ Spectacular example of using a building rooftop as a garden, Wu Dang, China.

▼ Creating shade: Bill Mollison's nursery in New South Wales, Australia, protected by multiple levels of plantings and multiple densities of shade.

➤ Raised-bed gardening has been practiced in China for many thousands of years. Variety of greens in raised beds in Sheng Nong Jia province, China.

◄ Starts emerging (lower center) in a hexagonal grid pattern, allowing more seedlings in the available space.

▼ A bounty of your favorite produce can be grown in a very small space. Here, an array of lettuces and greens occupies just a few square feet.

▲ Spiral patterns can be found in the "eye," or seed head, of sunflowers.

➤ Planting squash seeds for starts in a hexagonal grid using a simple chicken-wire frame.

▼ Natural windbreaks are preferable to artificial ones. Fruit trees and an annual planting of sorghum alter the potentially damaging prevailing wind patterns.

▲ Strategic planting of fruit trees minimizing the effects of the wind.

◀ Stacking: peach trees interplanted with squash, buckwheat, and vetch to give multiple heights that contour the level of the earth.

▼ Some spectacular results achieved by Alan York.

▲ Trees indicating water: large cottonwoods and fruit trees at the Seeds of Change research farm bordering the bosque of the Rio Grande.

◄ Alan York in front of one of his espaliered Asian pear trees in Anderson Valley, California.

► Alan York determining the form of his espaliered apple trees.

◄ Bill Mollison expounding in his library at home in Tyalgum, New South Wales, Australia.

► Elixir Farm Botanicals, set in the rolling landscape of the Ozark Mountains.

▼ Increasing the edge effect by creating islands inside ponds.

▲ Terracing on a large scale to create edge in the Wu Dang mountain area, China.

➤ Swales from the air: Mollison's artistic brush strokes on a terrestrial canvas.

▼ Dendritic branching patterns evident in the orchard's winter landscape.

▲ A "room" of pasilla chiles surrounded by black African sorghum growing at the Seeds of Change research farm.

◄ Weeds and grasses, here surrounding a patch of sweet potatoes, help retain moisture and condition the soil.

▼ Growing crops on a small scale in raised beds with a simple, practical network of sticks and twine to hold retractable shade cloth.

growth and add manure (as long as care is taken not to overgraze the land). They can be sustained on soil-building crops such as alfalfa, thus fulfilling a double objective. Additionally, animals such as chickens, ducks, geese, and pigs aerate the soil and eat noxious weeds and pests.

The Role of Humus and Compost

"Gardeners can create soils anywhere," says Bill Mollison. John Jeavons proved this point incontrovertibly, first at his test garden on poor land in Palo Alto, California, that belonged to the Syntex Corporation, and later at his hillside farm in Willits. He started with soils that Alan Chadwick described as "the worst possible." Jeavons began with the essentials: mixing humus-laden compost into the soil as well as bringing its nutrient content into balance. While noting that the process of building soil takes time and requires patience, Jeavons has demonstrated that "Grow Bio-intensive" techniques can achieve excellent soil and bountiful crops within as little as five to ten years.

Scoop up a handful of dark, spongy, porous soil from Jeavons' 1-acre Willits farm today, and you can smell the fresh woodsy aroma of fertility and of humus.

Humus, a generic term for raw organic matter in some form of decomposition, is the main source of food for soil microorganisms. It is variable in composition, depending on the nature of the original material and the conditions of its decomposition.

To forget how to dig the earth and tend the soil is to forget ourselves.

—GANDHI

Modern agricultural methods are based on applying man-made chemicals to land and crops, replacing the natural process of humus formation as the principal method for stimulating growth. This replacement is one reason why the effects of chemical agriculture are disastrous for soil, since humus is an essential element of soil fertility. Among the many benefits that humus provides are improvement of soil structure and texture (for example, by loosening dense, clay-type soils and binding light, sandy soils), and promotion of aeration. Humus attracts earthworms; releases nutrients to plants and beneficial microorganisms, improving plant yields; and retains water (up to six times its own weight, helping to make soil drought-, flood-, and erosion-resistant). Humus also reduces the stress on plants in extreme climates by providing nutrients, buffering soil from excesses in acidity or alkalinity, and preventing toxic elements (such as small amounts of heavy metals) from being absorbed by plants and soil organisms. Humus improves the structure of the soil while nourishing it. Healthy soil in turn produces healthy plants that can better resist disease and pests.

Jeavons describes the process by which plants are nourished by humus, extracting the nutrients they need from the water/ soil particle interface: "As plant roots grow through the soil in search of nutrients, each plant root is surrounded by a 'halo' of hydrogen ions, which are a by-product of the roots' respiration. These hydrogen ions also carry a positive electrical charge. The root actually 'bargains' with the humus, exchanging some of its positively charged hydrogen ions for calcium, magnesium, manganese, copper, zinc, and other charged nutrient ions bound to the surface of the humus. An active exchange is set up between humus and roots, the plants 'choosing' which nutrients they need to balance their own inner chemistry."

Creating humus and maintaining a relationship between soil and humus content is a dynamic recycling process that helps keep biological activity in the soil at an optimal level; it is a key to effective soil management. This biological activity, in which enzymes break down humus, is called humusification. Ideal conditions for this "virtuous circle" of humusification are relatively high soil aeration (by cultivation), adequate moisture (by irrigation), good pH, and trace mineral nutrients. However, it is important to keep the relationship between soil and humus in balance or nutrients will be lost and the dynamic process will become stagnant.

Composting to Build Humus

Building humus, and thus soil, is most efficiently and cheaply done by the natural means of composting, the fermentation and decomposition of organic material that can then be recycled into the soil. It is a sustainable process through which elements such as carbon, nitrogen, phosphorus, calcium, potash, and numerous trace minerals can be returned to the soil from decomposed plant materials, manure, and other organic nutrients.

Composting occurs naturally by means of animal waste (including earthworm castings) and in the natural decay of plant and other organic material on the ground and in the soil, such as root matter and mi-

Discovering Hidden Treasure

In the early 1970s Alan Kapuler found himself living in the Siskiyou Mountains of southwest Oregon. Entering a new, unique ecosystem, he undertook to learn as much about the local flora as possible. His horticultural interests focused on food plants, and he constructed a modest greenhouse with available materials in which he began to germinate seeds of lettuces, onions, tomatoes, cabbages, and other brassicas. He had observed the destruction caused by clear-cut logging in the montane area above him and set out to plant small "nook" gardens in this area. The first need in this type of on-site gardening is fertile soil.

Alan quickly found that planting seeds in soil of low fertility resulted in small plants of low vigor and insignificant food yield. He began ranging the hillsides searching for deposits of topsoil and loam, the magic high-humus growing medium. Fallen and rotting trees were a mecca for organic matter useful in amending alluvial sandy loams deposited in the twists and turns of streambeds. He looked under cottonwoods, alders, conifers, willows, manzanitas, and madrones for the consequences of centuries' worth of deposits of leaves, bark, and twigs. Only under maples was the soil deep and fertile; on the steep slopes where creeks run intermittently, maples and yews are good indications of water close to the surface. Closer to year-round creeks, under the expansive Oregon bigleaf maples (*Acer macrophyllum*) that were between 50 and 150 years old and reached a hundred feet into the sky, Alan found the most beautiful, soft, fragrant, moist, and fertile soil in the whole forest, laced with fungal hyphae. The annual deposit of soft, huge maple leaves had left a legacy that he used to grow his seedlings and to amend the wild garden soils. He had looked, understood his locale, and found a treasure.

croorganisms that die and decompose. This process, of course, has been occurring for millions of years, and can be observed by taking a stroll through any densely wooded area and examining the forest floor. Controlled or man-made composting, however, accelerates the natural process and proves beneficial in two main ways: by feeding plants and by enriching the soil. It also allows us to avoid the environmentally unfriendly alternative of discarding compostible organic matter in landfills. Landfills are usually compacted and therefore airtight, preventing decomposition; this results in organic matter actually leaching toxins that can contaminate groundwater. Currently, up to one-third of household waste in landfills in the United States is made up of organic, compostible materials.

Fortunately, household composting is a growing trend as people realize the value of this material to the environment and the soil and the simple contribution they can make by "recycling" it back to their gardens; it is estimated that at least six million households are actively engaged in composting their own organic waste. Even in urban areas, kitchen scraps can be composted in a small backyard, or taken to a compost center or community garden. You can buy low-maintenance home com-

posting worm barrels to take care of waste and generate nutrient-rich worm castings, or you can make your own with a plastic trash can and simple materials and tools (see *Start with the Soil*, by Grace Gershuny). It's a great way to get kids involved in the process, and they'll have fun feeding the worms and seeing for themselves how waste can be turned into riches.

On the most pragmatic of levels, by improving plant yields, saving water, preventing erosion, and obviating the need for store-bought fertilizers and supplements, composting is the least expensive gardening technique to build humus and soil. Managing compost is simple and rewarding, and takes only a few minutes per week.

The Dynamics of Composting

The decomposition process of composting is carried out by the same spectrum of naturally occurring bacteria, fungi, and other soil organisms (described on pages 83–86) that feed on the carbon content of the compost. The diversity of organisms present is directly correlated to the degree of variety in the composting materials, so the more types of compost, the better. In turn, organism diversity creates superior compost (and therefore soil) and improves the plants' resistance to pests and diseases.

Recycling Everything

John Jeavons sees a future in which the entire world has gone organic and everything is recycled. "Organic fertilizers are just human waste substitutes—a year's worth of human waste contains approximately all the nutrients needed to grow all the food one person needs for one year. Recycling of glass, food, aluminum, and paper is fine, but it's incomplete on its own— what we need to add to it is *living recycling,* the safe and proper *and legal* recycling of our entire biological waste stream. It can be done; we have the information and the technology we need to do it. We just need to develop the will to do it."

The organisms in compost create heat as they digest the materials, and the higher the temperature of the compost, the more rapidly it breaks down.

Composting requires the presence of both air and water, so the microorganisms can breathe and take in moisture. Too much of either is detrimental to the process of decomposition, but a damp, aerated compost pile is ideal. Materials should be added in such a way that there are pockets of air, but not arranged so loosely that there is too much. The amount of time for composting to be completed will vary greatly depending on the volume of compost, the climate, moisture, and the types of materials used. The average length of time to allow for the process to cycle is three to six months. In planning ahead, bear in mind that compost is most effectively used in the spring, when preparing the soil for planting.

The three essential components of compost are green vegetation, rehydrated dry (brown) vegetation, and soil. These components can be added in even proportions. Green vegetation provides nitrogen for the microorganisms that break the compost down. Green ingredients include fresh grass clippings, recently pulled weeds, leaves, flowers, kelp, and kitchen scraps. Appropriate kitchen scraps include fruit skins, peels, and cores; vegetable parts; tea leaves; coffee grounds; stale bread; and nonmeat leftovers. Meat, oil, and grease attract digging animals and should not be included in the pile.

Brown vegetation provides carbon, a vital food source for microorganisms. These materials include dry (old) grass clippings, weeds, leaves and flowers, and woody stems; also, paper towels and straw. The brown vegetation should be hydrated (watered) so that it breaks down more easily.

Good-quality topsoil with active microorganisms accelerates the decomposition while keeping it stable. These microorganisms break down complex compounds in the compost into a form that plants can assimilate. These compounds also contain antibiotics, vitamins, and enzymes that protect plants from disease. Adding soil also helps retain moisture and minimize odors.

Keep domestic pets away from the compost. The feces from meat-eating animals such as dogs and cats may contain disease-producing organisms. Certain other items should be added with caution. Weeds and diseased or pest-affected plants should be added only to "hot" piles that are decomposing rapidly (with an internal temperature of at least 130 degrees Fahrenheit). Some pernicious plants such as Bermuda grass, morning glory, and ivies *(Hedera)* should be completely dried and chopped up finely before being added to the mix. Thick or fibrous material should also be chopped up before being added. Poisonous plants, such as hemlock and castor, and acidic or toxin-bearing tree leaves, such as bay laurel, eucalyptus, juniper, pine, and walnut, can disrupt and distress the soil organisms and should be added sparingly.

Composting Techniques

At Willits, John Jeavons creates magnificent abundance by systematic composting to create humus. While Jeavons agrees that there are many ways that work for composting as long as certain general principles are followed, his success in building soil provides the best example to follow. Start by choosing a location that is conveniently placed for access from the kitchen (for waste disposal), to water, in case extra moisture is needed, and to the garden site where the compost will eventually be needed. Compost materials can be collected in a pile, as Jeavons does, or confined tidily in a bin, barrel, or frame. There are a number of wire, wood, or plastic containers on the market, or you can make your own. For example, you can cut off the bottom of a plastic garbage can, drill a few air holes in the sides, and bury the bottom 1 or 2 feet in the ground. You can also make a small enclosure with wire fencing; a 12-foot length of 3-foot-high medium-gauge 2- by 4-inch fencing secured in a circle will hold more than a cubic yard of compost.

With smaller quantities of compost, it is also possible to use the "pit" method (or sheet composting), which involves digging a hole to a depth of about a foot. The diameter of the hole will depend on the volume of the compost materials on hand. The organic matter is combined with at least 8 inches of soil and buried in the ground. The pit method works best in sandy soils and drier climates; with other conditions, you run the risk of flooding the ground with too much water during wet weather. A few bales of hay will also serve to create a barrier to surround your compost.

If compost is piled, place it on soil, not a paved surface, and do not site it next to a fence or building, which in time will begin to rot. Adequate drainage is also a factor to consider when locating a compost pile. Jeavons recommends a minimum pile size of 1 cubic yard (with base dimensions of 3 feet by 3 feet, and 3 feet high). Larger piles may result in more rapid decomposition, which may be advantageous in cooler or hotter climates; there, a pile of at least 2⅓ cubic yards (4 feet by 4 feet by 4 feet high) will best insulate the heat generated by the composting process. The decomposing process will lead to shrinkage, so expect your compost to diminish from its original size.

Once you have decided on the location and size of your compost area, Jeavons recommends digging the ground on which the compost is to be placed to a depth of a foot or so, to help aeration and drainage. Then place a 3-inch layer of rough materials, such as twigs, small branches, rose prunings, or corn or sunflower stalks on the ground; this will help keep the pile aerated. Next, layer the compost as you would a lasagna, starting with a 2-inch layer of rehydrated dry brown vegetation, an equal amount of green vegetation, and then a layer of soil. The thickness of the layer of soil will vary with the type of soil that you use. For example, with heavier clay soils, thinner layers (about ¼ inch) will give better results. (If the compost is sited in a location covered with perennial crops or plants, it may not be practical to add soil, since you cannot easily remove soil from such covered land. Layering your compost in approximately equal proportions of green and brown materials will provide an ideal carbon-nitrogen ratio of about 25 to 1.)

After adding each layer, water lightly to keep the compost evenly moist; too much water will drown the microorganisms, and too little will decrease activity. Layering compost requires significant amounts of brown and green vegetation at a time. If you generate only small quantities of such material, building a compost pile spontaneously as waste becomes available will also work, although it may take longer to cure and may have a carbon-nitrogen ratio that uses these nutrients less efficiently. Whether or not you use soil as one of the layers, covering the top of the pile with a little soil will help keep flies away and reduce odor.

Jeavons describes three techniques to speed the decomposition of compost, although in doing so, he says there is likely to be less cured compost in proportion to the materials added than by letting time take its course. One method is to increase the amount of nitrogen added relative to carbon by adding more green vegetation. Alternatively, increase aeration by periodic turning of the compost with a spading fork, turning the materials on the inside toward the outside, and vice versa, making sure the materials are sufficiently moist. (Never turning compost can also work, but complete decomposition takes longer.) Third, increase the surface area of the materials added by breaking them up; for example, broken-up twigs will decompose faster than whole ones.

It is most desirable to balance the components of compost, as adding too much green vegetation will cause the decomposition process to occur rapidly, producing unpleasant odors, while too much brown vegetation will impede the decomposition process, preventing the compost from becoming warm enough. However, some gardeners and farmers, including Howard-Yana Shapiro, prefer using cold compost piles that decompose more slowly through the action of anaerobic bacteria. These piles are composed mainly of dense brown vegetation, and the higher levels of carbon produced in the humus boost soil fertility. Tests by Jeavons and his associates at Ecology Action indicate that cold compost piles may produce more total cured compost per unit of composting materials.

Adding limited amounts of nutrients (or "condiments") such as finished compost, rock dust, and/or ashes from cooking fires or from the home fireplace can further increase the quality of the compost. Such additives should be sprinkled in sparingly, and in some cases not at all, depending on your soil type. To meet particular soil requirements, such as pH and nutrient levels, Jeavons' methods can be adapted to create special compost "recipes," with plants such as stinging nettles and fava beans making up much of the initial green vegetation.

Biodynamic gardeners and farmers, in pursuing the goal of maximizing food nutrition, take a slightly more interventionist approach to composting. The biodynamic approach aims at producing the highest possible quality of humus in order to create optimum soil fertility. Practicing biodynamic gardeners such as Alan York use homeopathic compost starters and activators (or "teas") that stimulate compost activity synergistically; the role of these biodynamic preparations, says York, is "to guide the decomposition process into an end product that has a stable nature to it." Six different preformulated biodynamic compost preparations, available from the Josephine Porter Institute, are made from medicinal herbs and plants such as yarrow, chamomile, dandelion, stinging nettles, valerian, and oak bark. These are then fermented over a period of time to develop their enriching and growth-stimulating properties. The preparations (or "preps"), once purchased, are then mixed with water and applied to compost with a watering can.

Studies of the effects of these preps show that even tiny amounts (such as *1* teaspoon to *10* tons of compost) make a noticeable and beneficial difference in the aroma and texture of the compost. They also even out fluctuations in compost temperature, accelerating the composting process. They further the growth of uniquely helpful bacteria found rarely or in low amounts in most composts, such as those that mobilize phosphate, fill nutrient cycle gaps between major soil organisms, liberate calcium and magnesium, and provide proteases and lipases to break down large molecules.

Two other biodynamic sprays made

with dried cow manure and silica are typically applied directly to the soil and to growing plants, respectively. The soil spray fosters beneficial biological processes in the humus, while the plant spray stimulates plants to make use of the many life forces in their vicinity: in the ground, in other plants, and in the air and sunlight. "The thing that's significant about the quality of the growth that results from biodynamically treated soil is that the cell structure of the plants has a completely different nature, with a tighter and denser growth habit, making it less susceptible to disease and insect problems," says York. "For example, a healthy plant builds up a very thick, waxy layer. When a fungus lands on it, it has to secrete a certain amount of acid to break through it. The thinner the layer of wax, the easier it is for the fungus to penetrate it. Fungi are totally dependent upon temperature and moisture, and anytime one of these is lacking, it's over." Diseases and insects attack weak, nutrient-poor plants as well.

These biodynamic sprays have been demonstrated to increase organic matter in soil and plant root density, resulting in better crop quality and thus yield. They also facilitate the exchange processes of organic matter in humus, positively regulating the relationship between plants and soil nutrients. Other benefits include easier potash absorption in the soil, reduction of fungal diseases, and stabilization of the amount of nitrogen in manure.

Specific Plant Recommendations for Growing Compost

John Jeavons, among others, suggests that to attain sustainable soil fertility, you should consider growing certain crops not only for food, but for the carbon and nutrient value they provide when composted. Such crops include fava beans, wheat, sorghum, oats, and cereal rye. In milder climates, these crops can be grown during the winter. Some compost crops, such as vetch, fix nitrogen in the soil, further improving its quality (an important advantage for growing tomatoes and corn especially, which need large amounts of nitrogen), as well as provide carbon and nitrogen for composting.

The most important goal for composting is to provide carbon. "Carbon, to use the analogy of fire, is the fuel," says Alan York. "If you want to keep the biological flames going, then carbon is the fuel that converts nutrients from minerals into forms that plants can take up." This is an issue close to John Jeavons' heart as well:

"Our goal is to improve the organic matter content of the soil to four percent or more to maintain soil fertility, and we want to do this on a closed-system basis," says Jeavons. "No system is totally closed, thank heavens, but we want to approach it as best we can. We feel that in order to do that, we're going to have to grow about sixty percent of our area on an ongoing, rotational basis in compost crops that produce large amounts of carbon and often, a significant amount of calories. Those compost crops can produce food to eat, like corn, and in some instances income, but you need a lot of carbon to maintain a proper humus level in the soil."

A related form of composting used by many gardeners utilizing similar plants is "green manuring," which is particularly effective for unworked soil. The method for green manuring involves growing nitrogen-fixing cover crops such as clover, vetch, alfalfa, beans, other legumes, buckwheat, lupins, and grasses that help loosen the soil naturally. Digging them into the soil shortly before maturity primarily provides nitrogen. These plants decompose rapidly, and planting can be done as soon as a month after the green manuring has taken place. In addition to making valuable nutrients more available to the soil, these cover crops insulate the soil from extremes of temperature, wind, and rain, inhibit weed growth, and help prevent erosion. With green manuring, one of the most important factors is to compost or dig the plants under before they go to seed, or they may return as unwelcome weeds.

Maintaining and Using Compost, and Bed Preparation

There are certain climatic considerations to bear in mind for maintaining your compost. In hotter climates, compost piles should be covered with straw, wood chips, or plastic to help them retain necessary moisture; siting the compost pile under the shade of trees helps, but avoid certain trees, such as pine, juniper, black walnut, or bay laurel, which produce inhibiting acids. In wetter climates, it helps to cover the compost with straw or plastic to prevent it from becoming too waterlogged. Remember also that the greater mass of a large compost pile retains heat and moisture better than a small one, although the decomposition process will naturally slow significantly in winter.

There are several indicators that the composting process is complete and that the compost is cured and ready to use. The original components of the compost should be unrecognizable; the mixture should be an even dark brown or black in color, with a fine, crumbly texture; there should be an absence of any heat in the compost; and there should be a woodsy smell, like a rich soil—sweet, with no odor of decomposition. Do not let cured compost sit for too long, as it will continue to evolve from humus into topsoil, and many of its nutrients will be lost. If you cannot use it straightaway, cover it to protect it from the elements and to keep its moisture enclosed.

Compost is most valuable mixed into soil prepared for spring planting, and it can also be used as a soil preparation before sowing a lawn, as a loosely worked-in topdressing or mulch for flowers, shrubs, and trees, and for potting seedlings and plants. It makes a good fall soil preparation spread on the soil before adding mulch. "Ultimately, our goal would probably be to add compost before each crop," Jeavons advises. "And we do add compost before each crop during the really active growing season from mid-April through early August. We optimally add half an inch to one inch of cured compost (including fifty percent soil) for a four-month growing season. We usually don't add compost for our compost crops that

we plant in October for the slower growing season; we assume that the compost residue and nutrients that are still in the soil are enough."

John Jeavons again provides the best example for using compost and preparing soil for planting. Jeavons has demonstrated that his biointensive, sustainable mini-farming and gardening methods build up the soil up to sixty times as fast as would occur naturally. This method of organic farming is based on two horticultural techniques popular in Europe during the nineteenth and early twentieth centuries. The first, the French intensive technique, involved growing closely spaced crops on 18 inches of organic (horse) manure. The concentrated spacing provided a "living mulch" that retained moisture and inhibited weed growth. Seedlings and plants were grown under glass during the winter to give them an early start. The second system, biodynamic agriculture, was formulated and developed in the 1920s by Rudolf Steiner, the Austrian educator and philosopher. He attributed the decline in crop yields and their nutritive value in Europe to the introduction of chemical and synthetic fertilizers and pesticides, which did little to control pests and diseases but instead seemed to disturb the natural balance so that other problems multiplied. Steiner's theories involved the use of balanced, gentler organic fertilizers and the focus on a holistic approach to agriculture. A key in the biodynamic system is the recycling of all organic materials, especially compostible matter and manure, to maintain and improve the fertility of the soil. In the biodynamic model, conservation of all resources, not just nonrenewable resources, is of paramount importance.

Biodynamic and French intensive gardening methods were introduced to the United States by Alan Chadwick, an Englishman and former thespian who studied under Steiner. Chadwick applied the techniques to developing a 4-acre organic student garden at the Santa Cruz campus of the University of California. He was able to convert a poor clay soil into a fertile garden within three years through application of organic compost, and by employing a full range of techniques, Chadwick achieved yields four times those of commercial agriculture.

Jeavons' approach involves growing crops on raised convex beds, 3 to 6 feet across, and soil preparation is pivotal. The soil in these beds is loose, not compacted, so that air, moisture, warmth, nutrients, and the root structure of plants can penetrate its structure. By contrast, in traditional garden or farm rows that are spaced about a foot or more across, periodic irrigation washes away soil, microorganisms, and nutrients, and temperature fluctuations are greater. Soil is compacted between the rows, further impeding aeration and plant growth.

Jeavons estimates that a properly prepared and maintained bed of 100 square feet can yield enough vegetables and soft fruit during a four- to six-month growing season to sustain one person, depending on crop preferences and growing patterns (a 50-square-foot bed will yield the same over an eight- to twelve-month growing season). Most of the labor required is involved in preparing a raised bed (soil preparation, fertilization, and planting) for the first time: between five and ten hours. After the beds are planted, they can be maintained with an average of about fifteen minutes of work per day. After the first crop, only about four hours will be required for soil preparation, fertilization, and planting, because the soil will have better structure.

Building soil quality takes time and strength, and it requires patience. However, good soil may take only five to fifteen years to build using these methods, and building your own skills and powers of observation also requires similar development.

Soil Preparation for Jeavons' "Grow Biointensive" Raised Bed

In his book *How to Grow More Vegetables*, Jeavons outlines the necessary initial springtime preparation for a raised bed of *100* square feet:

🌿 Mark out the bed area with stakes in each corner, connected by string.

🌿 Soak the area for two hours with a sprinkler. Let the area dry and rest for two days.

🌿 Loosen the soil 12 inches deep with a spading fork and remove the weeds.

🌿 Water gently by hand for five minutes and let the soil rest for one day. If there are large clods of earth, wait a few days for natural breakup to occur.

🌿 Improve soil texture by adding sand to a clay soil, or clay to sandy soil. Add no more than 8 cubic feet (or a 1-inch depth), mixing in to a depth of 1 foot with a spading fork.

🌿 Spread 4 cubic feet (to a maximum of 8 cubic feet, or a 1-inch depth) of cured compost (including 50 percent soil) to a bed with good soil.

🌿 Water gently by hand for five minutes and let the soil rest for one day.

At this point, the bed is ready to be dug. An essential technique of Jeavons' method is double digging the soil in the bed. Where most gardeners would dig through the soil to a depth of 9 to 12 inches at most, or the depth of a gardening fork, Jeavons prepares the soil twice as deep by removing the first foot of soil and aerating the second foot or so before returning the top layer of soil.

DOUBLE DIGGING~

The object is to loosen the soil to a depth of 24 inches to allow aeration and proper water flow, and to enable plant roots to extend adequately, thus maximizing plant nutrition and growth. Loosening the topsoil will also benefit seedling growth. In preparing a bed for the first time, however, a depth of 15 to 18 inches will suffice; the action of nature, microorganisms, worms, and plant roots will make double digging progressively easier after the first season. After the next few years, it may be sufficient to surface-cultivate the top 2 inches of soil, preserving the structure of the deeper soil. It is always possible to test-dig a small area to see if the deeper soil is sufficiently compacted to warrant double digging to loosen it again. Digging by hand may be more labor-intensive than using a rototiller, but it will harm earthworms and other soil organisms far less and will not leave a hardpan.

There are five basic tools you will need for double digging. The first is a *wooden digging board* to stand on, which allows you to avoid standing directly on the bed and compacting the soil; instead, the board evenly distributes your weight. A piece of ⅝-inch plywood measuring 2 by 4 feet works well. You will also need a good-quality *D-handled digging fork* and *flat spade*. These tools allow good posture while digging as well as leverage. However, if you have back problems or other physical challenges, long-handled tools may be better. The other tools are a *rake* and a *wheelbarrow* (or 5-gallon plastic buckets) for moving soil.

Assuming the bed is *100* square feet, in a configuration of *5* feet wide and *20* feet long, dig a trench with a spade *1* foot wide and *1* foot deep across the narrow end of the bed. Remove the soil by wheelbarrow or in buckets and make a pile for use in compost or to fill in the last trench in the bed, at the end of the process. Then loosen the soil in the bottom of the trench with a fork to a depth (ideally) of another *12* inches. Only go as deep as the fork allows, and if this is less than *12* inches, don't worry; you don't want to strain your fork or yourself, and at least the soil will be easier to double dig

the next time. If the soil at the bottom of the trench is dry, water the loosened soil.

Then dig a trench the same size and in the same way directly behind the first one. As you dig the trench, move the soil forward

Once you build soil, you want to keep it alive.

—JOHN JEAVONS

into the first trench rather than removing it entirely. Loosen the soil in the second trench with a fork, and water if necessary. Continue this process until a series of *1*-foot-wide trenches has been dug the length of the bed, raking the surface soil to create an even bed every three or four trenches or so. You will probably not need to add the soil you removed by bucket or wheelbarrow at the beginning to the last trench, as the slightly increased volume of the newly loosened, aerated soil will compensate.

Jeavons estimates that this initial double-digging process in compacted soil will take up to four hours for a bed of *100* square feet. A beginner can expect to take a little longer; do not rush double digging, and if you have back problems or other health concerns, it is best to consult your physician before you start. Think of double digging as valuable exercise! Besides, it will require less digging and effort later on, and plant yields will be far superior to those from unprepared or briefly prepared soil.

The final steps of bed preparation are:

☑ **Once the entire bed has been double dug, level the surface of the bed with a rake, adding the soil you removed from the very first trench if necessary.**

☑ **Water gently by hand for three to five minutes and let the soil rest for one day.**

☑ **Depending on the type of soil (as indicated by a soil test), sprinkle organic fertilizers such as alfalfa meal, oyster-shell flour, phosphate rock, or granite dust over the bed, without treading on it.**

☑ **Spread a 1/2-inch to 1-inch layer of cured compost (including 50 percent soil) over the surface of the entire bed. Without treading on the bed, sift the organic fertilizers and cured compost into the top 2 to 4 inches of soil with a spading fork.**

☑ **Standing on the digging board, you may need to gently press down the topmost layer of soil all over the bed to remove excess air.**

The bed is now ready to plant, preferably as soon as possible. For successive crops, the procedure is far simpler. If undertaking an autumn planting, the soil will require only single digging (to a depth of 1 foot) and no addition of compost or fertilizer. The following spring, double dig the soil again, exactly as before, to a depth of 2 feet. Rake the bed to level it and water gently for three to five minutes. Add any organic fertilizers or trace minerals and a 1/2-inch to 1-inch layer of compost, mixing into the soil with a fork to a depth of 3 or 4 inches. If needed, gently compress the soil using the digging board before planting.

There are variations on this double-dug bed preparation theme. For example, the *complete texturizing double-dug* process can be used to improve soil quality more rapidly by adding compost farther down in the soil. It is a one-time process, and is especially effective for heavy, compacted clay soils. Remove the top 12 inches of soil in the trench, as before, and add an inch of cured compost (including 50 percent soil) to the top of the loosened soil in the bottom 12 inches of the trench. The compost is then mixed into the loosened soil, and the rest of the double-digging procedure is then followed, as above.

The goal of double digging, however, is to create a good soil structure. Once this is created, Jeavons points out that the soil needs only to be surface-cultivated—loosened 2 inches deep—before fertilizing, composting, and planting.

Mulching

Another method of adding humus to the soil and protecting it is by mulching. Using materials such as straw, hay, tree bark, wood chips, bean husks, grass clippings, sawdust, leaves, or seaweed as mulch serves a number of purposes. In addition to building soil over time, mulch protects the ground from the elements—sun, wind, rain, snow, and frost—and allows it to retain moisture better, an especially important factor for sandy soils. It also inhibits weed growth and soil erosion. Mulch is best applied in the spring, once the soil has had a chance to warm up. It should be kept a few inches away from the base of plants, to avoid cutting off air and encouraging rotting of plant matter with retained moisture, and it should not be applied too deeply, or it may harbor pests. Avoid non-organic mulch such as plastic sheeting or gravel, which will not add to the fertility of the soil. Jeavons' approach instead uses a "living mulch" of closely spaced plants in order to produce similar functions as the mulch described above, while preserving the carbonaceous materials for the production of the all-important compost.

Undoubtedly the most interesting application of permanent mulching as a means of building soil is the natural-farming method of Masanobu Fukuoka, described in Chapter 8. While Fukuoka does compost limited amounts of organic household waste for his kitchen garden, he regards the effort involved to do this on a large scale as too much like hard work.

Rotation

Soil can be further improved by rotating crops. Growing the same plants in the same part of the garden year after year will exhaust the soil of nutrients and encourage pests, weeds, and diseases, while a rotation of different crops will help maintain the nutrient balance. Ideally, nutrient-demanding crops such as beets, cabbage, corn, lettuce, potatoes, squash, and tomatoes should be followed by less demanding or soil-enriching crops, such as legumes, carrots, garlic, onions, and turnips. Likewise, deep-rooted crops should follow those with shallow roots, so that nutrients are extracted from the same soil at different levels from year to year. In general, plants in the same family should be grouped together. The next year, avoid planting even family members in the same soil, to avoid pest or disease pathogen buildup. Rotating green manure cover crops (page 97) is an excellent method of building soil in a methodical way. Biodynamic gardeners often prefer to rotate plants according to whether they are leaf vegetables, root vegetables, fruits, or flowers, so the demands on the soil vary from year to year.

Landscaping and Erosion Control

If building soil and fertility are the keys to a healthy and sustainable system, it is equally important to protect these gains once they have been established. One of the priorities of permaculture and its founder, Bill Mollison, is to minimize soil loss, and this can be achieved in several integrated ways, especially by planning and by anticipating events that might precipitate soil loss. For example, good soil in a particular location should be taken into account when siting and landscaping, and planting should be done in a way that is site-appropriate. Species should be grown that are suited to particular conditions; for example, rocky areas with little soil can support almond or olive trees, while poorly drained areas will benefit black currants. Similarly, acid soils are suitable for strawberries, blueberries, potatoes, and endive, while alkaline soils will support grasses and green manure crops, avocados, beets, cabbage, onions, and lettuce. Attempts to grow trees or crops in inappropriate locations will most likely fail, creating barren soil that is at risk of washing or blowing away.

Mollison plants sites of potential erosion such as steep slopes, embankments, and gullies with fast-growing local species. Erosion can also be controlled by terracing and placing barriers such as logs or hay bales across slopes to catch silt and water. Planting on the slope behind the logs or above the terraces solidifies the landscape. His system of designing swales to catch and store water and the planting of trees close by to reduce salt buildup further contributes to soil conditioning. Swales are another means of preventing soil erosion, and in dry areas they collect silt, making them ideal planting areas.

Another of Mollison's most important techniques is to avoid cultivating bare soil, which damages the microorganisms in the soil and risks causing more extensive soil loss through wind or water erosion. Instead, he advocates planting exposed soil with plants, trees, and/or shrubs. These create shade, retain moisture and minimize evaporation, buffer the soil from extremes of temperature, and form a beneficial "bubble" of carbon dioxide. Mollison's techniques for soil conditioning and aeration include using tilling implements, such as a fork or chisel plow, that loosen but do not turn the soil, thereby minimizing transpiration and subsequent loss of fertility. Chisel plows are being used increasingly in the United States, Europe, and Australia. The "shoe" of the plow opens the soil beneath the surface and lifts it without turning the soil over. Moisture and air can then penetrate, and plant roots grow better; seeds can be planted directly into the plow furrows.

Alan York also cultivates as infrequently as possible. He says: "Cultivation destroys the organic matter and humus in soil, and this is necessarily detrimental. On the other hand, uncultivated pastures build organic matter at the highest rate of all—they are the premier soil builders. In the wild, grasslands are the most productive realm on earth—when it comes to the amount of organic matter, minerals, and soil depth, nothing compares."

Fukuoka avoids weeding by tillage or with herbicides because weeds can contribute to soil fertility and keeping the natural order in balance. Moreover, simply by not cultivating the ground, the number of weeds naturally drops significantly. By sowing seeds in the same fields as standing crops, the seeds grow and take hold before weeds have a chance to establish themselves. In addition, Fukuoka controls weeds by using clover as a ground cover and mulching with straw. He also allows ducks or chickens to graze through and fertilize the fields.

Last, Wes Jackson, at the Land Institute in Kansas, advocates learning from the natural system of the prairie and covering the soil—ideally with new crops of herbaceous perennial seed producers. Jackson, like Mollison, York, and Fukuoka, recognizes that untilled land is better off, in terms of erosion and nutrients, than plowed land. Among the benefits of his model of perennial polyculture are the protection and preservation of the soil and improvement in crumb structure through root action, increased porosity and nutritive value, and reduced soil loss.

BY APPLYING THE SOLUTIONS OF THE master gardeners, it is possible to reverse the devastating soil loss that has occurred in our lifetimes. It is necessary to begin on a small scale, and enough small successes can form the foundations for bigger solutions. The first lesson these gardeners can teach us is to learn by observation, and to understand the nature of the soil we each live on. Then it is possible to apply the many techniques that have already been developed to improve and build life-giving soil.

4

water:

Doing More with Less

As humans, our physical composition is approximately 70 percent water. Coincidentally, this is about the same proportion of the planet that is covered by water. We can survive for only a few days without water, yet less than *1* percent of the world's total is fresh, unsalinated water, the type upon which most terrestrial life depends (a further 2 percent or so is fresh water frozen in the polar ice caps). Fruits, plants, and trees are still more highly water-based (about 90 percent), and even comets chasing through the universe are composed mainly of water. Water is an invaluable and limited resource that is essential to life—it is the lifeblood of the land and one of the principal limiting factors for plant growth.

The importance of water is evident in the etymology of the word itself. The word for "water" in Persian, and the first word in

---

Do not the unbelievers see...
that by means of water we give life
to everything?

—THE KORAN

---

the Persian dictionary, is *ab*. From this root comes the word *abad*, meaning "abode," and *abadan*, meaning "civilized." It seems that no civilization has ever been conceived without good water (or soil), past or present.

The global water crisis threatens not only health and well-being but survival itself, and it is a situation that has been created in large part by commercial agricultural practices and industrial negligence. As in the case of soil, there are solutions that can be implemented in your own home and garden as well as on a broad governmental scale. You have it within your power

to demand the necessary changes in perception, practice, and policy that will safeguard and protect the future of our planet.

LIKE SOIL, WATER IS USUALLY TAKEN FOR granted, and yet its ability to act as a solvent, dissolving mineral matter and nutrients in the soil, is the key to providing energy to sustain all forms of plant life. Soil and water are symbiotic preconditions for growth: Soil provides the medium in which plants can extend their roots and absorb water. Plants draw in water for cell growth, and they also transpire water; some plant roots extend many feet below the surface, and as a result, soil also dries to greater depths than bare soil. At the same time, soil covered by vegetation is more resistant to the erosive force of rain and flowing water because plant roots bind the mineral particles of the soil together. But despite their entwined relationship, water, unlike soil, cannot be "built"; there is only so much of it, and we can work only within the natural limits of the water's cycle or we face shortage and catastrophe.

Almost 50 percent of the public water supply in the United States is taken from submerged groundwater—either springs, wells, or aquifers (the remainder is drawn from surface water). Aquifers are water-bearing layers of porous soil or rock that lie at variable depths, overlaying imperme-able strata, and contain groundwater in sufficient quantities to pump. Aquifers us-ually take millennia to form, and water moves through them slowly, at a rate of a few feet per day or per year. For example, the water in the aquifer beneath London is estimated to be twenty thousand years old. Because of the slow rate of movement, and because of the anaerobic nature of aqui-fers, pollutants and toxins that reach these sources of groundwater disperse and break down only very gradually, if at all. The rate at which water pumped from aquifers is recharged or replaced is highly variable; where the rate of extraction exceeds re-placement, the aquifers are said to be "mined." This is occurring very rapidly, particularly in parts of the arid western United States, where water is so scarce that the groundwater being pumped today is precipitation that fell several thousand years ago and will take tens of thousands of years to replenish.

Water is volatile, constantly moving and recycling itself in a continuous flow. Evaporation occurs mostly from the oceans into the atmosphere. There it is stored in clouds and eventually falls back to earth in the form of precipitation. Some of this water is directly absorbed by plants, and through the process of transpiration, mois-ture evaporates from foliage and returns to the atmosphere. The rest of the precipita-tion that falls on land either is absorbed into the soil to feed plants and replenish groundwater or runs off to join streams, rivers, or lakes that eventually empty back into the ocean, thus completing the cycle.

Given sufficient rainfall, water moves down until it reaches porous underground rock, where it forms groundwater; the up-permost level of groundwater is the water table. Where the water table is sufficiently high to emerge on the surface in a valley or depression in the land, it forms a surface stream or river; if it is forced upward to the surface between impervious strata of rock, it forms a spring. Surface streams and rivers are therefore closely correlated to water stored in the ground.

Water is the most important plant nu-trient, and it is needed in prodigious amounts; to produce 2 pounds of plant dry matter, approximately 200 gallons of water are required in the root zone. More than 125 gallons (or 1,000 pounds) of water are required, on average, to produce 1 pound of fresh corn using commercial agricultural methods in the United States. When water falls on the soil, it moves downward because of gravity and capillary action. Gravity will pull water downward through the spaces in coarse soils, while in denser soils, water may be pulled downward, toward the dry soil, by capillary action. Capillary action occurs because water tends to cling to the surface of solid substances; this is why water can be drawn upward, against the force of gravity (like wax in a candlewick), as well as down. Sandy soils, because they are porous, will drain quickly after rain, and only the capillary water remains, clinging to soil particles. Clay soils drain more slowly, because of their density. Whatever the type of soil, once plant roots take up the available moisture and the soil dries further, more water is necessary to keep plants alive. Plants, like people, are dependent on large amounts of a resource—water—that is renewable only over an exceedingly long time span or, in some cases, is essentially nonrenewable.

The Scale of the Water Crisis

Water is in short supply in eighty nations of the world, and clean drinking water is no longer freely available to most of the planetary population. The World Health Organization estimates that in developing countries, over 60 percent of those living in rural areas and one-quarter of urban dwellers have no access to safe drinking water. It is estimated that a quarter of a million people die worldwide every year from drinking polluted water. In her book *Clean Water*, Karen Barss reports that up to two hundred million people in seventy countries worldwide are affected by parasitic waterborne diseases such as schistosomiasis and *Cryptosporidium* infection, while 75 percent of all human disease (typhoid and cholera in particular) is caused by untreated water.

One of the crises in our global water supply is being caused by human intervention in the environment, and especially massive deforestation programs that are radically changing rainfall patterns. Over one-third of the world's original forest cover has been cut down to meet agricultural and industrial needs. At one time, large areas in North Africa that are now covered by the advancing Sahara Desert were verdant forests and arable land, before deforestation and poor farming practices destroyed the delicate balance of the ecosystem. In Bolivia, land erosion and drought caused by deforestation around four hundred years ago, when the vast forests were felled to fuel the melting of silver and gold ore, continue to contribute to a legacy of oppressive poverty.

As Al Gore points out in his book *Earth in the Balance*, the plight of modern-day Ethiopia is directly attributable to un-sustainable land management. Just forty years ago, 40 percent of the country was covered by forests; now the figure is just 1 percent. Rainfall disappeared with the felling of the forests, leaving a desertified wasteland. Drought, famine, civil war, and economic turmoil have resulted.

Changing the patterns of rainfall and creating the conditions for massive water shortfalls and desertification are one side of the equation. On the other side—the demand side—the situation is also bleak. Globally, we are using five times as much water as we were in 1950. In the late 1970s the U.S. Water Resources Council reported that a water crisis was likely before the end of the century, due mostly to the fact that agriculture consumes over 40 percent of all water pumped for any purpose (this

figure is as high as 80 to 90 percent in some western states), while a further 35 to 40 percent is used to cool electric-power-generating plants (the remainder is divided between industrial use and domestic water supply). The situation is actually more critical today than had been predicted. Total water use in the United States averages

Nobody can be in good health if he does not have all the time, fresh air, sunshine, and good water.

—FLYING HAWK, OGLALA SIOUX CHIEF

1,400 gallons per person per day (which is over double the average in Europe). The Environmental Protection Agency (EPA) estimates that nationwide, use of ground-water is increasing by 25 percent every ten years.

The value of water is certain to escalate. Some predict that access to supplies of clean water will lead to war, sooner rather than later; 70 percent of the world's 214 major river systems are shared by at least two countries, and 12 are shared by five or more countries. Already the value of land is often linked to the yield, viability, and potability of its groundwater or surface water supply. In buying property, access to an adequate and reliable water source is now a prime concern.

One problem contributing to the shortage of water is that our system of modern agriculture regards water as a limitless and cheap renewable resource when in fact it is being relentlessly depleted without sufficient planning for conservation and replacement. About one-eighth of all cropland in the United States is under irrigation, and as much as 75 percent of fresh water worldwide is used for crop irrigation (at least half of which is lost through evaporation, runoff, or leakage); this simply is not sustainable.

The rapid depletion of water in underground aquifers has occurred (and is continuing unabated) particularly seriously in California and in the western plains states, where the Ogallala Aquifer, stretching from Texas northward to Nebraska, supplies rich farmland—and up to 20 percent of all U.S. cropland. In the case of the Ogallala Aquifer, once the largest store of groundwater known to exist on the planet, more water is pumped per year than the entire flow of the Colorado River. The aquifer's recharge rate is very low; in fact, it is eight times slower than the withdrawal rate. Its water table is dropping by 3 feet per year, and it has been estimated that the aquifer may have only thirty to forty years' supply left. Secondary problems of groundwater depletion include erosion and land subsidence; in Texas and Florida, sinkholes are not uncommon for this reason. In the San Joaquin Valley of California, fifty years of overirrigation have caused an area the size of Connecticut to subside by up to 30 feet.

Another major problem created by current irrigation methods is the accumulation of salt in valuable arable topsoil. This is particularly serious when dry or desert areas are irrigated, as the soil, which receives little rainfall, contains significant quantities of unleached salts. Irrigation and waterlogging cause these salts to rise to the surface, suffocating the roots of plants and destroying the soil as a growing medium. When the soil dries, the ground becomes hard and impenetrable, and the salts wash away to enter the surface water cycle. The same effect is created in locations such as the Grand Valley in western Colorado, where water is pumped from the Colorado River, which has relatively high levels of salinity to begin with. Crop yields have fallen sharply (by up to 30 percent on irrigated land) and equipment loss has occurred because of corrosion caused by salt. This phenomenon is nothing new; it is a major reason the "fertile crescent" of Mesopotamia, fed by the Tigris and Euphrates Rivers, became barren centuries ago. Up to one-third of the world's irrigated farmland is affected by problems of salinization, and the problem is particularly severe in Australia, the Indus Valley, and the Nile Valley of Egypt, where 30 percent of arable land has been affected since the Aswan Dam was built in the 1960s. In contrast, salinization is much less of a problem in areas of high rainfall, where salts are regularly flushed out of the soil.

Further, overirrigation (which occurs mainly in dry climates) aids pesticides, herbicides, and fertilizers to run off into surface water and groundwater and ultimately into our drinking-water supplies. Overirrigation also leaches away nutrients from the soil, depleting fertility.

In addition to a declining supply, we are witnessing a rapid decline in the quality of water. Although water quality in the United States is officially regulated by the EPA, it only monitors levels of sixty or so water contaminants, out of the hundreds of thousands that exist, and it openly acknowledges that these standards are constantly violated. The EPA estimates that about half of all public water supplies do not meet federal health standards. Much of the water treatment and delivery infrastructure in the United States and other nations is old and obsolete, and cash-starved municipalities typically lack the funds to upgrade and improve them. The National Resources Defense Council believes the American public is being deliberately misled about the scale of the problem and water quality standards, and that penalties for water violations are very rarely enforced.

For all life, water is necessary.

—STERLING B. HENDRICKS

AGRICULTURAL CONTAMINATION OF water sources is a major cause of pollution. In her seminal book *Silent Spring*, Rachel Carson warned of the indiscriminate destruction caused by unrestricted pesticide use. Despite the impact of that work, the use of agricultural pesticides continues to increase. The U.S. Department of Agriculture (USDA) estimates that 2.5 billion pounds of pesticides are used in the United

States every year. It has further been estimated that in the United States, two-thirds of all pollution entering rivers and over half the pollution entering lakes can be attributed to agriculture.

Current gardening practices contribute to the problem as well. In the United States alone, gardeners spend an estimated $1

When the well's dry, we know the worth of water.

—BENJAMIN FRANKLIN

billion per year on pesticides that are just as toxic as their agricultural counterparts. Ironically, the results of such massive application are no different in the long run from those documented in commercial agriculture: no significant improvement in yield, and a long-term depletion in soil fertility. Besides, pesticide application is inevitably self-defeating, as pests eventually develop resistance: Over 440 species of insects and mites and 70 types of fungus have developed immunity to the specific pesticides formulated to kill them.

An upstream community's wastewater is a downstream community's contaminated drinking water. Pollution that leads

to bacterial or viral contamination results in diseases such as typhoid and cholera. However, chemical contamination of the water supply may take years, even decades, to manifest in the form of human cancers, diseases, and illnesses caused by a depleted immune system.

Although the natural cycle of water works to cleanse the supply in the long run, we humans are creatures of the short term. Unfortunately, all over the globe, water is being polluted far faster than nature can cleanse or replenish it.

Solutions to Our Water Crisis

The only safe water for humans is water that is safe for other living organisms. Just as testing your soil is the first place to start in understanding what needs to be done to improve it (page 81), so it is beneficial to have your water professionally tested. In addition to analyzing pH and hardness, the contaminants to be tested should include lead, nitrates, chlorine and fluoride (if on a municipal system), biological contaminants, herbicides, pesticides, iron, and sulfates. In certain locations where radon or heavy-metal pollution might present a problem, such as in areas with granite bedrock, landfills, underground storage tanks, or mining activity, the water test should check for appropriate contaminants. Various home water filtration and treatment systems, ranging from the simple to the sophisticated, can be installed to purify contaminated water. Testing your water for contaminants is essential for making a decision on the most appropriate system.

Gray water—the wastewater from sinks, showers, and baths—can be cleaned biologically by means of a series of natural filters and through the action of bacteria. This can be done on your own property even if you have limited space. The gray water can then be reused productively. There are several techniques and materials that can be used in series, such as gravel, sand, and charcoal.

Bill Mollison has established permaculture systems that complete the water purification process by passing the water through a watercress bed (to remove nitrates and dyes) and a carbon trickle filter consisting of burnt rice, oat, or wheat husks. A number of experimental systems for cleaning and purifying even heavily polluted water exist; the story of one particularly challenging example is well presented in a *1996* children's book, *Chattanooga Sludge*, by Molly Bang. The technique described, bioremediation, developed and pioneered by John Todd, uses microbes to feed on contaminants and break them down into harmless by-products, and it has been used successfully in Los Angeles and other communities in California.

Homeowners and gardeners can take a number of diagnostic and preventive steps to safeguard the quality of their water and that of the community. The most obvious is to avoid using toxic fertilizers and sprays on your land. For those on a well system, it is important to consider the likely flow of water to the well, taking into account the slope of the land and surrounding topography. Nearby landfills and farmland are more obvious potential hazards to the quality of the well water, and it is important to undertake your own research on what is being dumped, which sprays or fertilizers are being used on crops, and whether leaching and runoff are likely to affect your water supply. It may be necessary to let other neighbors know of potential problems, to educate them on the consequences of these problems, and to organize an appropriate response.

A further consideration is whether a septic system lies above your well and in the path of water flow. If so, it may be prudent or necessary to relocate the site of the septic system. Recycle what you can and take care to dispose of potentially toxic materials correctly, especially any substances (motor oil, for example) that might leach into groundwater. Another preventive step to protect your water is to avoid burying or burning trash or waste anywhere close to a source of groundwater, or in the path of its flow.

In addition to determining water quality, taking steps to cleanse it, and taking preventive action, there is a range of actions that we can take as individuals to better husband our water resources. The three main principles regarding water in Mollison's permaculture system are, first, to maximize "harvesting" and retention of water; second, to recycle water as many times as possible, thus minimizing the amount of water used and needed; and third, to keep it clean by means of biological filtering.

The first step in maximizing water is to conduct a water audit of supply and usage. How much water comes onto your land, and where does it come from? How much water do you use, and for what purpose? How much water is wasted, and why?

Water-Saving Strategies

IN THE HOUSE:

✿ **Plumb the kitchen sink, washing machine, bathroom sinks, and baths or showers to a gray-water system that irrigates the garden or orchard.**

✿ **Use phosphate-free detergents so that gray water can be safely used for irrigation. These detergents are available in many natural foods supermarkets and stores.**

✿ **Fit low-flow taps, faucets, and shower heads, available at most plumbing stores.**

✿ **Replace washers on dripping taps.**

✿ **Fit low-flow toilets or place bricks in the cistern to displace some water and thus reduce the amount used per flush.**

✿ **Flush less often.**

✿ **Stop unnecessary use of water by using sink plugs for rinsing dishes in the kitchen or washing hands.**

✿ **Limit the number of times you wash dishes; use a dishwasher once a day at the most, and use it only when it is fully loaded.**

✿ **Wash only full loads of laundry in the washing machine.**

✿ **Wash the car less frequently, and when you do, use buckets rather than a hose, preferably while it is standing on the lawn so that the grass needs less watering, and use nontoxic soaps.**

✿ **Forsake the swimming pool. Mollison**

suggests turning it into an aquaculture system for raising fish and/or shellfish, and swimming at the beach or in rivers.

IN THE GARDEN:

✘ Use mulch extensively to reduce evaporation of water from the soil (see page 103).

✘ Use shade netting where appropriate for the same purpose.

✘ Water the garden in the morning to give the water time to be absorbed into the soil before the sun evaporates it.

✘ Water at intervals—at least one day between waterings.

✘ Water the garden by hand as much as possible to avoid overwatering and unnecessary runoff.

✘ Match plant species to your particular site. In arid regions, plant trees and shrubs that require little or no additional water other than normal precipitation.

✘ Store as much water as possible in productive biomass—plants or animals—on your land or in your garden. The denser the vegetation, the more water is stored, especially compared to bare ground.

✘ Improve the humus content of the soil, which will increase its water-retention ability (see previous chapter).

IN ADDITION TO SAVING WATER, MOLLI-son describes a number of strategies for harvesting and storing water for the home and garden. The main objectives of the strategies are to:

✘ Minimize the amount of water that runs off the ground and leaves your property without having been used at least once. Any water that does escape is wasted. A primary objective is to increase the degree to which water penetrates the soil. Increasing the soil's water-retention capacity also serves the dual function of improving your soil (see previous chapter).

✘ Slow down the water flow and divert excess water at the point where it originates (or as close as possible), or catch for use later. But most important, keep it on your property!

✘ Reuse the water on your property as much as possible, for example, by recycling and filtering gray water (see page 115).

Harvesting, Holding, and Storing Water

As Bill Mollison says, "Nowhere on earth is short of rain. Everywhere is very short of storage." Most precipitation simply escapes; Mollison estimates that 88 percent of precipitation in a chronically dry country such as Australia evaporates or runs off the land no matter where it falls, flowing unharvested and untouched back into the sea. There are a number of techniques for capturing water and storing it for domestic or livestock use, and/or for irrigation. It can be caught from the roof of your house and other structures in gutters and directed by drainpipes into storage tanks. (The top layer of water from the tanks should be diverted to the garden to avoid contamination by dust, industrial pollution, roofing materials, or birds). Alternatively, water can be collected on the ground in ditches or swales, culverts, and small dams, beginning on the highest slopes. These can then feed lower-lying areas by means of contour banks or diversion culverts that carry the water down and across slopes to other dams, ponds, or tanks (wherever possible, natural contours should be used to your advantage). Tanks, ponds, or dams can also be used to hold household gray water.

One of the key methods Bill Mollison uses to hold and store water is terraforming or landscaping—specifically, the creation of swales or ditches. Their purpose is to intercept the flow of water moving down sloping land, to hold it, and to act as absorption beds. Swales not only increase groundwater, reduce water runoff, and prevent soil erosion, but also boost the soil's water retention by as much as 75 percent. They should hold runoff for hours or days, until the water has a chance to infiltrate the soil at a slower rate.

Swales take the form of long, level (or nearly level) hollows or excavations of varying width; they are built sequentially, one above the next, along contour lines so each one catches the overflow from the swale above. If the lowest swale overflows during periods of heavy rain, then in theory there are not enough swales. On steeper property, swales should be deeper and terraced more closely.

A vital part of swale design is the planting of trees and plants on the downslope swale mound or bank. Water-loving crops that put out a prodigious amount of ground cover, such as squash and melons, can be profitably grown in these areas. The action of the roots of these plants and the gradual buildup of humus from leaves and other plant matter will increase the soil's rate of absorption of the water stored in

---

For we must needs die, and are as water spilt upon the ground, which cannot be gathered up again.

—II SAMUEL, 14:14

▲ Closely spaced crops growing in raised beds at Jeavons' biointensive demonstration farm. Note the cloches with removable tops, used as a semipermanent growing environment for tomatoes.

Double digging: loosening the soil at the bottom of the trench with a sturdy gardening fork.

◄ Double digging: watering the loosened soil at the bottom of the trench before moving on to double-dig the next section and cover the trench with soil.

► Double digging: excavating a trench with a spade across the narrow end of the bed. Note the digging board, which allows the gardener to avoid standing directly on the bed.

◄ Even in the depths of winter, "cold" compost piles are alive with activity. Pictured is one of Howard-Yana Shapiro's many anaerobic compost piles.

◄ Even amounts of the three essential components of compost—green vegetation, soil, and brown vegetation—by weight.

▼ John Jeavons' layered compost, containing nitrogenous (green) material, carbonaceous (brown) material, and soil. A compost pile in an advanced state of curing can be seen in the background.

▶ The steam rising from Alan York's compost pile on a chilly fall morning signals the teeming activity within and the heat generated by the decomposing material. York uses biodynamic teas to activate the microbes.

◄ Kitchen scraps and compost can be fed to worms in an enclosed bed, like this one. The worm casings make wonderful potting soil for starts, and worms can be transferred into the garden from time to time.

Chemical agriculture. ➤

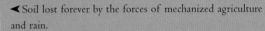
◄ Soil lost forever by the forces of mechanized agriculture and rain.

▼ Effective backyard terracing on a slope demonstrated at John Jeavons' minifarm.

▲ This seriously eroded Bolivian landscape, used for grain farming, has barely enough soil left to produce even a modest crop.

◄ Soil lost forever by the forces of mechanized agriculture and wind.

▲ River water is the silver thread of life and is essential for human activity. Especially in times of drought and in dry regions (such as the region of Bolivia pictured here), human civilization and agriculture seek its richness.

◄ John Jeavons' fertile one-acre biointensive demonstration farm, set on a hillside in Willits, California.

▲ Centuries-old Peruvian terracing has kept erosion at bay to retain the scarce arable soil.

▶ Alan York examining the richness of the organic matter in the soil at his orchard.

◀ Wheat patch grown by John Jeavons both for the grain and for its carbonaceous material (straw and chaff) when composted.

▼ Dried, salinated soil in a conventional cotton field in California.

▲ John Jeavons in front of his beloved madrone tree on his biointensive demonstration farm in Willits, California.

▼ Overall view of crops occupying raised beds, three to six feet across, at Jeavons' demonstration farm.

the swales and prevent waterlogging. Furthermore, in planting close to the moist swale areas, it is possible to take advantage of the collected water and minimize the amount of irrigation required, thus preserving water. In drier regions, this biomass will reduce the accumulation of salt because it will prevent repeated evaporation. Ideally, in addition, trees will shade the swales, further reducing water evaporation.

Mollison recommends that swales be set at a distance of between three and twenty times the average swale width, depending on the amount of rainfall and soil type. Thus, if the swales are 3 feet across and rainfall is greater than 50 inches a year, Mollison suggests a distance between swales of 9 feet; where rainfall is less than 10 inches, they should be 50 to 60 feet apart. Unlike dams, swale banks should not be compacted, so that water absorption by the soil is maximized, and their beds can be loosened and even filled with a layer of gravel or sand to achieve the same purpose.

This swaling technique can be applied equally well in the urban environment. For example, gutters can be placed across sloping cement driveways to slow the flow of water as it drains away and to divert the water flow toward lawns or plants on either side. Contouring paths so they wind gently between flower or plant beds will likewise divert runoff productively.

Tanks are a common and practical means of water collection in countries such as Australia (Mollison's homeland), but they are rare in the United States and Europe, and even in countries such as India, where rain is only seasonally abundant but clean drinking water is scarce. Tanks can be made of galvanized metal, plastic, concrete or cement, wood, or clay. They should be completely screened or covered to prevent leaves and other foreign material from collecting, and to avoid insect problems, such as mosquito larvae. (Alternatively, Mollison recommends introducing certain types of small fish to counter insects.) Algae will collect on the bottom or sides of tanks, but they are harmless and serve the purpose of filtering the water. To avoid disturbing them, the outlet pipe should be at least 2 or 3 inches above the bottom of the tank. Water destined for drinking should be passed through a carbon or ceramic filter system. A gray-water holding tank can save as much as 30 percent of total water usage for a family of four.

Different types and designs of dams are recommended for particular uses and landscapes; for example, saddle dams set in hollows of hilly areas for storage or wildlife use; horseshoe or ridge-point dams set on level ridges of a downslope, for similar uses; keypoint dams in valleys for storing irrigation water; and contour dams for irrigation or control of floodwaters in gently sloping areas (for more information on types of dams, diversion drains, and so on, see *Permaculture: A Designer's Manual,* by Bill Mollison). Essential dams (supplying household water or placed to prevent erosion, for example) may be lined with rock or concrete if the land is sandy and porous. If the soil is composed of at least 40 percent clay, the earth should be sufficient to hold the water. Any pond or dam also offers the potential of aquaculture.

The diversion drains that redirect runoff water or connect dams and tanks may be simple earth ditches, but using impermeable materials such as stone, concrete, or piping (culverts) will maximize water retention. The holding areas they lead to should in general be approximately one-twentieth the area of runoff to which they are linked. In dry or arid areas susceptible to occasional high volumes of water or flash floods, it is important to devise an overflow system that will divert excessive water without eroding the landscape, especially on steeper slopes; using grassed or paved spillways will accomplish this.

Another means of holding water, on flat ground as well as sloping land, is mulching (see page 103). Mulching reduces evaporation, and in protecting the soil from the detrimental effects of the sun, wind, and water, it minimizes erosion and avoids extremes of temperature. Mulch also retains water and moisture, allowing it to be absorbed by the soil more slowly, thereby reducing runoff, and it prevents or reduces the growth of weeds, which compete with other plants for water.

Using Water Efficiently

Another approach to conserving water in a garden setting is provided by John Jeavons at his hillside farm in Willits, California. "When we first started this project, a number of us recognized that we really liked home-brewed beer, so we decided we'd figure out what was the smallest area we'd need to grow all the hops and other ingredients for beer. We looked up the information and found out the average beer consumption per person in the United States, and we concluded then and there that there wasn't enough time, land, water, and other inputs to sustainably grow this amount of beer. We could grow some of it, but not all of it, and we did not want to deplete hundreds or even thousands of years' worth of soil and water for an unsustainable process.

"Once you start to become responsible on a closed-system basis for raising your own food, you get to see things in a different light. "Grow Biointensive" minifarming and gardening use water three to eight times more efficiently, and in some cases even better than that. So if everyone in California had been practicing gardening and agriculture this way, the more than six years of drought that affected the state in the late *1980s* and early *1990s*, for example, would never have happened, because one year's worth of water used conventionally could have produced food for several years biointensively."

One of the aims of Jeavons' work is to solve the problem of growing food with natural rainfall only, since *80* percent of agriculture worldwide does not have the option of using large-scale irrigation. He devotes a number of beds to experiments in dry-farming, or natural-rainfall, techniques: testing for viability of plant varieties, optimal spacing, soil composition, and so on. He and his associates plant the

beds just before the rainy season and at (or just before) the end of the rainy season, when the moisture in the soil is at a maximum, and do not water them thereafter. He experiments with thin mulches of straw or shade netting to minimize evaporation

> Water is good; it benefits all things and does not compete with them. It dwells in lowly places that all disdain. That is why it is so near to Tao.
>
> —LAO-TZU

and to protect some of the plants from the sun. Sometimes Jeavons simulates these conditions at other times of the year—by watering the beds to the same extent that the rainy season would provide moisture—in order to gain the necessary information on dry-farming techniques.

John Jeavons' methods, and especially his double-digging technique (see pages *100–102*), enable the soil to hold more water because of the enhanced air-pore space that is created. This also has the advantage of creating a medium in which biological activity is encouraged. The double-dug bed-preparation process (pages *100–102*) involves generous watering at each step, ensuring that the soil begins with adequate moisture, so that far less is required later. Jeavons regards his raised beds as a type of terraform, in the same vein as Mollison's permaculture landscaping but on a smaller scale—they are effectively "basins" for catching water and retaining nutrients.

Further, Jeavons' emphasis on building

Teaching Our Children About Sustainability

"We need to have the things we believe in introduced through the school system, when our kids are growing up," says Alan Kapuler. "The active thing we can do, in addition to gardening, is to introduce gardening in our schools, so our kids are encouraged to touch, nurture, and work with plants and soil."

soil and composting provides a key to saving water in the garden. Jeavons notes: "Compost alone can reduce water consumption up to seventy-five percent; that is, you can end up using twenty-five percent of the water you would use without compost. Then, with the miniclimate and humidity 'bubble' created close to the ground by biointensive close-spacing techniques, you can save even more water, up to an additional fifty percent. Add in the effect of having the correct nutrients in the soil available to the plants, which can reduce water consumption by up to seventy-five percent on top of that, and you can grow certain crops such as zucchini under optimal conditions with as little as three percent of the amount of water per pound of food produced that you might use with other techniques. We've done close to that."

In dry regions, Jeavons sometimes advocates triple digging beds to a depth of 36 inches rather than the 6-inch average in normal agriculture. Triple digging creates 50 percent more air-pore space in the soil, and that can help hold water. A good crop can be grown with just *10* inches of water retained in the soil. To retain *9* inches of water in a triple-dug growing area, you would need about *20* inches of natural rainfall. In a dry region that receives as little as 5 inches of rain per year, therefore, you need to take the rainfall from an area three times larger than the one used for growing crops and add it to the growing area's rainfall for a total of 20 inches of rainfall introduced in the growing area. For this purpose, Jeavons is experimenting with water catchment systems, thin mulches, crop spacing, and crop varieties that can grow well with minimal water.

Taking Action

On a broader level, simple solutions exist and obvious policies can be implemented to alleviate issues of water shortage and pollution. A key to effecting such change is education: teaching your children, other family members, neighbors, and friends about the issues. Perceptions and practices have to change, which requires the active involvement of the individual; implementation must begin in and around your own home. It is just such actions by citizens' groups that have led to the restoration of Chesapeake Bay on the East Coast, for example. Various civic groups are working together to educate the public and to promote individual action for preserving the bay, and these groups have also involved local municipalities and enlisted their support and resources to effect change.

A massive increase in the demand for organically grown produce would obviously contribute greatly to the reduction in use of polluting chemicals, herbicides, and pesticides. Already some large agribusiness concerns are experimenting with or beginning organic programs, proving that it can be done. By supporting companies that do this, you can vote for change with your dollars!

Agriculture is truly sustainable only if it is practiced within the limits of the local watershed rather than solely according to the dictates of the market economy. However, this equation requires a willingness to change our consumption habits and to change the way that agriculture is perceived. It also requires us to reevaluate the prices that should be paid to reward practices that give priority to sound water conservation and protection. Specifically, sustainable organic gardening not only seeks to create habitats, but also points to the desirability of variety of land layout in high-catchment areas: a mixture of forest, arable land, and grassland, which provides the optimal mix for absorbing and storing precipitation and preventing runoff that might lead to erosion. It also uses practices that do not pollute our water tables, streams, rivers, and oceans. It stresses the role of crop rotation and composting in humus development to enhance water retention.

Ultimately, we will receive clean water only when we collectively demand it. Let your elected representatives know that current practices are unacceptable. Write them letters, send faxes and e-mail, and telephone them to demand change. The National Academy of Sciences has reported: "There exists some technology or combination of technologies capable of dealing with every hazardous waste so as to eliminate concern for future hazards." Most of these technologies are commercially available; if they are not being used, it is because producers and users of pollutants choose profit over ethical and prudent behavior.

Demand ecosanity and the abolition of unsustainable water subsidies; demand instead the introduction of "depletion" quotas or taxes, especially in dry regions, for water and other nonrenewable (and even renewable) resources. In the western United States we must address—sooner rather than later—the unregulated,

short-sighted population expansion and water-intensive farming practices that are encouraged by public subsidy. These trends must be discouraged and even reversed, since water resources are being irrevocably depleted. Subsidies should be given instead for dry-land farming and for growing crops using techniques such as drip irrigation.

Our opinions must also lead the campaign at the local level to demand strict enforcement of clean-water regulations. We must look around us, and each of us must demand of our local officials close monitoring of industrial waste and the installation of power-station and heavy-industry smokestack scrubbers to minimize sulfur emissions and thus significantly reduce acid rain. We must insist on tough standards for auto exhaust, starting with our own vehicles, limiting carbon monoxide and nitrogen oxide emissions.

Meanwhile, as homeowners, we can replant our water-thirsty lawns with site-appropriate plants that thrive without lots of water—or maintenance, for that matter. We can set up or get involved in recycling projects that will ultimately save water and reduce pollution, switch to solar power and support other forms of "clean" power such as harvesting the wind, use non-toxic cleaners in our homes, install home waste filters and gray-water tanks, and follow the other suggestions for the garden and home that this chapter has offered.

As individuals or small groups, we can ultimately make a difference on a global scale. A perfect example of this is local and community tree planting, which can have an impact far beyond the local environment. In John Jeavons' words, "If everyone in the world planted just twenty trees and took care of them each year on an ongoing basis, and did this for five years, we would produce the world tree base we need in order to properly reforest the earth. If we don't, we will be in serious difficulty." In Australia, Bill Mollison has small teams of individuals who can plant up to five thousand trees per day, or twenty-five thousand per week.

Mollison is well aware of the positive intervention we can make in the water cycle by means of local topographic design. For example, he points out that cloud formation, humidity, and rain are affected by "condenser" tree lines, forested windward slopes, vegetation in general, and even minor topographical variations. It has been calculated that up to 40 percent of the rainfall in parts of Tasmania and Sweden is attributable to wind and clouds flowing over ridges forested with trees in excess of 20 to 30 feet in height. "Condenser" tree lines are most valuable on coastlines that lie in the path of afternoon or night breezes flowing from the sea to the land; for example, on subtropical trade-wind coasts, or the California coast. Conversely, absence of these trees could result in drought not only on the coastline but for a substantial distance inland. Massive but perfectly feasible plantings—and, conversely, the reversal of large-scale deforestation, especially in delicate and vital ecological areas such as the rain forests—can affect rainfall patterns significantly and on a wide geographical basis.

Mollison also describes methods of "creating" or encouraging rainfall by cloud seeding; the benefit outweighs any pollution we might see. Cloud seeding has been shown to have wide impact when done under certain favorable climatic conditions in locations such as over strategic down-wind hills. (In the same vein, it has been shown that local rains occur close to specific factory smoke emissions.) However, Mollison points out that once initiated, such effects cannot quickly be stopped, and ground storage systems must be planned ahead of time and be of adequate proportions to reap the benefit. Whether the solutions are effected at the micro or macro level, the knowledge and technology exist for all of us to safeguard our supply of water and to keep it clean.

IN SUMMARY, A KEY TO REVERSING THE trends of depletion and pollution of water is widespread understanding and awareness of the issues. It is only when we realize as individuals within our larger society that water is not limitless in supply, that it is not a completely and instantly renew-

able resource, that we will embrace the simple solutions that master gardeners such as Bill Mollison and John Jeavons have expounded and pioneered. At the same time, we must understand that our current methods of commercial farming and industrial practices are poisoning our water. As a race, we are soiling our own nest and are rapidly making it unlivable. We are creating and permitting the use of toxins and poisons that we, our children, and our neighbors are ingesting. Each of us, in our homes, gardens, and beyond, can take meaningful individual action to preserve water and to protect its quality. For the future of the planet, these actions must be taken now, by all of us, each and every day.

5
kinship gardening:
Fostering Biodiversity

Each of us bears a responsibility for maintaining our planet's unique and beautiful diversity for future generations. As gardeners, this means taking individual action to preserve the wealth of ornamental, medicinal, and food plants, as well as those wild species with no currently known use. As native inhabitants succumb to human intervention, plants are becoming extinct on a widespread and drastic scale. The United Nations has estimated that up to *15* percent of all plant species face extinction by the middle of the twenty-first century. Scientist and author E. O. Wilson estimates that 20 percent of all species on the planet could disappear within the next thirty years. Still other botanical experts predict the extinction of up to 25 percent of all species within our lifetime. Regardless of which of these estimates is closest to the true level of loss, the result, as Wilson observes, is that "what humanity is doing now in a single lifetime will impoverish our descendants for virtually all time to come."

This precipitous loss of biodiversity, for which humans and their impact on habitat and the environment are largely responsible, has chilling ramifications for the health of the ecosystem as a whole and for the human food chain in particular. Plant diversity is vital in ensuring the future of our food supply. Biodiversity can be thought of as a "bank" of genetic material that can be drawn on by us and future generations to improve crop quality and yields, and to cope with changing environmental conditions. Diversity provides species that can grow in different climatic conditions, terrains, growing seasons, and altitudes, and it constantly provides resources for keeping ahead of continually evolving pests and plant diseases. Variety, after all, is the spice of life, and the dazzling choice that diversity offers in our food plants is preferable to the homogeneous food that results from standardized monocrops.

The tendency in large-scale modern agriculture around the world is toward uniformity and standardization of landscapes rather than diversity. Emphasis is placed on productivity through monocropping and maximization of yields, and the technology employed is inherently destructive. We have witnessed a tremendous loss of wildlife habitat from the creation of huge farms with fields strictly for production, the widespread use of herbicides and pesticides, indiscriminate logging, the transformation of wetlands and other marginal areas of huge diversity into arable farmland, and urbanization. We are confronting an ecocrisis, and the trend puts us on the path to catastrophe.

Half of the food grown in the United States today is produced on just 4 percent of all farms in the country, and these are almost exclusively planted in monocrops. This trend is due in large part to the exodus from the farms to the cities since World War II; by 1990, less than 2 percent of the country's population lived on farms, compared to 23 percent fifty years before. Because farms today are large modern agricultural businesses that plant single crops with genetic uniformity, much of our food is based on little diversity.

The dangers of reduced genetic diversity are clear. The Irish potato famine of the mid-nineteenth century was caused by the fact that only a few types were grown in Ireland, and those types had minimal, if any, genetic variability. In *1845* and *1846*, with the Irish population almost completely dependent on potatoes as a staple, famine resulted when a potato blight rotted the entire crop in the ground. Up to a million people (or one in eight) died, and another million or more emigrated.

Similarly, in the United States in the late *1960s*, southern leaf blight destroyed as much as *15* percent of the largely homogeneous midwestern and southern hybrid corn crop, at a cost of more than $*1* billion. Resistance to the blight was achieved only by introducing the genes of various types of Latin American and African corn. However, despite this lesson, the potential for disaster remains. Paul Raeburn, in his book *The Last Harvest*, observes: "Each of the million cornstalks that springs from the rich soil of the U.S. corn belt is nearly an identical twin of every other one. You do not have to be an expert to see it. The corn plants are of identical height and shape. The ears are indistinguishable. Each has the same genes for leaf size and stiffness of stem.

"By focusing on a handful of the very best varieties, grain-belt farmers continue to squeeze ever better harvests from their fields. But there is a downside to this concentration on the same few corn varieties. Never before have so many millions of acres around the world been covered by plants that are so nearly identical. American farmers, part of one of the most productive agricultural enterprises in history, are waging a genetic gamble. They are 'betting the farm' in a way they never intended. Many are not even aware of the risks they face."

Genetic manipulation to produce pest-resistant but identical corn on such a widespread scale may seem to work in the short term, but nature's inevitable and continued mutation is likely to rebound on the farmers. Raeburn concludes that the pests and diseases "will exact their biological revenge. Seed companies and farmers ought to take a lesson from Las Vegas. You can keep a winning streak going for a long time. But in the end, the house always wins."

Similar problems affect America's gardens. They can be seen in the often mundane actions of gardeners to "tame" the wilds of their backyards, replacing native plants with popular but inappropriate species for their locations. Readily available seeds or plants are offered, selected, and grown without thought given to diversity, and the natural habitats of animals and their food supplies are destroyed, leading to whole local communities of plants, animals, and insects disappearing from their native locales. As gardeners, we face the reality that the major seed companies effectively control which seed varieties are available, a situation reinforced by consumer demand for uniformity and predictability. Moreover, the biggest seed companies in the world today are owned by multinational corporations who largely do not sell seeds as their primary business. Of the ten largest, three are primarily chemical companies and one is a pharmaceutical business.

It is in the vested interests of some of these major seed companies to offer a limited variety of seeds, some of which have been genetically developed to *require* chemical application; specifically, those chemicals also produced by the company. The trend in gardening, as in farming at large, has been away from the historical practice of individuals saving their best seeds, often family heirlooms, for future planting. Increasingly, the large multinational seed companies control the production and sale of seed, in part to return their development costs and also to reap the profit annually. The priority for these companies is profitability and market share, an understandable but tragic primary goal in today's world; they are not interested in preserving biodiversity despite the fact that such a foundation for a business could be profitable (not to mention essential for the human race).

Sara Stein touchingly documents the disappearance of diversity in her immensely readable book *Noah's Garden:* "I'm lucky to have spent my childhood summers among woods, streams, meadows, and marshes, but most suburbanites have never searched for frogs' eggs, caught fireflies in a jar, or peeked into a grassy nest of adorable baby mice. As the years pass, fewer and fewer people will long for the call of bullfrogs. Today's children, growing up on lawns and pavements, will not even have nostalgia to guide them, and soon the animals will be not only missing but forgotten."

The same trends are apparent in the

gardens and yards of our towns and sub-urbs. Stein describes the scene in her part of the northeastern United States: "There are lawns (few species, many individuals), foundation plantings (count the kinds—yew, yew again, more yew, and a rhodo-dendron), ground covers (pachysandra, maybe juniper). Everywhere is impatiens [jewelweed], named for its impatience to throw its numerous seeds…. Count the kinds of street trees; ten fingers will do. Count the aphids on the roses; the digits of all the neighborhood's inhabitants are not enough…. Diversity of species is a form of safety in numbers—not numbers of individuals, but numbers of ways in which each individual's prodigious reproductive power is modulated by conflicts of inter-est among all the individuals with which it shares the land. The more species there are, the less likely it is that any one of them will get out of hand."

It is hard to disagree with Stein when she writes, "Our intelligence, however pro-digious we like to think it is, is trivial com-pared to the accumulated wisdom of the hundred million species that make up the earth's biosphere. Since each microbe, ani-mal, and plant possesses some minute por-tion of the know-how that makes the whole earth work, the loss of any species

erases some portion of organic intelligence, and leaves the land more stupid."

Kinship Gardening

Alan Kapuler, Ph.D., biologist, botanist, and Research Director of Seeds of Change, the Santa Fe–based organic and heirloom seed company and organic food company, has devoted much of the last twenty-five years to devising a strategic plan for preserving plant diversity and examining how this plan translates into garden design and the choice of plants for our gardens. His strategic plan—kinship gardening—represents a road map to the gene pool of the plant world, providing

One touch of nature makes the whole world kin.

—WILLIAM SHAKESPEARE, *Troilus and Cressida*

a guide to the plants we need to save to preserve biodiversity for future genera-tions. Kinship gardening is an innovative concept that supports in a practical way the conservation of plant diversity. If done on a massive scale cooperatively by indi-vidual gardeners, it would make possible the preservation of our living inheritance. Kapuler's concept developed from the realization that our homes and backyards can and must play an important role in preserving diversity. We need to grow and care for as many different kinds of plants as possible. Indeed, Kapuler believes that "a solitary yet committed individual or family can energetically work to create an alternative to the widespread ecological destruction by developing a collection of diverse plants."

Alan was captivated by the wonder of plants and their diversity at an early age. He received a degree in biology from Yale University before he was twenty and later a doctorate in molecular biology from Rockefeller University. He became fascinated with the historical process involving botanists—many great, many unknown— who collected plants all over the world and catalogued and described them. He was particularly interested in analysis of the relationships between plants and the complex grouping of plants into families. Then, when he began gardening himself, he started to save seeds. One of his first interests was tomatoes, to which he was attracted by their diversity. He grew cherry tomatoes, salad tomatoes, tomatoes that made good paste, tomatoes high in beta carotene, and a wide range of other tomatoes that were rare or unusual. After a few

years, he realized there was a limit to how many varieties of tomatoes he could manage (and wanted to grow), especially as he was particularly interested in growing as many of the other known vegetable and fruit crops as he could. From there, his interest turned to other members of the same family—Solanaceae—which includes potatoes, eggplants, peppers, groundcherries, tobacco, and petunias, among many others.

As a biologist, Alan realized that this relatively small but vastly important food plant family was one small piece of the huge fabric of diversity, and that this fabric, which is our heritage, was progressively shrinking. While he knew little about the fabric as a whole at this point, Alan appreciated its importance and determined to make it his life's work. As he succinctly puts it, "In order to preserve diversity, one must first know its structure.

"Computer buffs learn early on about the 'save' command. Most of us lose an important document or records of untold hours of accumulated work before it becomes an ingrained habit to take care of what we have done. Strange that it may take computers to show us what we must do to take care of the biosphere in which

▲ The denser the vegetation, the more water is stored, especially compared to bare ground. A river of plant material covering an orchard floor.

◄ Without the benefit of shade netting, similar effects can be achieved with rudimentary plant materials, such as in this nursery in Honduras.

▲ Using these elementary tools, a Permaculture crew of five can plant as many as five thousand trees a day, twenty-five thousand a week, and well over a million trees in a year.

▲ Shade netting diminishes the amount of direct sunlight, therefore keeping the plants and soil cooler and reducing evaporative transpiration.

➤ Contour banks and culverts on Bill Mollison's property move water gradually down a slope.

➤ A backyard perennial kinship garden in New Mexico showing a collection of over four hundred specimens, including malvas, cacti, nitrogen-fixing plants, araliaceae, mints, and sages.

▲ Even in times of
serious drought, swales
still exhibit their ability
to hold moisture and
nourish life. This
photograph was taken
at the Permaculture
Institute in the seventh
year of a drought.

◀ Sweet potatoes pro-
ducing prodigiously in
the microclimate of a
moisture-holding swale.

◄ Aerial view taken of swales at the Permaculture Institute in New South Wales, Australia. Many of the swales empty into a system of ponds and dams.

► Rinsing fermented tomato seeds to cleanse the pulp from the viable seeds.

◀ Crushing ripe tomatoes as a preliminary step before fermenting and wet cleaning.

➤ Brassicas from selected varieties going to seed.

▼ Bagging sorghum seed heads at the Land Institute, Kansas, to control random movement of pollen.

▲ Studying Torpedo Red bottle onions in the field to select for their desirable archetypal characteristics.

◄ Selecting open-pollinated red sweet corn at the Seeds of Change research farm.

▲ Biodiversity in the back garden: beauty, habitat, and a healthy ecosystem at the micro level.

◄ One can examine a kinship of mints in a very small space.

◄ A small section of the Seeds of Change kinship garden focusing on the agave family demonstrates different colors, textures, heights, and shapes.

▶ A small sampling of the amaranth gene pool.

▼ Part of the kinship garden succulent collection. When growing different species of plants in the same family together, an infinite variety of likenesses and connective characteristics becomes apparent.

we live. Daily, moment by moment, we are losing the diversity that has survived and accumulated during the billions of years of biological life on this planet. The loss, dimly appreciated by most of us, is only the more tragic within the perspective of the wonder and loveliness of life.

"From the perspective of a single human lifetime, it takes a while to appreciate the magnitude of billions of years of uninterrupted biological evolution. As a species we are strongly dependent on the plant kindom." (Kapuler refers to "kindom" rather than "kingdom" to indicate the relationship of kinship domains rather than a hierarchy or monarchy.) "The gene pool is the collected set of biological experience stored in organisms inside the cellular chromosomes. It is the source of organisms. It is our past and future. We inhabit a rapidly changing present. Little more than one hundred years ago there were no cars, no home electricity, and no computers. One hundred years from now we may see the continued profound reduction in the diversity of living creatures. It is a good time to plant gardens enriched in the still available genetic diversity."

Kapuler's work is driven by the loss of plant diversity and the extinction of plant species. Amplifying this trend is the fact that certain valuable heirloom (and even recently bred) food, medicinal, and ornamental cultivars are losing favor with seed companies, and are becoming increasingly unavailable. Kapuler's research increased his awareness that food and medicinal plants cluster in the same genera, and these genera have lost species. "Among plants, about half of the species are endemic to small regions. While they may be great in numbers in those locales, they grow in only a few places in terms of the whole planet. For example, the coast and giant redwoods of California and Oregon.... About a quarter of our genera that have locally distributed species are at risk of extinction.

"For example, seed supplies for more than eighty percent of the known genera of daisies are very scarce or unavailable," remarks Kapuler. "References to the predominantly rare and obscure genera and species are in the scientific botanical literature. They are not included in any of the popular, common, or available texts used by horticulturalists or gardeners." Without a structured approach to preserving these species, they may well be irrevocably lost. Kinship gardening also empowers us to witness evolution and in the process to

Guide to Taxonomic Terms

Taxonomy, the science of naming organisms, dates back to Aristotle; modern taxonomy was developed in the eighteenth century by Carolus Linnaeus. The immensity of plant diversity is one of the most difficult things to comprehend, yet with Dahlgren's mapping system, it is simplified so that the individual plant can be seen in terms of the whole. ✵ Classifying plants on an ascending hierarchy of categories, each *species* (defined as a group of individual plants or cultivars that share many characteristics and interbreed freely) clusters to form *genera* (groups of plant species with similarities in form and general appearance, growth habits, and cultural requirements). Genera in turn fit together to make *subtribes* and *tribes*. These groupings form *subfamilies* and *families* (groups with similarities in flower and fruit form), and they group to form *orders* of plants. Groups of orders organize to make the final categorization of *superorders*. Thus, for flowering plants, there are approximately 280,000 species that exist within 14,600 genera, grouped into about 200 tribes (and 3,000 subtribes), 540 families, within 106 orders, which in turn are organized into 32 superorders.

learn about diversity and to be involved in its conservation—no small ideal.

A Road Map for Diversity

Kapuler's kinship gardening approach, which he describes as "a new kind of gardening," is based on the work of the eminent Danish botanist Rolf Dahlgren, who in the mid-1970s first mapped in great detail the complex and extensive interrelationships between angiosperms—flowering plants—beyond the family level. Dahlgren organized the kinship relationships of all flowering plants into a single layout or map using a multitude of traits, and he filled innumerable gaps in knowledge in the way plant life fits together as a whole. (Sadly, Dahlgren was killed in a car accident in 1989.) Kapuler and the Swedish biologist Olaf Brentmar amended and extended Dahlgren's mapping format to include all plants, including members of the other major divisions in the plant kindom, as follows:

↙ **Angiosperms**—Flowering plants with roots, stems, leaves, and well-developed conductive tissues. They produce seeds within a closed chamber. By far the most numerous group of plants and the most important to humans, as virtually all our food plants and common garden flowers are angiosperms.

↙ **Mosses**—Quite possibly the first land plants; small, nonflowering green plants such as liverworts and hornworts.

↙ **Psilophytes**—Spore-bearing vascular plants—whisk ferns—with only two genera; one is tropical, native to Mexico and the Caribbean, the other an epiphyte distributed throughout the South Pacific and Oceania.

↙ **Club Mosses**—Also known as ground pines. Also among the first land plants. More closely related to ferns and horsetails than mosses; most types are tropical.

↙ **Horsetails**—Rushlike perennial herbs with conspicuous joints.

↙ **Ferns**—Nonflowering vascular plants that reproduce by spores.

↙ **Cycads**—Large subtropical and tropical seed plants related to conifers, with the appearance of palms or ferns. Fossil evidence shows them to be common in prehistoric times.

↙ **Gingko**—Also known as the maidenhair. The sole surviving species of a group of ancient plants. A slender ornamental tree with fernlike leaves.

↙ **Gnetophytes**—Tropical gymnosperms. Mostly trees native to Africa and woody vines native to Asia.

↙ **Conifers**—Mostly evergreen trees and shrubs that bear their seeds and pollen on separate scale-structured cones.

IT IS ESTIMATED THAT THERE ARE BE-tween half a million and one million doc-umented species, varieties, and cultivars in the plant kindom; of these, we can identify about 280,000 species of angiosperms, or flowering plants. (It is believed that per-haps about 90 percent of all plants that grow on the planet are known to us and have been classified. Unfortunately, some of the remaining 10 percent or so will be-come extinct before they can be identified.)

While most botanical texts focus on species, genera, and families, Kapuler be-lieves that to fully comprehend the scope of plant development (and thereby to construct a road map for diversity), it is important to understand the connections between plant families and their larger in-tegral units. The bibliography for this chap-ter (at the end of the book) contains most of the necessary information for flowering plants (angiosperms) as well as some of the other divisions; Kapuler's works are an excellent place to start.

Within the division of angiosperms, for example, Dahlgren identified 540 fam-ilies, 106 orders, and 32 superorders. Kapuler observes that although habitats are disappearing and species going extinct,

knowledge of the structure of the plant kindom allows us to make a representative subset of the vanishing diversity. Dahl-gren's mapping system is the best format we have for understanding the connec-tions within and between the major plant groups. Dahlgren's system provides an organizational structure for building gar-dens based on kinship (also referred to as "sampling gardening" by the J. L. Hud-son seed catalog), giving us the practical means for achieving a representative sample of the plant kindom in our own gardens.

Planting for Diversity

A stunning diversity of plants can be grown in our gardens and greenhouses, on our decks, and even in a window box or two. Seeds can be obtained from companies seeking to perpetuate diversity, such as Deep Diversity, Seeds of Change, Seed Savers Exchange, Native Seeds/SEARCH, J. L. Hudson, Seedsman, Exotica Rare Fruit Nursery, Oregon Exotics, Prairie Moon Nursery, and Elixir Farm Botan-icals (see Resources on page 221). "One can do something very significant in a very small space," notes Kapuler. Specifically, he advocates that we each take a group or family of our favorite plants, research them thoroughly, and plant them in a phylogeny, or evolutionary pattern reflecting their developmental history. Some people collect orchids, others roses. Many of us have small collections of cacti or succulents. Kinship gardening is about actively and thoroughly investigating a particular botanical area and specializing in a diverse collection of closely related plants—not just randomly collecting or planting a favorite species.

Kapuler points out that if just one million people around the world tended a single species in their family for generations, as has been done in the case of heirloom beans in the United States through Seed Savers Exchange, we could distribute the half million or so known plant species twice over. Kapuler wishes passionately that large numbers of people would become engaged in a kinship approach, and that they would garden more to learn more. "Wouldn't it be marvelous if every town and city in the country had a town or city garden? Then, residents and visitors alike could walk in and see the diversity of the local wildflowers and plants, and learn which are the rare and endangered species.

"Understanding diversity will rely on gardens organized genealogically," says Kapuler. "Conservation will rely on gardeners whose kinship gardens become the sanctuaries for diversity and the vehicle for learning. Kinship gardening can be viewed as the experimental science of horticulture. Botanical scientists, by providing analytical genealogies that illustrate the structure of the many plant groups, and gardeners, by maintaining living collections of plants, are essential allies. This combined endeavor allows us to understand which species, genera, tribes, and families need to be collected and maintained. This much-needed human feedback loop is essential for the conservation of diversity to succeed."

Kapuler believes that creating and maintaining gardens that contain and demonstrate the marvelous fabric of interrelationships are of major importance. These gardens, notes Kapuler, would be "conservatory in design and didactic of genealogy. As we eliminate some species, others become chosen to become enhanced, sometimes enormously." Kinship gardening provides a framework for systematically sampling the diversity of the gene pool of the plant kindom. Garden beds can be planted in such a way that the layout is coevolutionary—biogenetic neighbors are planted together to emphasize their long-term kinship and to provide a living view of the course and consequences of evolution. It also draws attention to the many species and families that, while integral to the gene pool, are rare, or may have been little used or considered by our civilization (especially if they are incidental to our food and fiber production system), or are difficult to cultivate.

Models of Kinship Gardening

According to Dahlgren, there are 32 super-orders of angiosperms. Angiosperms are particularly significant, because almost all of the plants providing us with food and medicines belong to this group. With

> In order to preserve diversity, it helps to have a working model of its structure.
>
> —ALAN KAPULER

about 280,000 species of angiosperms, how does the individual gardener determine which plants to grow? There are several alternatives. One would be to grow only the rarest and most endangered species you could find. Another option would be to grow representatives of each superorder in its own bed, requiring 32 beds of whatever size the available space

allows. Three of the superorders and 15 of the 106 orders are exclusively tropical, requiring a greenhouse, and 14 of the orders are aquatic, requiring ponds or water containers. Outdoors, in the temperate zone, 28 of the 32 superorders and 93 of the 106 orders can be grown. Alternatively, you could grow representatives of a single superorder that happens to contain your favorite plants, and specialize in a particular family or species.

For example, let us suppose you particularly enjoy eating garlic, onions, leeks, and shallots. These plants all belong to the allium family, in the angiosperm superorder, the Lilianae, which in terms of species happens to be the largest of all the superorders. (See Diagram 3.) So you might decide to grow as many types of garlic as you possibly can, or alternatively, as many representatives of the genera of the allium family as possible, with the aim of maximizing diversity. Another approach would be to grow representatives of the other orders within the Lilianae superorder, which include orchids, lilies, irises, pineapples, and yams.

As a more specific example, let us assume you love lilies, gladioli, or irises. Within the lily order there are eight fami-

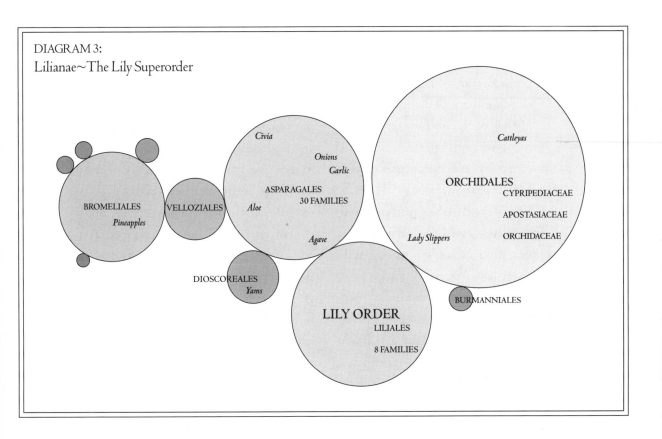

DIAGRAM 3:
Lilianae~The Lily Superorder

BROMELIALES
Pineapples

VELLOZIALES

DIOSCOREALES
Yams

Civia

Onions
Garlic

ASPARAGALES
30 FAMILIES

Aloe

Agave

LILY ORDER
LILIALES
8 FAMILIES

Cattleyas

ORCHIDALES

CYPRIPEDIACEAE

APOSTASIACEAE

Lady Slippers   ORCHIDACEAE

BURMANNIALES

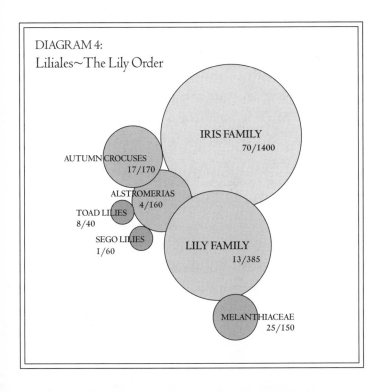

DIAGRAM 4:
Liliales~The Lily Order

IRIS FAMILY
70/1400

AUTUMN CROCUSES
17/170

ALSTROMERIAS
4/160

TOAD LILIES
8/40

SEGO LILIES
1/60

LILY FAMILY
13/385

MELANTHIACEAE
25/150

DIAGRAM 3:
Rolf Dahlgren advanced our understanding of all plants by analyzing traits such as cells, biochemistry, pollinators, and cohabitators, as well as flowers, leaves, stems, and bulbs. The bubble mapping system is a shorthand for organizing these myriad traits and relationships into a working model for planting in beds. The relative sizes of the bubbles represent the number of species that fall within each group.

DIAGRAM 4:
The first figure shown is the number of genera within each family; the second is the number of species. Note that the bubble map can be further extended to show relationships among the subfamilies, tribes, and subtribes within each family.

lies. (See Diagram *4*.) Table *1* shows some of the available representative cultivars in each family of the lily order that can be grown together in a temperate climate, and their main use (as ornamentals, medicinal plants, food plants, or herbs).

Likewise, within the Asparagales order of the Lilianae superorder, there are thirty families, which include species such as the aspidistra, lily-of-the-valley, garden asparagus, agave, aloe, tuberose, yucca (Joshua tree), red-hot poker, spider plant, harebell, hyacinth, amaryllis, snowdrop, and daffodil.

These examples demonstrate how, as individual gardeners taking responsibility to grow these coevolved plants together, we can preserve for future generations the treasure of the gene pool that has taken billions of years to evolve.

In collaboration with Swedish biologist Olaf Brentmar, and based on Dahlgren's work, Kapuler has also analyzed the remarkably large and diverse Asteraceae, or daisy family. There are *23,000* species in more than *1,600* genera and *14* tribes, including coneflowers, zinnias, marigolds, lettuce, chicory, burdock, sunroots (Jerusalem artichokes), dahlias, thistles, cosmos, sunflowers, asters, dandelions, calendulas, and chrysanthemums.

Most gardeners plant some of these species for food, for their beautiful flowers, or for their medicinal qualities. Which of this vast array of diversity should gardeners grow? Whether you have a tiny garden, a set of pots arranged on a deck, patio, or fire escape, or reserve a single bed in a larger garden, one can select one member of each of the *14* daisy tribes to construct a coevolutionary kinship learning garden. Alternatively, a gardener focusing on a single tribe such as sunflowers (Heliantheae) would have representatives of the *17* subtribes and *16* groups (within the subtribes), giving *33* kinds for an accurate genetic sampling of the sunflower tribe.

Exploring the Carrot-Ginseng Alliance

A further area of study for kinship gardening conducted by Kapuler is the carrot-ginseng alliance (the two families that make up the Araliales order of angiosperms), plants with an ancient history of human use as both food and medicine. (See Table *2*.) These two families include *489* genera and *4,611* species. Many botanists have considered the carrot-ginseng alliance to be closely related to the daisy alliance (Asterales), and numerous plants in both orders share common characteristics. Research continues into the natural kinships between these orders.

TABLE *1*
Some Representative Plants in the Lily Order

	FAMILY	GENUS AND SPECIES	COMMON NAME	COMMENT
1	Iridaceae	*Crocus sativus*	Saffron crocus	Medicinal
		Gladiolus x hortulanus	Garden gladiolus	Flower
		Iris x germanica var. florentina	Orris root	Medicinal
		Iris tenax	Wild iris	Endemic ⚘
2	Geosiridaceae	*Geosiris aphylla*	Earth iris	⚘ ⚘
3	Colchicaceae	*Colchicum autumnale*	Autumn crocus	Medicinal
4	Alstromeriaceae	*Alstromeria aurantiaca*	Chilean lily	Herb
		A. haemantha	Herb lily	Herb
5	Tricyrtidaceae	*Tricyrtis sp.*	Toad lily	Herb
6	Calochortaceae	*Calochortus elegans*	Sego lily	Food
		C. tolmiei	Pussy's ears	Endemic ⚘
7	Liliaceae	*Camassia quamash*	Camas lily	Food
		Chlorogalum pomeridianum	Wild potato (soaproot)	Cosmetics
		Lilium columbianum	Oregon lily	Endemic ⚘
		Medeola virginica	Indian cucumber root	Food
8	Melanthiceae	*Xerophyllum tenax*	Weaving grass	Endemic ⚘
		Melanthium virginicum	Bunchflower	Herb

⚘ Endemic—(local); because these plants are found only in one specific
  bioregion, they are by definition endangered

⚘ ⚘ Single species of leafless herb found only in Madagascar

Kapuler notes that "the words in our language, the chronicle of nations, the naming of plants testify to our long-term interaction with aromatic herbaceous plants that we now call umbelliferae or 'umbels,' in reference to their generally flat-topped flower spikes, which hold a multitude of small florets on a flat plane. In deciphering Linear B, the Mycenaean language of Crete, one of the first words to be decoded was the Greek for 'coriander'.... In fact, the umbels are the archetypal plant family. Their biological similarities provided support for the concept of biological families akin to those of humans and other mammals.

"As we are folk who eat carrots, parsnips, parsley, cilantro, celery, chervil, caraway, and cumin, umbels are familiar to us. As we are gardeners, herbalists, and biologists, angelica, asafetida, sweet cicely, skirret, Alexander's salad greens, English ivy, ginseng, gotu kola (a salad green and ayurvedic herb), and yampah (an edible root native to the Pacific Northwest) inhabit our backyards and flower beds, our kitchens and our cuisines. Nutritionally, the simple amino acid alanine is found in high concentrations in both carrots and ginseng. Although most of these plants are European natives, some come from Asia and others from North and South America." The greatest area of biological concentration of these plants is the confluence of Asia, Africa, and Europe—the so-called Fertile Crescent of the Tigris-Euphrates basin area bordered by Turkey, southwest Russia, and Afghanistan.

Kapuler notes that the old and venerable history of carrots, ginseng, and their relatives is a particularly interesting one, filled with contradictions. "Many names have come to us referring to these plants. Different people have routinely used different names for the same plants. Similarly, many times the same names have been used for different plants. This has led to a second-, third-, and fourth-growth jungle of names, references, identifications, and confusions. The plants themselves have clusters of close relatives, which makes identification difficult.

"Here in the Pacific Northwest, there are at least seventy species of desert parsley, genus *Lomatium*. It is the rarest and most diverse representative of the umbel family in our bioregion, and virtually none of the species are in cultivation. Yet indigenous peoples used them for food and medicine, revered them, and held them in great respect. The genus had been predicted by Luther Burbank as the progenitor of im-

TABLE 2

The Families, Subfamilies, and Tribes of the Carrot-Ginseng Alliance

	# GENERA	# SPECIES	EXAMPLES
1 | **FAMILY ARALIACEAE**			
Subfamily Aralioideae	**58**	**977**	
Tribe Aralieae	11	82	*wild sarsaparilla, ginseng*
Tribe Mackinlayeae	4	19	
Tribe Scheffleraeae	37	841	*English ivy*
Unassigned to Tribe	6	35	*Siberian ginseng*
2 | **FAMILY APIACEAE** (Umbelliferae)			
Subfamily Apioideae	**385**	**2,853**	
Tribe Ammineae	29	148	*caraway, ammi (bishop's tonic)*
Tribe Apieae	113	960	*dill, celery, celeriac, parsley, fennel, skirret, osha*
Tribe Cacaulideae	23	65	*cumin, orlaya*
Tribe Coriandreae	6	15	*coriander (cilantro)*
Tribe Dauceae	6	67	*carrot*
Tribe Echinophoreae	6	28	*prickly samphire*
Tribe Hohenackerieae	1	2	
Tribe Laserpiteae	9	69	*laserwort*
Tribe Peucedaneae	79	819	*lovage, parsnip, angelica, cow parsnip, asafetida*
Tribe Scandiceae	21	151	*chervil, sweet cicely*
Tribe Smyrnieae	41	305	*Andean carrot, Alexander's salad greens*
Unassigned to Tribe	51	124	
Subfamily Hydrocotyloideae	**35**	**532**	
Tribe Hydrocotyleae	11	372	*gotu kola, water pennywort*
Tribe Mulineae	19	155	
Unassigned to Tribe	5	5	
Subfamily Saniculoideae	**11**	**329**	
Tribe Lagoeceae	4	7	
Tribe Saniculeae	7	322	*eryngium, cilantro, tuberosa*

NOTE: A more complete breakdown of subtribes and database for species of the Araliales order can be found in *Peace Seeds Research Journal*, vol. 6, 1991 (Seeds of Change)

portant new food plants such as nutritious tubers and herbs, but the seeds are difficult to germinate and their rise to prominence will depend on kinship gardeners."

Kapuler finds it astonishing that, given their illustrious history and usefulness, these families of plants have so few genera in cultivation and that so few are available from seed companies. Their rarity, and our lack of skill in growing these interesting plants, makes them prime candidates for kinship gardening.

Kapuler hopes that "gardeners and conservationists will become more interested in collecting representatives, in saving seeds, and in organizing gardens that display the structure, diversity, and relationships among these plants. After centuries of taxonomy, we still don't have a natural

> # Saying is one thing and doing is another.
>
> —MONTAIGNE

framework appropriate to carrots, celery, parsley, parsnips, ginseng, sarsaparilla, and their kin. This portends the very important roles that gardeners will have in promoting understanding of plant relationships. In fact, conservation and relationship go hand in hand, and unless we take care of these biological treasures, herbaria replete with dead specimens will provide a record of the extinction of diversity."

Alan Kapuler Plants a Kinship Garden

After almost ten years of studying and writing about the working kinship model of the plant kindom, and after fifteen years of collecting thousands of diverse plants, Kapuler designed the layout for his own kinship garden and began planting in 1994. "To establish an intensely diverse, phylogenetically accurate, and taxonomically interesting kinship garden where the plants thrive is a demanding process," remarks Kapuler. Working with several friends, assistants, and volunteers, he planted his garden as a representative subset of the world's flora in a greenhouse on the Seeds of Change research farm just outside Corvallis, Oregon. This particular semitropical kinship garden environment is inside a metal-framed greenhouse measuring 30 feet by 90 feet, and 15 feet high, covered with a double layer of 6 mil polyethylene and inflated with two small squirrel-cage blowers. A minimum night temperature of 45 degrees Fahrenheit is provided by a natural-gas-fired heater along with two internal circulating fans. During the summer, circulation and cooling are provided by the doors at both ends and by rolling up the plastic at the very top of the end walls.

Kapuler notes the initial practical considerations: "There are an infinite number of possible gardens based upon the extraordinary variety of plants present on earth. However, there are limitations when one builds a kinship garden based on Dahlgren's layout. The first is the access to diversity: namely, what plants and seeds are available. The second is the constraints of your environment. Not surprisingly, these are the very same issues central to the development of life through evolution."

Kapuler describes the process of laying out the kinship garden: "Based on the map of the coevolutionary structure for the plant kindom, we established and labeled in the tilled plot, using wooden stakes, each of the thirty-two superorders of the flowering plants in its appropriate location. Before planting, we placed the diverse set of plants we had collected representing each superorder near its appropriate stake. To accommodate aquatic plants, we purchased three hundred-and-fifty-gallon plastic feed containers and sank them into the ground in the proper location to house the aquatic monocots and dicots.

"It is interesting, challenging, and daunting to discover that notwithstanding the immense amount of work that has gone into studying plants and establishing their kinship relationships, when it comes to making a garden representative of these studies, virtually nothing is known. Kinship gardening is a new area of biological research. My choice of plants for the initial garden was both historical and conceptual. For more than a decade, we had been collecting plants based on knowledge, curiosity, utility, fragrance, and happenstance. Survival and success of the plants we collected reflected our skill at horticulture, which in turn depended on the conditions in our other greenhouses and gardens.

"Ultimately, initial planting combined not only plants from our own collection but also those available from local nurseries, starts grown from seeds available by mail order and botanical gardens, the National Plant Germ Plasm System collection, and from collections we harvested in the wild. The first selection focused upon perennial plants that optimized diversity and already liked our local growing conditions. These plants were to be totem plants or representatives for the major groups. Thus a six-foot shrub of lemon verbena (*Aloysia triphylla*), a longtime denizen of our orchid greenhouse, was transplanted to the kinship garden as representative of the verbena family (Verbenaceae). Several five-foot papayas (*Carica papaya*, Caricaceae) were planted to represent the viola order (Violales). From Ecuador, we planted a cold-hardy custard apple (*Annona* sp., Annonaceae), basul (*Erythrina edulis*, Fabaceae, *Phaseolus* tribe), ice cream bean tree (*Inga feuillei*, Mimosaceae, *Inga* tribe), and a crown of the Andean carrot (*Arracacia* Apiaceae) as representatives of their respective orders in the magnolia, citrus, and carrot-ginseng superorders. At the unlikely location of a local store, I purchased an unlabeled pot containing a poor specimen of elegant aralia (*Dizygotheca elegantissima*, Araliaceae) as a representative of the ginseng family. It is now eight feet tall, in good health, and quite beautiful.

"Additionally, I planted seeds of the Australian blue lillipili (*Syzygium australe*, Myrtaceae), which grew into nice shrubs, and a seed of the rose apple (*Eugenia jambos*), which over the course of two years also has become a lovely potted shrub. Both species were eventually transferred from pots into the ground as representatives of the myrtle family, order, and superorder. We also had been collecting the lost crops of the Incas, plants that had been used by this culture but long since forgotten by modern cuisine and agriculture. We decided to use these plants, including the tamarillo (tree tomato), giant ground-cherry, Andean carrot, and yacon (a sunflower relative with edible tubers), as one of the aspects of the initial planting for their cultural and historical interest.

"One of the nicest early features of the kinship garden was the liberation of many potted plants from their tight and overgrown containers into a direct connection with topsoil. During the month of the initial planting, I had several fun and rewarding nighttime dreams in which the plants thanked me for facilitating their escape from pots! Nothing can replace the daily journey through one's greenhouse, hose and fog nozzle in hand, checking the success of transplants, the progress of growth, the development of flower spikes, the opening of flowers, the setting of seeds, and the maturing of fruits.

"As the more common families, orders, and superorders became represented in the kinship garden, locating representatives of rarer families, orders, and superorders became and continues to be more difficult. Furthermore, having acquired the seed, locating and placing plants combines botanical scientific knowledge, ecological insight, horticultural skill, and an intuitive savvy that Chinese people call *feng shui*. The aspects of shade and sun, soil quality, and water requirement all contribute to the growth and long-term success of the garden. Plants that initially do well don't necessarily survive the overwintering transition or some of the other ecological vicissitudes that occur during the cycle of seasons. Moreover, some vines need to be pruned back routinely to keep them from outgrowing their neighborhood, while others seed prolifically, becoming unexpected weeds.

"Basic tasks like weeding are important parts of maintaining the health, appearance, and utility of the garden. Cultivated beds of plants comprised of orders and/or superorders facilitate this and present the plants and their relationships in a clear, pleasing fashion. Well located and maintained paths also facilitate gardeners and visitors being able to take care of and enjoy the relationships held by the plants.

"Many times I am asked about problems with insects or other pests, or about how to successfully grow certain plants. Rarely has there been an insurmount-

able difficulty that the daily inspection of plants during watering has not helped eliminate. During our many years of greenhouse maintenance here in Oregon, the most significant plant destruction has come from mollusks. Nightly inspection with a flashlight is my simple cure. Pick 'em and remove 'em.

This is botanical horticulture in action; it is also conservation in practice. Botany students from the local university, Oregon State, have remarked that a few hours in the kinship garden did more for their understanding of botany than several years' worth of academic coursework.

—ALAN KAPULER

....

"After the kinship garden was planted with totem representatives for many of the major groups of plants, we decided to plant several annuals to fill out the area. In the cucurbits, we planted a single gourd plant that has white flowers (*Lagenaria siceraria*,

Cucurbitaceae) and two plants of a water-melon—citrus melon—used for making pickles (*Citrullis lanatus*, Cucurbitaceae). Among the daisies, we planted several marigolds. In the legumes, we planted several bush and pole beans. In the locale dedicated to the potato-tomato family, we planted several kinds of peppers, a large-fruited ground-cherry, a giant solanum, and a tree datura. Next to these, in the related morning glory family (Convolvulaceae), we planted some heirloom morning glories.

"Since part of the garden was rather empty and unplanted, we transplanted several kinds of castor beans, knowingly putting them in the 'wrong' place. I had reckoned that it would take several years to grow the basic kinship framework of the garden and that consistent with my other work of producing seed crops, it would be acceptable to use the space as needed while the longer-term goal was to establish everything in its appropriate kinship location. Thus, every once in a while an interesting seedling would arise, and rather than move it or remove it, we would leave it alone to grow, flower, seed out, and finish its cycle.

"Several times I mistakenly put plants in the wrong place entirely. For example, I thought that *Debregeasia edulis* was in the myrtle family, when actually it belongs to the nettle order (Urticales, Urticaceae). Two years later it was transplanted to the appropriate place. There is a certain patience essential for enjoying the process of watching the kinship garden evolve, develop, and thrive. Some of the errors have been as instructive as the victories.

"During the first year, several plants 'got away.' Most notable in this regard were the cucurbits. By early August of the first season, the gourd plant had made twenty- to thirty-foot runners and was threatening to overtake the whole garden. So we hung several twenty-foot-square pieces of netted shade cloth eight feet off the ground and encouraged the runners to climb onto the netting; we did the same for the watermelon runners. By the end of September, both plants had made a second tier, an actual second story for the garden, and more than fifty fruits matured during the next two months. We learned, however, not to plant rapacious annual cucurbits in the kinship garden."

During 1995, the second year of the kinship garden, several factors contributed to significant increases in its depth and diversity. Kapuler was able to purchase a fantastic collection of cacti, hundreds of kinds grown from seed. Likewise, he was offered extensive collections of succulents and gingers, covering a wide spectrum of families, genera, and species. In each case, these additions allowed for a more in-depth layout as family, subfamily, tribal, and superorder representatives were added to the kinship garden. Other acquisitions included a dwarf Cavendish banana and a beautiful China rose. Kapuler believes that with some luck, dedication, and perseverance, almost anyone can build a plant collection through contacts and acquisitions one makes pursuing this exciting interest.

Some groups that thrive in the temperate zone are noticeably absent from Kapuler's kinship garden, since the conditions in the greenhouse are semitropical. For example, the bellflower order and ranunculus superorder, which includes the poppies, are not included; likewise the dogwood superorder and major portions of the rose superorder, which includes the stone fruits, pome fruits, brambles, walnuts, chestnuts, and oaks. However, as the appropriate representatives are found, they too will be included; a temperate-zone kinship garden is in the planning stage.

Kapuler notes that there is always a place for an unusual, rare, or unrepresented group. Over the years, many plants get tucked away in a corner or on a bench and receive little attention because they fit in poorly within the larger groups that most of us collect. Since the kinship garden optimizes diversity, additions like this fit in and find a home much more readily than the more common plants that are easy to obtain and that are already represented.

"As for the future, I envisage a journey through the kinship garden that can be an unforgettable experience of the wonder and beauty of the plant kindom. During the years to come, the kinship garden needs to grow in many ways. We see that arching trellises will make it possible to create second and third levels so that upon entering the garden, one is surrounded at every turn by marvelous diversity and kinship strategy. As the trees and shrubs representative of the major groups become established perennials, they can become the home for epiphytes and sites for clusters of pots housing interesting relatives."

Most of all, Kapuler hopes the concept of kinship gardening will "take," and that diversity-based conservation gardens—"botanical arks"—will germinate all over the world. As he puts it with passion, "I urge you to look into gene pool diversity and grow a few friends!"

6

seed saving and selection:

Grow What You Like

Gardening is all about the interdependence of nature—and the independence to grow what you like to eat and what pleases your eye. Follow your passions by learning the basic tenets of seed saving and plant breeding. You will find yourself growing fewer monocultures in a garden of diversity, and tending to plants with greater resistance to disease and blight.

Boone Halberg, one of the world's foremost corn experts, is a sharp, witty, and gentle individual who works at the Institute of Technology in Oaxaca, Mexico. He is an expert in plant diversity, especially in the fertile Oaxaca Valley, southeast of Mexico City, which has been farmed continuously for over eight thousand years. Native cultures in the region today remain close to their agricultural heritage; ancient varieties of corn interplanted with squash and beans cover the rolling valley floor, and teosinte, the ancestor of corn, can still be found growing in fields. Halberg explains that Oaxaca has been a crossroads of plant and animal migration for millions of years. The region forms a unique continental bridge between the Southern and Northern Hemispheres, one that has allowed species to travel between the two. Halberg describes the process that has taken place over millennia whereby teosinte was most likely selected into what we know as our modern corn. Farmers have continually chosen varieties of corn for desirable characteristics such as size, flavor, vigor, nutrition, and beauty, and adapted their selection to their particular piece of property. Today, in the state of Oaxaca, there are eighty-five thousand farmers who grow corn, and they all have at least one of

their own varieties. Thus, there are a minimum of eighty-five thousand varieties of corn—true biodiversity.

In times gone by, gardeners and farmers saved their own seeds from the plants that they grew. Wild plants were domesticated and passed down through the generations, and crop diversity flourished, as it still does in Oaxaca. Seed saving used to be a necessity on a global level, and countless families brought their best and most familiar seeds with them when they emigrated to the United States. The inexorable move from farms and rural areas to the cities and suburbs over the past few decades has diminished the enormous diversity of this seed stock. Today, the major source of seeds is large seed companies, which, because of their size and the economies of scale that they operate with, are not well adapted to preserve and offer true diversity.

The number of seed companies has shrunk dramatically even during the last twenty years. Suzanne Ashworth observes in her book *Seed to Seed* that most of those going out of business have been, or are, smaller companies (often family-held endeavors) "that had been rich sources of unique varieties…. The collections being dropped, which sometimes represent the accumulated life's work of several generations of seedsmen, are often well adapted to specific regional climates and are resistant to local diseases and pests. Far from being obsolete or inferior, these may well be the best home garden varieties ever developed. It is entirely possible that half of the non-hybrid varieties currently available from seed companies could be lost during the next decade." This makes it all the more vital that we each take action to perpetuate the rare heirloom, traditional, and open-pollinated varieties that are available through organizations such as Seed Savers Exchange, Seeds of Change, and other sources of germ plasm listed on page *138* and in Resources on page *221*.

Most gardeners no longer save their own seeds, and most seed companies prefer hybrids because they are more profitable. The large seed companies, many of which are owned by large multinational chemical companies, tend to market proprietary, genetically inbred hybrids that are unique—and secret—in composition and production rather than more diverse open-pollinated varieties. Unfortunately, what

Patenting Plants?

Alan Kapuler has strong opinions on the patenting of specific plant lines by large companies. "I can't stand the patenting of stuff that is divine—it's not ours to own.

"We started a long time ago with systems that endorse violent behavior— the lion-eats-the-gazelle mentality. But we need to abandon this way of thinking, a way that's based on the idea of kingdoms, and replace it with thinking that's based on systems of kinship. We can take the gene pool we have and work with it to retool our ecology."

is good for the bottom line of these multi-nationals is not necessarily good for the independence of gardeners, for diversity, or for the security of our food supply. Most hybrids are unsuitable for seed saving because either they do not breed true or they are sterile. These traits place farmers and gardeners in a position where they must purchase new seeds each and every year. Hybrids also allow for ease of commercial harvesting, since the plants are genetically similar and tend to mature at the same time; however, this trait is usually not desirable for home gardeners who eat what they grow and generally need their crops to mature over an extended period of time. The genetic uniformity of hybrid plants also makes crops more susceptible to epidemic disease.

"Many of us remember our grandmother's seed jar and the paper bags of seed pods drying in the kitchen," writes Bill Mollison. "It is a public scandal that these seeds have now been patented or subjected to legal controls…. It is also scandalous that large multinational corporations have gained control over our main food plants via seed patenting. Without dedicated home gardeners, the diversity of seeds of our staple foods could not exist. Such seed resources are only safe in the hands of peo-

ple who save and grow them and eat their bounty." Fortunately, there are an increasing number of gardeners who save their seed from year to year.

Ashworth notes in *Seed to Seed* that "seed saving offers gardeners the opportunity to grow a bit of history in their own backyard. For thousands of years, seed savers have been the stewards and guardians of this valuable and irreplaceable genetic heritage….Vegetable gardeners must do everything in their power to maintain what remains, because extinction is forever." (*Seed to Seed* provides valuable reference information on a large number of vegetables and their seeds, including taxonomy, pollination characteristics and techniques, and general seed production, harvesting, and processing techniques.)

Seed Saving:
What to Collect and When

Whether you begin seed saving by being given (or tracking down) family heirloom seeds or by starting with a seed order from one of the sources given in Chapter 5, it is prudent to sow more seeds and grow more plants than you will need for eating. If you are growing outbreeding plants that cross-pollinate, clip the flowering part or remove the tassels (in the case of corn) of any plants that exhibit atypical or undesirable

A Conversation with Howard-Yana Shapiro

"I was a conscientious objector during the Vietnam conflict, and I was assigned to a series of African-American colleges in the South to work on their accreditation processes. While undertaking this work, I learned that everyone—black and white—saved seeds in the southern culture; in many cases, these were ancestral seeds of valued crops passed down through the generations. All this was very different from my frame of reference—I grew up in New York as a hip kid, or so I thought—and I realized then that I didn't really know anything. And I also realized that seed saving was the future. If these people had retained their culture and kept themselves alive by saving their seeds, then if I was to have any hope of remembering my culture in the future, I needed to turn to agriculture and take a hand.

"Later I became an anthropologist and studied culture, but I soon realized that I wasn't really interested in that—what I was really interested in was things like corn. I remember standing in awe in front of a field of corn. And that changed my life."

A Tribute to a Guardian of Garden Diversity

Curtis Showell is a tall, lanky farmer who lives on his family's land in Bishopville, Maryland; born in Virginia, he has lived in this area for nearly forty years. The land he works has been worked by several generations of his ancestors. "I got three bloodlines. On my dad's side of the family, I come from the Wooster Indians. On my mom's side, well, she is basically the same tribe Pocahontas was." (The third line is African-American.) With a wide interest in all of the cucurbits (except cucumbers), Curtis has amassed a world-class collection of seeds; it is a collection orchestrated by a self-taught genius. As a child, Curtis was taken with the growing of food. The family garden has always been a source of pride.

"I started out when I was a kid. I was about eight years old. A seed catalog came to our house, and we ordered seed for the family garden. The next year when the catalog came I noticed that some of my favorite varieties had disappeared out of the catalog. There wasn't a thing wrong with them. A lot of them were superior to these today. They had better flavor and their keeping quality was good. With some of the new stuff, the keeping quality is not that good and the taste is overrated. So I started collecting—no one else in the family, just me. I guess it was my instinct; after I had seen the disappearance of seed, I said I had better hold on to this here and stop wasting it. I have been collecting and growing ever since. I think they should be preserved for the next generation."

The list Curtis maintains is overwhelming: over a thousand varieties of squash and pretty close to a thousand varieties of melons. He uses the best criteria that any grower can when choosing which seed to collect and grow: taste. "I test them by eating what I grow and letting other people sample them too, to see if they agree with what I say. Of course, I have to pretty near shoo them away when the crops start to come in," Curtis says with a chuckle. In an age of ever-growing complexity, we are lucky to know gardeners like Curtis Showell. —*H.S.*

characteristics, or that are less vigorous, so they do not cross-pollinate or accidentally become plants yielding seeds to be saved (this process is called roguing).

Maintaining varietal purity is important. Pure seeds can be saved by isolating a single outbreeding plant variety from others so there is no risk of cross-pollination. The isolation distance varies from species to species. Isolation is difficult in communities where similar varieties are commonly grown in close proximity in adjacent gardens (so you may need to take your neighbors' gardens into account). Alternatively, to ensure purity, you can use techniques such as hand-pollination, physical barriers such as bagging or caging, or staggering plantings over time so that you plant a second crop as the first sets its seeds. Vegetables such as corn, lettuce, sunflowers, and annual umbels can be isolated this way, but it is important to have reliable information on the different maturity dates for accurate planning purposes. Alan Kapuler uses what he describes as ecostrategies to achieve isolation: that is, he plans his garden layout to do the job for him.

Once your plants are ready for seed harvesting, select the seeds of those plants that are free of pests and diseases and display desirable characteristics such as best flavor or high vigor. Make sure that these plants are marked or distinguished so that you, or members of your family, do not

> To own a bit of ground, to scratch it with a hoe, to plant seeds, and to watch the renewal of life—this is the commonest delight of the race, the most satisfactory thing a man can do.
>
> —CHARLES DUDLEY WARNER

harvest and eat them by mistake! Likewise, protect them as far as possible from birds and other natural predators. Of course, in some cases, such as tomatoes, squash, and melons, you can both extract the seeds and eat the fruit. Alan Kapuler is a great believer in "snibbiting," a wonderful way of "recycling" vegetables without waste. For vegetables such as carrots, turnips, and radishes, the roots can be eaten and the green tops (attached to the very top of the root) can be planted. They will then flower and yield seeds. Similarly, for onions and garlic, the bulb tops can be eaten and the roots (attached to the very bottom of the bulb) can be replanted to yield seeds.

In her book *Seed to Seed*, Ashworth makes a number of practical suggestions for plant selection in saving seeds. "Plant characteristics to consider during selection could include earliness, disease resistance, insect resistance, drought resistance, stockiness, vigor, color, lateness to bolt, hardiness, uniformity or lack of it, and trueness-to-type. Fruit characteristics that can be selected for include color, shape, size, thickness of flesh, productivity, storage ability, flavor, and many others…. Only plants that display good vigor should be selected to save for seed."

For example, with plants such as lettuce, brassicas, and root crops that bolt, or go to seed, at the end of their productive season, it is advantageous to select seed from those plants that are slow to bolt, thus extending their edible stage. After selecting individual plants with a prolonged leaf stage over a sufficient time period, it is possible to develop exclusively late-bolting varieties. In doing so, you perpetuate those plants that can be harvested for eating for as long as possible before going to seed.

One of the characteristics that gardeners care about the most is flavor. For those crops whose flavor you enjoy and that yield continuous pickings, such as peas or green beans, it is best to save the most vigorous bushes and leave them completely alone and unharvested until the pods are dried and the seeds are ready to save; meanwhile, harvest for food consumption the yield from the remaining plants. When lifting root vegetables for the winter, select the largest, healthiest, and most representative of the crop. With most fruit, size, flavor, appearance, and freedom from pests and disease are the main considerations.

Ashworth advises that population size is of paramount importance in seed selection: "To avoid decreasing the genetic diversity within a crop, seed should be obtained from the greatest possible number of plants that meet the selection criteria. Maintaining the genetic diversity within a population is the key to continued evolution and the ability of plants to adapt to varying environmental conditions." It is important never to select only the largest

A Conversation with Alan Kapuler

"I'm a child of the 1960s, of the peace and love revolution, and I lived for a while in a commune in Jacksonville, Oregon. One night I was cooking dinner at the commune. I cut the bottom off a bulb of garlic, threw it in the compost, and sautéed up the rest. Then I realized, how come I'm throwing away the part that's alive, the part that grows the roots? I realized in that instant how wasteful it was, and what violence it was to a living thing. By snibbiting—using the top of a head of garlic and replanting the bottom, which roots and grows again—you don't have to kill anything. Likewise, when I cut a squash open, it's important to save the seeds and grow them. You can eat with one hand and plant with the other, which is a marvelous thing to do.

"I realized that to change the world, the core issue is violence, whether the violence is done to the earth, to one another, or to the biosphere. They are all interconnected through the food system.

"So in preparing one meal, I realized that the food system was at the core of nonviolence. Nonviolence provides the answer; it holds the key to peace and love for all of us, and it is what still motivates my work."

or best-looking fruit for seed, which could create a bottleneck that eliminates most of the genetic variability in that variety. Ashworth suggests, "Instead, always strive to save an equal amount of seed from as many plants as possible that are the most true-to-type within the population."

In the case of outbreeding plants, in order to preserve diversity, it is best to grow a large number of plants and select seeds from each plant. Self-pollinated, inbreeding plants such as lettuce, beans, peas, and tomatoes contain relatively little genetic variability, and in theory, saving seeds from one or two plants is sufficient, although it is desirable to maximize genetic variability and select seeds from as many suitable plants as possible. Corn is at the other extreme; it is most prone to inbreeding problems and, as Ashworth points out, it "is highly sensitive to inadequate population sizes. Significant and irreversible damage can occur in a single generation if a large enough population is not grown."

In terms of specific numbers of plants from which it is desirable to save seeds and preserve genetic variability, Michael and Jude Fanton (who founded the Australian Seed Savers' Network) suggest at least twenty plants in the case of onions, leeks, and sunflowers; plant breeder Carol Deppe advises at least a hundred in the case of corn. For members of the squash family (cucurbits), at least five to ten fruits per variety, each from different plants, should be kept for saving seeds. While these numbers may be more than you need for your garden, you can use the rest as gifts for family and friends. There is a definite joy and satisfaction in sharing this harvest.

As for when exactly to collect seed for saving, Carol Deppe has a general rule that covers just about every fruit crop: Let the fruit ripen beyond table stage for as long as possible without its actually rotting, falling off, or being stolen by birds, squirrels, or other self-appointed sharers. The Fantons advise that for those plants whose seeds form the edible part, such as corn, beans, peas, and sunflowers, the seeds can be left on the plant until they are completely dry. In this case, however, take action in the event that wet weather sets in, or if predators such as mice and birds begin to attack the standing seed crop. In the case of plants such as lettuces, carrots, and onions, which let their seed fall on the ground when they are ripe, it is necessary to harvest them pro-

"From the Many, One, and from the One, Many"

Seed saving is the resource base of our society. Without it, there is no continuity in the cycle of life. To continue the cycle is to continue society, like raising a family; you hope your children will come of age in a better society. With seed saving and selection, the principle is to narrow down the desired characteristics from many plants to a single one, and then to grow out many more plants in a stable line from the one you have selected so these characteristics are passed on: This is the principle of "from the many, one, and from the one, many." Although populations are more successful at adapting than individuals, change occurs on the level of the individual rather than that of the population as a whole. Boris Pasternak wrote in *Doctor Zhivago*: "Gregariousness is the refuge of mediocrity.... Only individuals seek the truth." Those individual plants best adapted to our evolving environmental conditions are inevitably the ones that we select as gardeners.

—*Alan Kapuler*

gressively as they become ripe, especially in wet and windy weather. In general, plants are best harvested for seeds in the early morning, after the dew has evaporated, but when the pods and seeds are still too damp to shatter and scatter. They are best threshed in the afternoon, after the seeds and pods have dried out and can be easily broken.

Cleaning, Drying, and Storing Seeds

Seeds are cleaned in one of two ways: *wet processing* or *dry processing*. The wet-processing method is used for those seeds that are embedded in the damp flesh of fruits or berries such as tomatoes, eggplant, squash, and melons. Seeds that are dry-processed include those that are harvested from pods or husks that have dried in place on the plant, such as corn, beans, onions, lettuce, and most flowers.

Wet cleaning involves removing the seeds from the fruit and, where appropriate, letting the pulp, juice, and seeds ferment together as they would under natural conditions when the fruit falls to the ground and begins to rot. During this fermentation process, microorganisms destroy many seed-borne diseases, which is particularly important for plants such as tomatoes and

cucumbers. Next, the seeds should be washed vigorously in water to clean them and separate them from the pulp and juice. In general, fertile seeds sink, while sterile ones float. This process should be repeated until only fertile seeds remain. Then the seeds should be strained and cleaned under running water.

To dry the seeds, the best technique is to place them on fine mesh screens with wooden frames or to use a food dehydrator set at 95 degrees Fahrenheit (if you own a food dehydrator without a thermostat, be very careful and check the temperature closely). Do not dry seeds on paper, cloth, or nonrigid plastic surfaces as the seeds are likely to stubbornly stick to the surface. Spread out the seeds in as thin a layer as possible and dry as quickly as possible, in a warm but not too hot place, to prevent mold or germination. Stir the seeds occasionally and never dry them in direct sunlight, which might damage the seeds, or in a heated oven, although placing them in an oven with just the pilot light on and the door ajar is fine as long as the temperature remains below *100* degrees Fahrenheit.

With dry processing, the seeds are left to dry on the plants, but in rainy or frosty weather, the plants should be harvested and hung to dry in a garage, shed, or other suitable place. The seeds are then rubbed, threshed, or winnowed to separate them from the chaff—the husks, pods, petals, and other extraneous material covering or containing the seeds. Various techniques are used for winnowing, depending on the type of seed, but the basic method involves tossing the seed gently into the air from a container or basket and letting the chaff fall to the ground or blow away. Small fans or hair dryers with the heating element turned off are ideal for facilitating this process. Remember, fertile seeds are heavier and denser than sterile ones, so if using a fan, the ones that land nearer to the fan after being gently tossed in the air are mostly fertile, while those that land farther away are more likely to be sterile. With particularly light seeds or those with chaff that is difficult to separate, rubbing them through a suitable screen to separate the seed from the chaff is the best method. With smaller amounts of seed, you can swirl the dry seeds in a mixing bowl until the chaff separates to the surface and the seeds sink to the bottom. Large quantities of dried seed pods such as beans and peas can be placed in a sack and trampled to separate out the seeds.

Storing seeds is the most crucial aspect of seed saving apart from selection and breeding. In the absence of rodents, woven

---

For further details on harvesting, cleaning, drying, and storing seeds, consult the Seeds of Change catalog, Suzanne Ashworth's book *Seed to Seed*, Appendix F of Carol Deppe's *Breed Your Own Vegetable Varieties*, and *The Seed Savers' Handbook*. (See the Bibliography.)

---

baskets are ideal seed-pod storage containers; as Ashworth observes, "Many traditional Indian baskets are woven with seed collection specifically in mind. Baskets allow the air to circulate around the seed pods, which encourages further drying. Paper bags, cotton feed sacks, and cardboard boxes are also commonly used to collect seeds and seed pods.... It is best not to reuse bags or boxes, however, because seeds from the first collection often get stuck in their seams and can become mixed with a second seed harvest. Fruits, berries, and other seeds that are embedded in moist flesh are usually collected in plastic buckets, plastic deli tubs from the grocery store, and various kinds of bowls." Deppe likes to use onion bags and other types of mesh bag, and open paper bags. She also collects the cardboard trays used to ship soda cans to stores, and using the trays for this purpose is a wonderful way of recycling them.

Most vegetable and flower seeds kept in a dormant state in a cool, dry, dark, and airtight environment will maintain germination potential for between two and ten years. Some seeds, such as those of umbels and *Allium* species (which include garlic and onions), tend to be sensitive and should be planted the next year or kept in an airtight container in the freezer. "The greatest enemies of stored seeds are light, high temperature, and high moisture," advises Ashworth. "Seeds that are stored in fluctuating temperature and moisture levels lose their ability to germinate very quickly.... Always realize that seed vigor can be lost during storage well before the seed dies completely." Note that most seeds retain and need enough moisture (about 6 or 7 percent of their mass) that they are not *completely* dormant.

Since the perfect temperature for seed storage in most cases is about 40 degrees Fahrenheit, it is best to keep seeds refrigerated if possible (*Allium* seeds should be frozen at about -20 degrees Fahrenheit). Seeds that are *completely* dried can be frozen, which has the added advantage of killing any pernicious weevils or insects; however, it is important that the seeds contain minimal (but necessary) moisture, a condition that is easier to attain in many western states, for example, compared to other parts of the country. Squash seeds can be tested for dryness by bending them with your fingers. If they snap, they are sufficiently dry to store; if they bend without snapping, they require further drying. With all other seeds, drying overnight in a food dehydrator set at 95 degrees Fahrenheit is sufficient.

Before planting, bring the seeds to room temperature in their container and then expose them to the air for a few days to allow them to acclimate to light, humidity, and normal temperatures.

◄ Recordkeeping in the backyard: flagging crosses with marker ribbons. Note the fruit developing from the taped blossoms.

▼ Carol Deppe discusses a plant breeding project in her Oregon backyard garden.

◄ Building a backyard prairie.

Three stages of a plant breeding trial at the Seeds of Change research farm in New Mexico: bean plants at the beginning of the growing season; approaching peak season; and some samples of grow-out.

▲ Backyard research plot at the Land Institute containing examples of typical plants in Wes Jackson's perennial polyculture model.

➤ Alan Kapuler, Ph.D., research director of Seeds of Change, selecting marigolds.

▼ Chile breeding project: part of a trial of over two hundred varieties of chile at the Seeds of Change research farm to select for plant flavor and architecture, and resistance to drought.

▲ Above all, plant breeding should be fun. Carol Deppe's backyard playground, Oregon.

➤ The rich prairie of the American Midwest provides an instructive model.

◄ Examples of the extraordinary biomass of typical prairie perennial root structure.

➤ Daikon used as a plough to break up the soil and to deposit enormous amounts of vegetative material, which adds organic matter, allows water penetration, and feeds the soil microorganisms.

▼ Sweet potatoes used as ground cover, for root penetration, as carbonaceous material that adds organic matter to the soil, and as food.

➤ Chile seeds drying on a fine mesh screen with a simple window fan providing a light breeze to assist in the drying process. In the background, Southport White Globe onions selected for their shape and form.

▲ Daikon mulch. In Fukuoka's model, the seeds contained in the mulch sprout in the spring.

▶ Leek seed heads drying indoors in the fall to avoid inclement weather.

◀ Alan Kapuler in his seed room. Note the seeds saved in envelopes, plastic bags, paper sacks, buckets, and cartons.

▼ Breaking and rubbing flower heads to separate the seeds from the chaff.

◄ Preparing the male squash
blossom for hand-pollinating.

► Hand-pollinating the
female squash blossom with
the male.

◄ Taping the female squash
blossom shut to prevent
further pollination.

► The taped blossom and
a marker ribbon for accurate
recordkeeping.

Another satisfactory storage method that does not require refrigeration is to place the seeds in a paper envelope and then in an airtight glass canning jar with a rubber seal. Some seed savers recommend using a zip-top plastic bag in the same way, but Deppe counsels that seeds (especially peas and beans) can suffocate in a sealed plastic bag, just like any other living thing, unless they are completely dry. Beans and peas should therefore be stored in plastic for up to two or three months only.

The Beginner's Two-Minute Drill for Seed Saving

Definitions

INBREEDER (I)

Self-fertile. A single plant or a pair, one female and one male, that will set fertile seeds. Many varieties (such as lettuce) can be grown near one another, will not cross, and the seeds will breed true.

OUTBREEDER (O)

Must cross to a neighbor to make fertile seeds. Varieties (sunflowers, for example) need to be separated or they will intercross. Separation can be done by timing of flowering, by distance, or by ecological layout. There are two kinds of outbreeding: one between varieties within the same spe-cies, and the other between varieties of different species. Thus varieties of *Cucurbita maxima* will all intercross with one another. *Cucurbita maxima* varieties will not cross with *Cucurbita pepo* varieties.

MIXED (M)

Can set fertile seeds by itself but prefers to outcross if possible—basil is an example. Most plants are this way. Needs isolation for seed saving.

ANNUAL

Plant completing its growth, flowering, and fruiting in one cycle or season.

BIENNIAL

Needs two cycles or seasons to go from seed to plant to seed. Examples are onions and brassicas. These are more difficult to obtain since they require additional attention in terms of weeding, cultivation, fertilization, and overwintering.

PERENNIALS

Generally take one year or more to flower and make seeds, and then do so for years.

WET PROCESSING

Fruits are fermented in water; fertile seeds

sink, are dried, and stored in a dry, cool place out of direct sunlight. Cucurbits (squash) and solanums (tomatoes, eggplant, and so on) are examples of seeds processed this way.

DRY PROCESSING

Seeds mature and dry out as the plant matures. The heavier seeds are generally fertile and the lighter ones sterile; by fanning in a breeze, the chaff blows away. The denser, fertile seeds are stored in a dry, cool place out of direct sunlight. Brassicas, beans, and corn are examples of seeds processed this way.

To make fertile seeds, which is the packaging of DNA for survival, the critical mineral is phosphate. The bases of DNA (and RNA) are held together by sugar-phosphate links. Of all garden amendments and fertilizers used to stimulate plant growth, phosphate is the most important for producing fertile seeds.

The Vegetative Seeds

One group of garden plants selected by people for many generations are propagated from bulbs, tubers, corms, and cuttings. They need a different storage setup compared to seeds stored in a dry state.

ALLIUMS

Onions and shallot bulbs and garlic rosettes are best stored in a dry, cool place (35 to 40 degrees Fahrenheit), out of direct sunlight. Duration of storage depends on the variety and on proper curing at the end of the growing season and after the harvest. Replanted onions will flower to give top seeds. Top seeds from hard-stalk garlic can be treated like cloves.

POTATOES, SWEET POTATOES, AND JERUSALEM ARTICHOKES

Whole tubers can be kept in a cool, dry place out of direct sunlight, or held in damp peat moss in the refrigerator.

Top Seeds

ANNUALS

Dry Process: Amaranth (M); basil (M); beans (I); broccoli (O); cilantro (M); corn (M, prefers O); dill (M); lettuce (I); marigolds (M); mustard greens (I, some M); nasturtiums (M); peas (I); poppies (M); radishes (M); soybeans (I); spinach (M); sunflowers (O).

Wet Process: Capsicums (I, some O); cucumbers (M); eggplants (M); gourds (M); ground-cherries (I); squash (M); tomatoes (most I); watermelons (M).

BIENNIALS	PERENNIALS
Dry Process: Beets (M); Brussels sprouts (M); cabbage (O, some M); carrots (M); cauliflower (M); celery (M); chard (M); Chinese cabbage (O); endive (I); fennel (M); kale (M); leeks (M); onions (M); parsley (M); parsnips (M); radicchio (I); turnips (M).	*Dry Process:* Cardoon (I); globe artichoke (I); rhubarb (I); rosemary (M); sage (M); thyme (M).
	Wet Process: Asparagus (I).

7

plant breeding:
Garden Trials at Home

Every gardener should be a plant breeder.
—Carol Deppe

Carol Deppe is a Harvard-trained geneticist, science writer, and author who believes passionately in the need to expand our food-crop base, and she sees this goal as largely dependent on the contributions and involvement of backyard gardeners and small-scale farmers. "Developing new vegetables doesn't require a specialized education, a lot of land, or even a lot of time. It can be done on any scale. It's enjoyable. It's deeply rewarding. You can get useful new varieties much faster than you might suppose. And you can eat your mistakes."

Deppe notes that the heyday of professional breeding of garden vegetables, during the first half of the twentieth century, is over. Professional large-scale plant breeding did not exist before the field of plant genetics was understood and exploited, so that "commercial vegetable production was still largely a scaled-up version of garden production. Most vegetables were sold near the farms where they were grown. Commercial varieties often were similar or identical to home garden ones." Unfortunately, since *1950* or so, commercial vegetables have been produced by different methods and with different goals in mind compared to those produced in home gardens. Professional breeders have concentrated on the needs of commercial growers, and breeding for gardening has also dwindled dramatically. "Now the professionals have largely left the field," says Deppe, "and there is a vacuum. It's time for amateurs to move back in to fill that gap."

Deppe summarizes the complex subject of plant breeding when she states, "Only ten methods have accounted for more than ninety percent of the accomplishments of plant breeding, both ancient and modern. They are finding and evaluating germ plasm, maintaining germ plasm (seed saving and clonal propagation), selection, making F1 hybrids, using F2s, inbreeding, outcrossing, backcrossing and recurrent backcrossing, using new mutations, and doing wide crosses (to generate entirely new species or mixes). You can do them all." Deppe's book *Breed Your Own Vegetable Varieties* covers all of these methods, and while this chapter focuses on finding and evaluating germ plasm and selection (because these are the foundation for everything else) as well as plant trials, details of the other methods are necessarily left to Deppe's book.

Novice amateur plant breeders should begin with one or two types of vegetable they like to eat—not least because you are likely to end up eating a lot of it before you are finished! Among the characteristics in vegetables that expert breeders look for are flavor, early maturity, disease resistance, vigor, growth pattern, size, color, shape of fruit, and overall beauty of the plants. One of the most important aspects of plant breeding is keenness of eye: While interesting and unusual genetic accidents happen all the time, they are often only recognized by attuned observation.

Part of the fun of plant breeding and a major reason to practice it is that you can pursue your own goals and enjoy the freedom it entails. "Backyard gardeners can afford to gamble," says Deppe. All that is needed for some lesser-known or new vegetable to escape its current obscurity is for some gardener to work with it and to start circulating the results. After all, the major food crops in the world evolved through the work of amateurs long before the era of professional plant breeding. Professionals may have perfected numerous varieties and broadened our choices, but they were not the ones who domesticated and developed the crops in the first place. Deppe's experiments with squash and mustard greens (see pages *184–187*) provide good examples of how amateur breeders can themselves set the ball rolling. Further, organizations such as the Seed Savers Exchange (see Resources on page *221*) and regional seed exchanges preserve and distribute seeds of varieties that are not commercially available, including those developed by individual gardeners and plant breeders.

If you are interested in marketing a new variety that you have developed, advises Deppe, "most of the smaller, family-owned, or alternative seed companies are happy to introduce varieties bred by amateurs. In most cases, you should approach just one seed company.... By the time you've developed a good new variety, you'll often know which seed company to offer it to. Look first to the companies from which you buy seed. If you like what they're doing, they might like what you've done, too."

Some gardeners are concerned that they need to allocate a large amount of productive space to breed plants. However, the beauty of backyard breeding is that, even for plants that take up a relatively large amount of land, such as potatoes, you can choose the scale of operation. You can make as few as one or two crosses, or five, ten, or more; for smaller plants that take up less space, you can usually evaluate dozens, hundreds, or even thousands in an area of a few square feet or in a small garden bed.

Designing Garden Trials
Seed saving, variety maintenance, and plant breeding all depend on being able to eval-

Finding and Maintaining Sources of Germ Plasm

Five of the most important sources of heirloom and endangered seeds are the Seed Savers Exchange, Native Seeds SEARCH, J. L. Hudson, Seeds of Change, and its sister company, Deep Diversity, a planetary gene pool resource and service (see Resources on page 222). The Exchange was founded in 1975 by Kent and Diane Whealy after they were given some family heirloom seeds that had originated in Bavaria four generations previously. They began a search for other heirloom varieties and started the organization that, through its membership of over eight thousand, is perpetuating rare and endangered seeds. If you have heirloom seeds, or wish to try some yourself, join the Exchange (write to Seed Savers Exchange, 3094 North Winn Road, Decorah, IA 52101). Members and nonmembers alike can make use of their invaluable publications.

The Garden Seed Inventory, by Kent Whealy, is a starting point for information; it is available from the Seed Savers Exchange. It provides a complete list of seed companies in the United States and Canada, as well as the varieties of seeds offered by these companies. The Seed Savers Exchange also produces the *Seed Savers Yearbook,* published each winter, which lists the thousands of noncommercial varieties of vegetables and fruit, listed by about eleven hundred members, available to members of the Exchange.

Another great source of information on seed companies worldwide is *Cornucopia: A Source Book of Edible Plants,* by Stephen Facciola, available from Seeds of Change. It lists rare as well as common varieties of edible plants worldwide, how they are used, and where to find their seeds.

Deppe praises the work of the U.S. Department of Agriculture–Agricultural Research Service (USDA–ARS) National Plant Germ Plasm System, whose role is to collect, maintain, and distribute germ plasm and information to plant researchers. USDA–ARS collections are organized in regional centers. Although Deppe cautions that curators are not all of the same mind when it comes to their willingness to assist backyard plant breeders, she suggests that most are likely to help with reasonable requests.

uate plant material as well as growing methods. Deppe describes two basic types of garden breeding trials: the first involves comparing several varieties under constant conditions, while the second seeks how best to grow a particular variety or crop, which involves testing a single variety under different conditions. "Many projects combine both objectives, simultaneously trialing various varieties and various methods. Garden trials of varieties as well as methods are central not just to plant breeding but to all good gardening." Deppe points out that while garden trials are scientific research, requiring good design, execution, and evaluation, they are also about just playing around and satisfying your curiosity. Above all, they should be fun. Most of the time they will yield edible results.

Deppe emphasizes the importance of three general rules when designing trials: RULE #1: *Adopt an adventurous mind-set.* Trials can satisfy your natural inquisitiveness, and they can be worked into the routine of gardening, so that whenever you plant, you can use it as an opportunity to conduct a trial. They don't have to be large-scale, but it helps to have fun with them. Surprisingly few people do them at all, so you are already ahead of the game by trying things

out. Don't try to do things uniformly—it will keep things much more interesting. For example, if you are growing a new variety of corn, you won't know the correct spacing because of the specifics of your particular garden: the soil, the amount of sunlight and shade, the weather conditions, and so on. If you plant corn at one uniform spacing and density, the best possible information you can get is how corn does at that particular density, which may not be the best at all. On the other hand, it is just as easy to plant or thin to give a variable spacing. Most of the row can be planted at the density you think will work best, but if you leave one end of the row relatively sparsely spaced and the other more densely spaced than the rest, you will get a lot more information. Evaluate the vigor of the plants and the size of the cobs accordingly.

Another way of exercising this adventurous mind-set is for every time you try something, also try the principle of *not* doing it. For example, leave organic fertilizer off one row (or vary the amounts applied) and evaluate the differences. Deppe learned a valuable lesson by not inoculating some of her legumes one year. After further trials, she concluded that it didn't make any difference if she inoculated or not. She is not certain exactly why this is so, but she suspects it has something to do with her microclimate in central Oregon.

RULE #2: *Don't make a big deal out of things.* By all means try elaborate experiments if you wish, but remember that simple and easy experiments are also very useful. And don't be intimidated—scale your trial to suit you. This rule applies particularly to record keeping; Deppe recommends that you keep appropriate records so that you can evaluate the information and use it another year, but you don't need to be fanatic about it. Just keep the information you are likely to need another year, and don't make record keeping into a chore. Ideally, keep a file on each crop variety, and keep your files in chronological order. Record what you need to, not everything. The most important information includes the variety of the plant being trialed, sources of seed material, planting and maturity dates, and general weather conditions during the growing season. It's a good idea to keep a detailed record of what you planted where, as garden markers can often mysteriously go AWOL. Finally, record excuses that might affect the results—for example,

that you tilled the soil later than you expected, or weed or pest infestation patterns, or reasons why the control did better.

RULE #3: *Use controls.* This is crucial. Without controls, trials are not interpretable or meaningful. Trials are not just doing something new or different. A trial is a comparison of two or more things, at least one of which should be familiar or a favorite variety of yours. Otherwise, unfavorable results might have more to do with the weather or some other external environmental factor. Try keeping the environmental conditions similar for all the plants being studied; for example, soil and shade should be the same. Sometimes it helps to have more than one control; you might try a classic or popular variety for comparison, even if it doesn't really appeal to you on its own merits. And, for example, you can compare F1s, recent open-pollinated varieties, and heirlooms in any of a variety of crops. Refer to Deppe's book for details on trial design.

Remember, you don't have to find everything out or get the results you are looking for in the first year. Deppe says: "It's often most efficient to do a small, crude trial the first year, then do a much better one the following year[s]. Whenever you are planning to evaluate many varieties and invest major effort, a small trial that is a subset of the major one can be used the first year to help shake down your experimental design and eliminate problems with both the principle and the practice. It's often better to do a number of small trials in different years than just one massive trial in one year." That way, weather variations, different beds, and somewhat different methods can be evened out.

In planning the plant breeding trials, Deppe suggests that where you are growing out an F1 or F2 hybrid, or other material derived from a cross, you should also grow out a little of the two original parents for comparison. Seed from hybrids always yields some plants with unexpected characteristics, and these can be better interpreted if you can refer back to the parents to compare the inheritance patterns involved. In addition, says Deppe, "Whenever you evaluate the disease resistance of experimental material, try to include at least one variety known to be resistant to the disease and one variety known to be sensitive to it as controls."

Deppe is frequently asked about the virtues of holding blind trials, where the plants are arranged so that you don't know which are which until after the trial and subsequent evaluation. She says blind trials are "most important when you're worried that your opinions or biases might influence the results or when what is being analyzed is very subjective. Blind trials usually aren't necessary in gardening work and are not always possible (as when varieties look different, for example). In addition, they spoil the fun of being able to watch and understand the trial as it is happening, although one case where I frequently use blind trial is for evaluation of flavor. I don't bother growing the plants blind, but arrange things so that I don't know which plant the material to be tasted came from until the tasting is done and the results recorded."

Evaluating Trials

In evaluating trials, it is necessary to take a number of factors into account. For example, superior spacing and more available sunlight can cause a particular plant to do better than others that are genetically similar. For example, plants often do better when growing at the edge of the bed. You might want to take these differences into account and evaluate only the plants growing in the middle of the bed for a more accurate reading.

Although a general, subjective impression of performance is often sufficient, general impressions can sometimes be misleading, says Deppe, especially when it comes to yields. It is often necessary to take at least some measurements. When it comes to collecting quantitative data, Deppe often measures and records certain individual plants rather than all of them, listing them, for example, as "up to 7 inches in height." "The performance of the best plant is especially important because it represents what the variety is capable of under my circumstances," says Deppe. Conversely, "the worst plants aren't as meaningful because in many cases they were just unlucky (for example, that's where a cat dug)."

Alternatively, Deppe measures the best plant, the worst (to create the range), and then the median, or the plant that is better than half and worse than half. Usually she prefers to record qualitative information, or general impressions such as "about the same as the control" or "a little better than the control." Chance will affect trial results, and the fewer the plants in a trial, the

more significant will be the effects of chance. It takes a large number of plants to see small differences, but most trials are concerned with establishing large differences. "Most good gardeners develop an excellent feel for what kinds of results are meaningful," counsels Deppe.

After conducting your trials, the evaluation process comes next. Consider carefully whether the answers you got and what you learned were directly relevant to the questions you set out with. "Thinking about a trial afterward is often the most important part," advises Deppe. Ask yourself whether the answers you got were those to the questions you thought you were asking; often they are not. Review flaws and limitations in the trial (whether under your control or not), and take them into account. Take note also of any unexpected results. Then, once you have analyzed your results, decide what to do with them. For example, decide whether or not to grow a certain variety the next year, or to grow more of something, or to grow it under different conditions or in a different way. Or decide to try additional trials the next year.

"In making your final judgments," says Deppe, "consider the bigger picture. If an open-pollinated variety that hardly any-one grows does almost (but not quite) as well as the fancy hybrid that everybody grows, maybe you should choose the open-pollinated variety. You can save its seed if you need or want to. In addition, when you buy the seed, you are probably supporting a small grower and a family seed company; when you buy the new hybrid, you are probably supporting a multinational giant. If a rare variety does as well or even almost as well as the common one, maybe you should grow it just because of its rareness. By growing it, you help to preserve it and the information about it. And by growing something different from your neighbors, you might not get their pest or disease when it sweeps over the whole area; your variety might be resistant…. Whenever you grow something different from your neighbors, you are contributing to the agricultural biodiversity of your country, your region, and your neighborhood. This is part of the bigger picture."

Finally, bear in mind that things sometimes go wrong and you won't get the results you hoped for or expected. Don't get discouraged: If you pay attention, you will learn *something* from the trial. Deppe says that whatever else, the worst experiences sometimes make the best stories!

Mr. Burbank gets unusual hybrids because he crosses great numbers of flowers and uses much pollen. He is skillful in the technique. He also dares. He has no traditional limitations. He knows no cross that he may not attempt. He has not studied the books. He has not been taught. Therefore he is free.

—LIBERTY HYDE BAILEY (1901)

At the most trying times, try to keep a sense of humor—and remember, there's always next year.

Reproduction and Basic Selection
The basic observation involved in plant breeding, says Carol Deppe, is that offspring tend to resemble their parents. Selection is only one of many plant-breeding

Human understanding of plant reproduction was undoubtedly complicated by the fact that plants are much more sexually diverse and versatile than people. A profound advance in plant breeding came about with the realization that most plants, like people, have fathers. With plants, as with people, it may not be entirely obvious who the father is. Flowers are the reproductive organs of the plant. The plant that produces a seed is clearly the mother of the seed. You can watch the seed-containing fruit develop from the flower on its mother. That the seed has a father isn't necessarily obvious.

—CAROL DEPPE

techniques, but it is the most important. Some plant-breeding projects involve only selection, and even when other techniques are used, selection is invariably one of them.

Some plant species are largely self-pollinating, some are cross-pollinating, and some are in between. Peas, for example, are highly self-pollinating. The pollen is usually shed and fertilizes the flower before the flower ever opens. Spinach is completely cross-pollinating because male and female flowers are on separate plants. With squash, separate male and female flowers grow on the same plants; sometimes they are self-pollinating, other times they are cross-pollinated by bees or other insects. With corn, the male flower (the tassel) and female flower (the silk) are on the same plant and are self-fertile, but usually cross-pollinate. Cabbage and many relatives in the brassica family have flowers with both male and female parts, but have biochemical mechanisms that prevent self-fertility.

The other major form of plant reproduction is cloning, which is vegetative rather than sexual reproduction. For example, roots or cuttings send up new shoots, or plants send out runners that then become distinct (but genetically identical) plants. Tubers such as potatoes and sweet potatoes, fruit trees, garlic, Jerusalem artichokes (sunchokes), and strawberries are all exam-ples of plants that easily clone vegetatively.

"Selection practiced without any understanding of plant reproduction often isn't very powerful," cautions Deppe, "because if you don't understand the role of pollen, when you try to save seed from the best parents, you are actually only choosing good mothers. Each seed has a father too. In the species that are largely inbreeding, when you select good mothers, you are automatically selecting good fathers. But for species that are largely outbreeding, when you select good mothers, all you have is good mothers. You don't know who the fathers are; they might be undesirable.

"Suppose, for example, that you have a patch of melons of a variety whose seed you are saving. The variety is one of your favorites, but you would prefer a somewhat larger fruit size. So you try to select for large fruit size by saving seed from the largest melon in the patch. When you grow the seed out the next year, the melons aren't particularly big. In fact, they don't even look like the same variety. Something has gone wrong. Actually, several things have gone wrong. You were trying to use the basic rule of selection by saving seed from the best, but you made four important but common mistakes.

"First, you assumed that the melon is the offspring. It isn't. It doesn't result from fertilization with the pollen; it is just part of the mother. Second, you assumed that the seed would carry genes that would generate melons like the one they started out in. But they don't necessarily, and they didn't. Third, you didn't choose the best father; you didn't know who the father of your seed was. Finally, you didn't necessarily even choose the best possible mother plant…. The size of a melon is affected very much by whether it is the first melon on the plant or a later one, for example, and by how many melons there are altogether…. The flower that gave rise to the fruit was probably pollinated by a bee that had just visited a flower from a completely different variety—one growing in your neighbor's garden, for example.

"Whenever we try to save seed or do selection," counsels Deppe, "we need to choose both the female and the male parents. That means we need to control pollination. In strongly inbreeding plants, such as peas, we don't actually have to do anything, because left to her own devices, the mother plant also contributes the pollen. So if we choose a good mother plant, she is also the father plant. Selection is very easy with inbreeding plants; we just save

Rainbow Inca Corn: One Example of Plant Breeding

Alan Kapuler's very first breeding project, which produced Rainbow Inca corn, occurred when he was living in a commune in southern Oregon, growing vegetables. Carol Deppe tells the story: ✍|"Rainbow Inca didn't start as a breeding project; it began as a spiritual act, a ceremony. Alan had grown a number of different varieties of corn the previous year, and he had chosen his twelve favorite ears of all the varieties. The ears were of all different kinds and colors—flour corns, native Indian corns, heirloom sweet corns, and other varieties. He shelled out the chosen twelve and planted the kernels all in one patch. He planted in rows, sowing all the seed of one type, then starting on the next, wherever he was in the row. The corn was all in one patch, in somewhat intermingled blocks."

Because of mole activity, Alan replanted randomly and at different dates, so that corn of various kinds was scattered throughout the patch. "This meant that all kinds of crosses could happen, even between very early and late types. He wasn't thinking about this at the time; it's just the way it happened. One of the corns Alan planted was an Incan flour corn with huge, flat white seeds and plants about twelve feet high. When Alan harvested his corn, the ears on his Incan corn were especially beautiful, and there were one or two colored seeds on each ear that represented pollination by a colored variety. There were yellows, reds, purples, and blues; solid colors, stripes, blazes, and spots; clear colors and iridescent ones. There were a hundred to a hundred and fifty colored kernels altogether. Alan picked the colored kernels off the ears and saved them.

"He planted about a hundred of the colored kernels the next year. When he harvested the patch, the ears showed an occasional crinkled seed, representing sweet types. The genes associated with sweet corn are recessive, so no crinkled kernels appeared in the original crosses involving the flour-type Incan mother plants. There were about forty crinkled kernels of all colors. Alan kept and planted the crinkled kernels the following year. His harvest was about five pounds of kernels, all sweet and of all colors.

"He selected for large, crinkled, flat kernels and planted a couple of ounces of seed. In subsequent years he continued selecting for large, fat kernels of all colors. He also selected for plant height of about eight feet instead of the ten to twelve feet typical of the original Incan corn (eight-foot plants were enough earlier in the season to be dependable). He also selected for ears that were lower on the plant—'so I could reach them,' he says. Lower ears are also larger, so selection for lower ears automatically selects for bigger ears and higher yield.

"Rainbow Inca sweet corn preserves the cytoplasm of the original Incan flour corn and a large amount of genetic variability derived from many sources. The kernels are of all colors and patterns, huge compared to any other sweet corn, and broad and flat. The plants are about eight feet tall. It's of late and reliable maturity here in Oregon (meaning that it would probably be considered midseason in most areas). It's undoubtedly been automatically selected for productivity in cool weather because of where it was bred; the flavor is excellent.

"Alan didn't realize that he had developed something special until he offered his Rainbow Inca through the Seed Savers Exchange and heard the reactions of those who grew it. It's excellent, unusual, unlike anything else, they said. Rainbow Inca is currently offered through Seeds of Change and remains one of the most unusual corns available."

seed from the best plants. With outbreeding-ing plants, however, whenever we maintain a variety, practice selection, or do any kind of plant breeding, we have to deliver the desirable pollen to the plant and exclude unwanted pollen. This means that before we can maintain any crop variety or develop any new ones, we need to know whether the plant we're working on is an inbreeder or outbreeder.

"When we practice selection," concludes Deppe, "we need to consider the entire plant, not just the fruit of the plant. We would choose a plant whose overall performance came closest to what we wanted and then either self-pollinate it or cross it to another, superior individual of the variety." Sometimes, in seed saving and plant breeding, the best specimens are selected; other times, we merely eliminate (rogue) or eat the worst specimens. Selection works, however, only when there is genetic variability for the characteristic we care about in the material we are starting with. If a squash variety, for example, is genetically homogeneous for fruit size, you can't get larger fruit size just by selection. You will probably need to cross that squash with another variety with bigger

fruits. Many breeding projects start with a cross; sometimes the cross is deliberate, and sometimes it is accidental or casual.

Creating New Varieties

One of Carol Deppe's projects came about because she likes the flavor of Sugar Loaf squash, a green-and-cream-striped type of delicata vine squash bred by Jim Baggett. Unfortunately, it has flesh that is only about half an inch thick and seeds that are hard to remove, which makes it a lot of work for comparatively little return. Deppe also loves the spectacular, intense, and completely different flavor of Jersey Golden acorn bush squash, which has thick flesh and seeds that are easily removed. In the case of Jersey Golden, the fruits are quite small and they do not keep very well. In Deppe's mind's eye, she envisioned a new variety of squash: a beautiful squash with the flavor and color of Jersey Golden, but with the oval shape and keeping quality of Sugar Loaf. Alternatively, she hoped to breed a squash with the flavor of Sugar Loaf and the thicker flesh and more easily removed seeds of Jersey Golden.

Deppe started out by crossing the two varieties of squash, which involved transferring the male pollen of one variety to the female flowers of the other, using the standard hand-pollinating methods used for seed saving. At the end of the season she harvested the fruit and saved the seeds, known as F1 hybrid seed—the first seed cross derived from crossing two different purebreeding varieties. The next year, Deppe planted six of these F1 hybrid seeds. All the plants gave golden-green speckled dumpling-shaped squash that were larger than either Jersey Golden or Sugar Loaf, with thicker flesh than either, and seeds that were easy to remove. The flavor was similar to Sugar Loaf, but even more intense.

This trial meant that Deppe could simply grow the F1 hybrid in order to have a thick-fleshed squash with Sugar Loaf–type flavor. However, because she also wanted a purebreeding variety with Jersey Golden flavor, she hand-pollinated the F1 plants to get the F2 generation, ate the fruit, and saved the seeds. The next year Deppe grew about fifty plants from the F2 seed. This time, she had all different kinds of fruit in every conceivable combination: some were golden, some green, others speckled or striped; some were acorn-shaped, others oblong or dumpling-shaped. Deppe will proceed by self-pollinating by hand the male and female flowers on the same plants that she has chosen, in order to produce a line of golden fruits with the desired characteristics. For another two or three generations, Deppe will self-pollinate the best plants from each line—it takes six generations or so to create a pure line. However, Deppe has enjoyed superior squash to eat right from the very first generation of the project. Her breeding project took up no extra space in her garden, as she would have grown both varieties anyway, and took no extra time beyond the thirty minutes or so it took her to extract the seeds and the effort in hand-pollinating the plants.

Another of Deppe's projects involved mustard greens. Her favorite variety is Green Wave, a vigorous overwintering type with thick, ruffled leaves that outgrows most weeds, and so can be broadcast with impunity, as it ends up swamping everything else around it. Raw, it is hot and fiery in flavor—too spicy for most humans, or, fortunately, for insects, deer, gophers, or other pests. As Deppe puts it, "Green Wave represents a superior agroecological concept for a cooking green: *It can be eaten only by animals that know how to cook."* Once cooked, Green Wave has a marvelous, rich, and uniquely flavorful quality, and the heat evident in its raw state is destroyed by the cooking process.

Unfortunately, though, Green Wave does not always overwinter in Deppe's garden. Even when it does, it does not grow well during the coldest months, so the leaves are not prime. Deppe decided that she needed a variation on Green Wave that overwinters without fail, and that is more vigorous in cold weather. Another mustard green called Green in the Snow can survive in temperatures as low as -20 degrees Fahrenheit and grows vigorously anytime that it's not actually frozen solid. Unfortunately, it has a narrow leaf blade and lacks the special Green Wave flavor. Deppe wanted a variety with the leaf and flavor of Green Wave and the overwintering quality of Green in the Snow.

As with the preceding example, whenever you want to develop a new variety that combines the characteristics of two other varieties, you start by crossing them. Deppe could have transferred pollen by hand from one variety to another, but instead she planted the two varieties in separate patches next to each other and relied on

the bees to cross-pollinate. Mustard (*Brassica juncea*) is largely self-pollinating; however, Deppe was expecting at least some of the plants to be crosses. At the end of the season, she harvested the dried plants of Green in the Snow and threshed out the seed. In October of that year, she broadcast the seed over an area of about 12 square feet, in between plants already growing around the garden. She knew most of the seedlings would be Green in the Snow, but she expected at least a few seedlings that were F1 hybrids crossed with Green Wave in the adjacent patch. Usually when you cross two varieties that differ in leaf width, the hybrid is somewhere in between, so Deppe was expecting to find the F1 hybrid seedlings against a larger number of Green in the Snow seedlings.

After a few weeks, Deppe could tell that about twenty out of the thousands of seedlings had distinctly broader leaves. She selected these twenty hybrids and hoed the rest away. When the hybrids grew bigger, they had a leaf size and flavor somewhere between the two parents, but in Deppe's opinion they were not particularly tasty. However, she did not let that bother her. The particular characteristics of the F1 generation reflect which genes are dominant, not which genes are present, so Deppe expected to be able to recover the flavor she wanted in subsequent generations. Despite a very hard winter that included a coating of freezing rain for several days and some hard frosts that killed the Green Wave, the hybrids survived and grew just as well as the Green in the Snow parent. The following year, Deppe planted the F2 seeds and obtained plants with different leaf widths ranging from the thin Green in the Snow to the thick Green Wave, and likewise, a broad range of flavor. Deppe plans to select for the flavor and leaf characteristic she wants in subsequent generations.

PLANT BREEDING AND GARDENING TRIals, like seed saving, are important ways in which we all can preserve our independence and secure for ourselves fresher and more nutritious produce. In Deppe's view, they also allow us to enjoy a direct, simple, and nurturing relationship with plants. A fortunate by-product of this process is that we are also preserving biodiversity. Plants and people have evolved together and shaped each other over thousands of years, and participating in this evolutionary process can be a spiritual experience. It is important that we are all *active* participants in maintaining and creating varieties for the future.

8

polyculture:

Eating in Every Direction

At the United Nations, there is a huge statue of a man full of purpose and muscle bent to the task of beating a sword, which does evil, of course, into a plowshare, which everyone knows will do good…. Yet the plowshare may well have destroyed more options for future generations than the sword.
—Wes Jackson

In his book *New Roots for Agriculture*, Wes Jackson writes that "nowhere is the ancient and long-discussed split between humans and nature more dramatic than in the manner in which land is covered by vegetation. To maintain the 'ever-normal' granary, the agricultural human's pull historically has been toward the monoculture of annuals. Nature's pull is toward the polyculture of perennials." Wes Jackson, president of the Land Institute in Salina, Kansas, has been working for over twenty years to resolve this dilemma and to reconcile these opposing tendencies. To this end, he has developed a new paradigm: natural systems agriculture, the centerpiece of which is his system of perennial polycultures. He follows in the footsteps of others, notably the great Russian geneticist N. I. Vavilov, who died in the 1940s, but the quest for such a sustainable system is more timely now than ever.

"I think we have the opportunity to develop a truly sustainable agriculture based on the polyculture of perennials," says Jackson. "At the Land Institute, we are working on the development of mixed perennial grain crops. We are interested in simulating the old prairie or in building domestic prairies for the future. If we could build domestic prairies, we might be able one day to have high-yielding fields that are planted only once every twenty years or so. After the fields have been established, we would need only to harvest the crop, relying on species diversity to take care of insects, pathogens, and fertility."

The Prairie as Model

As we have seen in Chapter 3, soil erosion is a major problem in most parts of the globe that are under cultivation, and desert-ification has affected large swaths of the developing world. In large part, these problems have been caused by commercial agricultural techniques, creating a vicious circle of destruction and loss. The rich prairie of the American Midwest provides an instructive model of how some of the most productive farmland in the world, with some of the most abundant soil to be found anywhere, is prone to appalling losses due to wind and water erosion. "When European settlers first broke the five-thousand-year-old prairie sod, they began a process of inexorable soil decline," remarks Jackson. The Iowa Department of Agriculture, for example, reported that by the early 1980s, half of the state's topsoil had been blown or washed away. The clock is ticking—without topsoil, crops will not grow, agriculture will not be possible, and our food supply will be severely compromised.

"The question today is, can we create a grain agriculture that reflects many of the characteristics of the original prairie ecosystem that made it sustainable?" says Jackson. In the perennial polyculture system that he proposes, a polyculture (rather than monoculture) of herbaceous perennial seed-producing plants—grain crops—provides permanent ground cover, like a pasture. Not only does Jackson's system heal and protect the soil, but the diverse polyculture of plants that can be selected increases productivity compared to a monoculture. Further, as we have seen in Chapter 5, such biodiversity reduces vulnerability to pests and diseases and creates beneficial habitat, to name just two of many advantages. As new productive perennial crops are developed by plant breeders, so they would represent a broad genetic base of disease resistance. This compares with what Jackson describes as "the current hard agricultural path, which promotes a genetic narrowing and therefore increased vulnerability to pests overall."

Perennial polyculture also has the potential to reverse the current decline in our genetic reservoir. "Population increase and intensive agriculture have reduced the amount of 'wasteland' where teosinte, the wild relative of corn, once lived," says Jackson. "For wheat and rice, too many of the old low-yielding but faithful varieties of various races and ethnic groups have been driven from the fields." These are members of the genetic bank that could beneficially be accessed now and then to introduce new germ plasm into crops made narrow by selection. Perennial poly-culture also increases soil nutritive value by fixing nitrogen and greatly reduces the amount of water used for irrigation. The ability of the soil to absorb and hold water is vastly increased, and application of chemical fertilizers, herbicides, and insecticides can be eliminated.

Just as Mollison's work on sustainable systems originated in his observation and

---

Let Nature never be forgot....
Consult the Genius of the Place
in all.

—ALEXANDER POPE

---

study of the self-sustaining ecology of the forest, so Jackson's work originated by studying the native ecosystem of the prairie on which he grew up and comparing it to fields of monocrops such as corn. Wendell Berry writes on the difference between the two paradigms: "The most noticeable difference is that whereas the soil is washing away in the cornfield, it is *building* in the prairie. And there is another difference that explains that one: the corn is an annual, the corn field is an annual monoculture, but the dominant feature of

Perennial Polyculture on a Garden Scale

Perennial polyculture is a system that can be applied in your small or large garden as well as to large tracts of farmland. It also applies to all ecosystems, not just prairie land, as the model can be adapted to the particular site as appropriate. Jackson is the first to explain that what's relevant is the thinking behind the system rather than the specifics; the important thing is to understand the reality of perenniality and to appreciate the features of natural ecosystems that promote stability. 🌿 Christian Petrovich, a Seeds of Change staff member at the New Mexico research farm, was formerly an intern at the Land Institute in Kansas who experienced firsthand the application of perennial polyculture to a backyard scale.

"In 1988 Wes Jackson packed his pickup with a shovel, a fork, and a bag of plant material and set off on a three-day trip to Nebraska, the Dakotas, and Minnesota to plant rhizomes and seed of the major candidates for perennial polyculture to see how vegetation and yields would develop from scratch over a period of years and in different environmental conditions. He returned to these ongoing experiments annually, and based on this preliminary research, in 1994 Wes sent me on a similar mission to plant thirty-foot-square sites at seventy-seven different sites in fourteen states. These sites were located in the backyards of members of the Land Institute.

"We rototilled the sites to prepare the soil for planting the seeds by hand onto the surface. Then we raked the seeds slightly below the surface and compacted the soil on top to ensure soil-to-seed contact. Finally, we mulched the sites. In each case, we planted eight prairie species—the four primary species identified for their potential by the Land Institute, and four secondary candidates that would support the establishment of a naturally functioning system. The idea was to see how the eight species would 'shake down' in each plot and whether they would form a stable community and a self-sustainable system. This process would take at least three years, because this is recognized as the minimum time needed for the plants to overcome initial conditions and self-organize without intervention into a stable perennial entity.

"It was an enormously inspiring grassroots effort undertaken by many people who have been influenced by the theories developed by Wes Jackson and the Land Institute. This ongoing effort isn't about professional plant researchers or the most innovative new data processing technology. It *is* about the implications of dedication to an exciting new concept and possibility that applies as much to backyard gardening as it does to prairie agriculture. It is about the consequence of care, when a human being, for their own private reasons, hears the faint whisper of a truth buried within, and despite all the reasons not to, decides to take the extra time they have and the extra space they have in their backyard to do their little bit, to construct a little piece of a far bigger puzzle."

Small-Scale Permaculture: A Michigan Miniprairie

Artist Linda Horn provides a vivid example of small-scale perennial polyculture that she pioneered on four acres of degraded former wheatland in southern Michigan. This is an area that still has tiny fragments of natural prairie left in the wild. Horn was inspired by a lecture given at the Chicago Botanic Garden in the early 1990s by Joyce Powers, owner of Prairie Ridge Nursery and president of CRM Ecosystems in Mount Horeb, Wisconsin. Writer and photographer Carolyn Ulrich describes the project:

"Powers had been poking gentle fun at the extremes sometimes required to protect gardens from the natural world around them. Horn took one look and quickly realized that a lifetime of barricading herself behind chain-link fences was not for her. She wanted to be in nature, not fight it. Horn's field seemed ripe for reversion to the sort of vegetation that would have greeted the European settlers in the mid-nineteenth century. Horn and Powers set to work.

"Powers selected a broad mix of seed that included perhaps forty species of native grasses, sedges, and forbs (flowering plants), selecting the appropriate mix of species based on such factors as geographic location, historic botanical records, soil type, slope and other site characteristics, microclimate, and the intended use of the site.... Plants began to bloom in 1996, much to Horn's delight. However, unexpectedly the field was first filled with gorgeous white daisies. While briefly enjoying their beauty, she knew they would have to be mowed—the seeds had been dormant in the soil, and if allowed to stay, the daisies would compete with the desired grasses and forbs. Three weeks later a diverse sea of green began to replicate a spring prairie as the seeds that had been planted began to emerge.

"'I knew right away that a prairie was going to provide a totally different rhythm and relationship to the land,' Horn enthused. 'Things are operating here that I won't even know about until they happen.' One part of the magic includes the intermingling of the plants to form an ecosystem, with the way their roots jostle and joggle to chart out territory belowground even more important than what transpires above. No less magical is the arrival of wildlife as birds and insects discover a newly created habitat. For Linda Horn these thrills are neverending."

the native prairie sod is that it is composed of a balanced *diversity* of perennials: grasses, legumes, sunflowers, etc., etc. The prairie is self-renewing; it accumulates ecological capital; and by its own abounding fertility and diversity it controls pests and diseases. The agribusiness corn field, on the other hand, is self-destructive; it consumes more ecological capital than it produces; and because it is a monoculture, it *invites* pests and diseases."

Jackson understands these differences and for these reasons advocates a permanent ground cover of diverse, complementary perennial plants. The perennials either can be adapted through breeding from traditional annual crops or are more productive strains of seed-producing perennials. Researchers at the Land Institute have emphasized the latter course to avoid the problems that have been bred into traditional grain crops such as dependence on chemicals, their use as a monoculture, and so on. Jackson has worked on developing a polyculture of wild species, choosing plants that are high-yielding (or that have this potential) and are mutually beneficial.

The challenge is to develop a polyculture of herbaceous food plants that combine the desirable qualities of perennialism and high yield. The most important issue

to be resolved in Jackson's system is that perennials do not concentrate all their energies into producing seed, or grain, unlike annual crops, as some is devoted to maintaining a vigorous root system through the winter and for beginning the growth cycle in the spring. Laura Jackson's Ph.D. research at Cornell revealed that seed increase can come at no cost to the plant.

"Prairie vegetation is a grass-dominated mixture consisting primarily of perennial warm-season and cool-season grasses, legumes, and composites growing oftentimes intermixed," explains Jon Piper, a Land Institute ecologist. "The diversity of plant species with complementary niches contributes in large part to the resilience of prairies in the face of climatic extremes. Differences in growth form, type of resource use, and seasonality allow these plant species to coexist. Under the ground, one plant may produce a deep taproot, whereas its neighbor produces shallow, fine roots. Some species, legumes primarily, fix atmospheric nitrogen in addition to taking up available nitrogen in the soil. Seasonal timing of resource use differs among species, thereby reducing competition for soil, water, and nutrients. Warm-season grasses and drought-hardy forbs are able to withstand the hot, dry conditions of summer.

Others, cool-season grasses and some forbs, persist by growing in the spring and setting seed before the onset of summer heat.

"Tight nutrient cycling is a sustainable feature of the prairie we would do well to emulate. Because most nutrients are tied up in living organisms and soil organic matter year round, they are not vulnerable to loss through leaching or erosion. In prairies, crucial nutrients are cycled seasonally within plants, stored in organic matter, or quickly taken up by plants and microbes once mineralized by decomposers in the soil.... As much as 60 to 75 percent of the prairie's total plant biomass occurs underground as roots, rhizomes, and crowns." Piper observes that climatic factors favorable to rapid growth and then drying of plant matter has led, over thousands of years, to the accumulation of soil organic matter via root turnover. In some prairies, between 30 and 60 percent of root biomass may turn over each summer, leaving a rich store of deep, dark organic matter that has made the highly productive U.S. grain belt possible.

"The few remnants of intact prairie serve as prime examples of inherently sustainable biotic communities in which complex webs of interdependent plants, animals, and microbes garner, retain, and efficiently recycle critical nutrients," says Piper. "Before we expend any more of our precious topsoil, we should consider a model for the future for our 'breadbasket' that mitigates soil erosion while providing edible seeds. Agroecosystems that are functional analogs of the prairie ecosystem should feature species adapted to local seasonal precipitation patterns, tight nutrient cycles, compatibility in resource use among species, soil preservation, and biological methods of crop protection."

Jackson's system of perennial polyculture has focused on four plants that represent different functional groups and guilds:

🌾 **Eastern gama grass**
(*Tripsacum dactyloides*), a warm-season grass—and a perennial relative of corn—is native to the region stretching from the southeastern United States and Great Plains southward into Central and South America. Its seeds are flavorful and nutritious, with 25 to 30 percent protein, but the plant currently has a low seed yield, only about 100 pounds per acre. However, research based on the introduction of a mutant gene has resulted in an in-

crease in seed number of from twelve to twenty times and a fourfold increase in seed yield by weight. It is not yet known what the limits for seed yield will be with concentrated breeding. Further, eastern gama grass has been discovered to fix small amounts of nitrogen, a characteristic that can no doubt be developed.

🌿 Wild rye grass

(*Elymus racemosus*), a cool-season grass, is a distant relative of wheat, rye, and barley. It is native to Eastern Europe (the Mongols once ate seeds from this plant), and it has been planted in the western United States primarily to stabilize sandy soils.

🌿 Illinois bundle flower

(*Desmanthus illinoensis*) is a nitrogen-fixing legume native to the Great Plains. It grows in a region stretching from Florida to New Mexico, and the seed contains 38 percent protein and 34 percent carbohydrate, suggesting considerable potential as a grain. Currently it yields up to 1,200 pounds per acre.

🌿 Maximilian sunflower

(*Helianthus maximillianii*) is a native to the grasslands of the Great Plains that ranges to the eastern seaboard and as far west as Texas and the Rocky Mountains. It yields 1,300 pounds per acre and the seed contains 21 percent oil, suggesting great potential as a grain or oil crop. The Maximilian sunflower also has the advantage of controlling weeds because of its allelopathic qualities; that is, it releases chemical compounds through its root system that inhibit the growth of other plants. Experiments conducted at the Land Institute confirm this significant allelopathic impact.

OTHER PROMISING PLANTS THAT CARRY considerable potential for perennial polyculture include the high-yielding, leguminous soybean; broomcorn millet, a perennial grass; sand dropseed, a native grass; wild senna, a legume; curly dock, a member of the buckwheat family; and the gray-headed coneflower. More than three hundred native and non-native herbaceous perennials have been grown at the Land Institute to determine their yield potential and suitability to the environment of the midwestern prairie. A further agronomic research inventory of 4,300 perennial grasses within six cool-season genera has also been studied over a period of twenty years.

One focus of the Land Institute's re-

A Conversation with Wes Jackson

"When I look back and think of my experiences and how I evolved my ideas on perennial polycultures, I am reminded of something Marshall McLuhan said: Imagine what it's like driving down the road but doing so while looking in the rearview mirror. You don't know where you're going; you can only look back and see where you've been. Even at the moment that you are at a particular spot, you don't know exactly where you are.

"I was born and raised on a farm, and it's becoming increasingly clear to me that I have more the mind of an agrarian than the mind of an industrialist. Unfortunately, the agrarian language does not resonate in a culture that has adopted the industrial paradigm. I also realize there is a very small minority of people who are still agrarians. Now, if you are an agrarian, you will abhor what has happened to the Kansas River valley where my extended family farms. This is a place where the fields I used to work are now occupied by a multistory factory and a forty-acre outlet for shoes. Roads have been built and numerous interchanges, and all of that rich, fertile land has been lost forever.

"Back in 1977, I sat down one day and made what I call a dichotomous key: an analysis of all the possible combinations of polyculture and monoculture, woody and herbaceous plants, annuals and perennials, and fruit/seed-bearing versus vegetative or foliage-bearing plants. Of course, I ended up with a whole bunch of combinations, twelve of which are practical. Of the rational categories, a polyculture of woody perennials bearing fruits or seed would be a mixed orchard; a polyculture of herbaceous annuals bearing fruits or seed would be a mixed crop system such as the corn-beans-squash-chiles system found in the Southwest or tropical Latin

America. A monoculture of herbaceous annual vegetative plants would be livestock silage crops, for example, and a monoculture of herbaceous perennial vegetative plants would be hay crops (legumes, grasses, and grazing crops). Interestingly, and crucially, I was struck by the one category that should exist but drew a blank: a polyculture of herbaceous perennials bearing fruit or seeds. That really intrigued me, not least because it is almost the opposite of our current high-yielding monoculture of annual cereals and legumes, and it gave me the spark that I needed to pursue the work in perennial polycultures that I have been developing over the last twenty years. It's become my life's work.

"Fruit and seed material is the most important plant food that we ingest; it's easily stored and handled, and highly nutritious. Unfortunately, none of our important grains are perennial, or when they are, as with sorghum, basically a tropical plant, they are not treated as such. If a few of them had been, we might not have so thoroughly plowed from the edge of the eastern deciduous forest to the Rockies. Where we did not plow or where we did plant back nature's herbaceous perennials in polyculture, our livestock have become fat on the leaf and seed products. Throughout this entire expanse, the mixed herbaceous perennials have not been cultured for the purpose of harvesting the seed except for the occasional times when collections were made to plant more mixed pasture.

"In the eastern tall-grass region, the European settlers substituted the domestic tall grass, corn. In the middle or mixed-grass region, they substituted a domestic middle-sized grass, wheat. My good friend Wendell Berry says that when we came across the North American continent, cutting down the forest and plowing the prairie, we never knew what we were doing because we never knew what we were undoing. We came with vision, but not with sight.

"Part of the problem of the Dust Bowl is that we tried to substitute the middle-sized grass in what was the short-grass prairie. The Dust Bowl followed the great plowing of the teens and twenties. When the dry winds blew in the thirties, the bad reputation of the region became firmly implanted on the American mind. All the work done by the Soil Conservation Service and others to prevent other dust-bowl conditions should be applauded. It is truly the work of thousands of diligent and dedicated people who have spent most of their productive lives thinking and working on the problem, but still the most sobering fact cannot be ignored: The soil is going fast."

search has been the phenomenon of over-yielding: the situation in which a polyculture of perennial crops yields more per unit area than their components yield in monoculture. "Overyielding may occur when competition between members of different species is less intense than competition between members of the same spe-

> Our meddling intellect
> Misshapes the beauteous form
> of things—
> We murder to dissect.
>
> —WILLIAM WORDSWORTH

cies, or where one crop species enhances the growth of another," explains Piper. "Canopies of neighboring crops might occupy different vertical layers, with tall crops tolerating strong light and shorter crops requiring shade or relatively high humidity. Crop species may have complementary nutrient requirements, as in mixtures of legumes and grasses, especially in soils where the nitrogen supply is limited. Finally, differences in the length of the growing period or in the seasonal peri-

ods of nutrient uptake among crops can promote overyielding. Where certain crops have been grown together for centuries, as in the maize-bean-squash polycultures of traditional Mexican agrarian cultures, intercrop compatibility has increased through coevolution."

One study at the Land Institute examined a series of monocultures and bicultures of wild senna, which does not fix nitrogen, and Illinois bundle flower, which does. Significant overyielding occurred by the second year of the experiment, and it appeared to increase with time. This study suggested the benefit to a perennial of association with a nitrogen-fixing species. It also showed that polycultures can counteract the trend observed with some perennials, of yield decreasing in later years. Another similar study examined overyielding trends of Illinois bundle flower and eastern gama grass. "In the first year in which gama grass produced seed, there was a 25 percent yield advantage in biculture based on average yields, and 19 percent overyielding based on best yields," recorded Piper. "In the next year, overyielding based on best results was 8 percent. These favorable results demonstrate that overyielding, typical in many polycultures of annual crops, can also occur in perennial polycultures and can occur in more than one year." Subsequent experiments with tricultures and with quadracultures—mixtures of three and four plant species respectively—are currently in progress, and suggest similarly exciting results, in part because of the distinct differences in soil, water, and nutrient uptake.

Further research conducted at the Land Institute on the effects of a polyculture of crops on the insect pest population confirms that this system tends to reduce the densities of insect pests compared to monocultures. "Crop diversity can provide physical barriers and masking odors that can interfere with colonization, movement, feeding efficiency, and reproduction of plant-feeding insects," Piper comments. "In addition, a polyculture environment often attracts great numbers of beneficial predators and parasitoids. Studies using annual grains and vegetables have demonstrated repeatedly that levels of insect pests tend to be reduced in polyculture relative to monoculture."

A good example of the Land Institute's work on developing perennials is the work on hybridizing sorghum. Grain sorghum *(Sorghum bicolor)* is native to the African continent and grown extensively as animal feed in the southern Great Plains of the United States. It is weakly perennial in tropical regions, but in temperate climates it is killed by frost. Researchers have crossed grain sorghum with a relative, johnsongrass *(Sorghum halapense)*, that is an overwintering, troublesome weed in the United States due to its underground rhizomes. They hope that by hybridizing the two types of sorghum, an overwintering, perennial sorghum can be developed.

The ultimate goal of ongoing research work is to achieve a polyculture of perennials with an average self-sustaining yield of 1,800 pounds per acre, or the equivalent of 30 bushels of wheat, goals that are not unreasonable given that corn yields have risen from 30 bushels per acre in the 1920s to well over 100 bushels by the 1980s, most of which is attributable to advances in breeding. "We are where the Wright brothers were at Kitty Hawk," writes Jackson. "I don't want to trivialize agriculture by comparing it to human flight, for I really do believe that our results to date and their implications are more profound for human civilization than the results the Wright brothers first achieved on December 17, 1903.

"Most of the new work on new crop development has involved the crossing of economically important annuals with some of their wild perennial relatives," Jackson continues. "There is a tendency for older patches [of perennials] to decline in productivity. It is well known that perennials provide a fair to good stand the first year and often a pretty good stand the second, but by the third year, production is headed steeply down. Though this is certainly a problem, we can't say for sure that this will always be the case and that this need be a biological law any more than an average of forty-bushel-per-acre corn in the pre-hybrid days was immutable biological law. It may have been a biological reality, but plant breeders proved it was not a biological law."

An interesting issue of plant breeding that concerns Jackson is why our culture has not yet developed herbaceous perennial seed crops. "New crop development has had relatively little attention in the history of our species since eight to ten thousand years ago when several generations of the most important revolutionaries ever to live on earth gave us essentially all of our crops and livestock. Of the thousands of seed-producing plant species known, fewer than one percent have been utilized by humans for food, clothing, and shelter. By and large humans do the easy things first, and so our crop scientists have improved the plants that have already demonstrated their amenability to cultivation.... We have logically questioned the wisdom of adding more plants when we are not fully utilizing many of the proven plants which are already available."

Jackson also believes that a sense of misplaced apathy has reigned since the 1930s and the days following the Depression and the legendary Dust Bowl of the Midwest. The formation of the Soil Conservation Service and the dramatic response of the Roosevelt administration to the problems of agriculture allowed scientists and laymen alike to turn their attention to other issues, confident that efforts to save the country's soil were in capable hands. There was little incentive to look elsewhere for answers or alternatives.

Natural Farming: Masanobu Fukuoka's Polyculture

A system that has similar ends to Jackson's perennial polycultures, even if the means are somewhat different, is Masanobu Fukuoka's "natural farming." Despite the name, this is a system that has complete transferability to a small backyard garden. The lineage of Fukuoka's techniques helps to explain the methods themselves. Over a period of centuries, traditional Japanese agricultural methods maintained the quality of the soil by adding organic compost and manure, by rotating crops, and by growing cover crops. Then, after World War II, Americans introduced chemical agricultural methods to Japan, which were less labor-intensive but did little to improve yields. However, the action of chemical fertilizers and pesticides rapidly weakened and depleted the soil, making crops increasingly dependent on chemical nutrients. The fertility of the soil was being rapidly mined.

Fukuoka's methods came out of a revelation that occurred while he was a young plant pathologist working for the Plant Inspection Division of the Yokohama Customs Bureau. Following a bout of exhaustion due to overwork and a high-spirited private life, Fukuoka's epiphany was to change his life. After spending a troubled night sleeping fitfully in the open overlooking Yokohama Harbor, he heard the sharp cry of a night heron in the early morning and it triggered his realization

that intellectual knowledge contributed nothing of intrinsic value, and that everything returns to nothingness. At that moment "true nature" was revealed, and in due course he returned to his father's citrus orchard and rice farm occupying a hillside overlooking Matsuyama Bay. There it occurred to Fukuoka that a "do-nothing" approach to farming would best match his new philosophy. He was inspired by the sight of a field he was passing that had been unplowed and unused for many years. Here, healthy rice seedlings were sprouting up through tangled weeds and grasses. Through experience, however, Fukuoka quickly learned the boundary between "doing nothing" and abandonment. He modified his approach to a natural way of farming, making work easier rather than harder, simplifying things, and working with the natural environment. Rather than doing nothing, he developed a philosophy and technique of *not* doing certain traditional things, such as plowing, composting, and fertilizing. Fukuoka realized that the land had become dependent on man's intervention because ever-changing and "improved" agricultural techniques had badly upset the natural balance.

Masanobu Fukuoka's philosophy is to

cooperate with nature rather than trying to improve on it or subjugate it. Fukuoka uses no machines, prepared fertilizer, or chemicals. He does not keep his fields flooded, create drainage furrows, plow the soil, or add compost or manure, yet his yields are comparable to, or greater than, those of traditional labor-intensive or chemical farming methods. Fukuoka harvests around eighty bushels, or more than five thousand pounds, of rice per acre from his fields, which have been unplowed in over forty years. One or two people can do all the work necessary for growing rice and winter grain in a matter of a few days. As Fukuoka observes, "It seems unlikely that there could be a simpler way of raising grain."

How, then, do Fukuoka's natural-farming methods work? One of the key techniques is to develop the soil while protecting it. He does not cultivate the soil and expose it to the elements. Instead, he lets the deep roots of an annual polyculture of plants penetrate and aerate the soil, a job made easier because it is not compacted by livestock or machinery. Fukuoka recognizes that the earth cultivates itself naturally through plant roots and the activity of microorganisms, earth-worms, and small animals. "As soon as cultivation is discontinued," notes Fukuoka, "the number of weeds decreases sharply.... Timing the seeding in such a way that there is no interval between succeeding crops gives the grain a great advantage over the weeds."

In addition, instead of adding fertilizer or compost, Fukuoka grows leguminous cover crops of clover in rotation and permanently mulches the soil with straw from grain crops of rice, rye, and barley. Fukuoka scatters his rice, rye, and barley seed in separate fields in the fall, the time when these seeds would sow themselves naturally, while his rice crop is still standing. Shortly afterward, he hand-cuts the rice crop, harvesting and threshing the seed and spreading the rice straw back over the fields as a mulch. In the early summer, he will harvest the rye and barley, again spreading the straw as mulch for the rice, which has begun to sprout after lying dormant through the winter. Allowing a prescribed number of ducks or chickens (about ten per quarter acre) to graze in the fields naturally provides enough manure to help the straw mulch decompose. One further beneficial side effect of straw mulching is that birds are prevented from eating the broadcast seed.

As the crops are growing, Fukuoka interferes as little as possible, except to cut back vegetation by hand to allow his slower-growing crops such as corn to establish themselves. Likewise, Fukuoka's polyculture orchard crops of sweet potatoes, buckwheat, mustard, soybeans, and daikon radishes topple over to add layers of mulch. Other vegetables such as cabbage, carrots, and turnips grow side by side with burdock and kitchen herbs, whose seeds he has mixed and scattered.

Using these natural-farming techniques, the fertility and structure of the soil in Fukuoka's fields improve each season. This contrasts with traditionally cultivated land that yields in direct proportion to the inputs of compost or manure, and the depletion in quality and fertility of land treated chemically. Fukuoka's methods have also proved that it is unnecessary to leave paddy fields flooded in order to grow rice; the ground cover and mulch can retain water and moisture just as effectively as extensive ongoing irrigation.

Most significantly, his system of natural farming means that crops can be grown this way on marginal land previously considered unsuitable.

AS WE HAVE DESCRIBED, WHILE WES Jackson's research focuses on large-scale perennial polycultures, the principles of the system can be scaled down to the dimensions of your garden and your particular ecosystem, using appropriate plants and food crops. Masanobu Fukuoka's parallel system of natural farming further demonstrates the practicalities of growing mixed crops on a garden scale that keeps the ground covered while replenishing and building the soil. Although Fukuoka does not use perennials, he sequences his plantings of annual crops and harvests them in such a way that the effect is similar to Jackson's model. Bill Mollison in his permaculture system also advocates rotations that yield similar results. This weight of expertise and experience drawn from working systems on three continents provides an irresistible model for gardening for the future of the planet.

postscript:
Practicing What We Preach at Seeds of Change: The Life and Times of an Organic Seed Company

> Though I do not believe that a plant will spring up where no seed has been,
> I have great faith in a seed.
> Convince me that you have a seed there, and I am prepared to expect wonders.
> —Henry David Thoreau

Seeds of Change is an organic seed company and organic food company based in Santa Fe, New Mexico, with research farms in northern New Mexico and Oregon. Until *1994*, another research farm was located in Gila, New Mexico. The stories behind the principals involved in the company, and how they do their work, shed interesting light on the way in which such a business not only sells seeds and foods but also seeks to further awareness of sustainable agriculture and socially responsible food production systems.

How did these principals begin to see their path in this work? For Alan Kapuler, director of research and one of the founders of Seeds of Change, it began in the early *1970s*, when he was in his thirties and first started to put together what plants he wanted to grow, and how. For Rich Pecorraro, former manager of the Seeds of Change Gila research farm, inspiration came as he passed out of his teenage years into manhood, making decisions about what he would eat and how he would grow it. Emigdio Ballon, director of agronomy, grew up in Bolivia and from an early age was taken by his grandfather on trips to collect plants and herbs from the wild. They would watch the birds and small animals in the milpa and choose what to eat first, then second, and so on. For Howard-Yana Shapiro, vice president of agriculture and commercial, his mission began as soon as he could walk on his grandparents' farm, seeing his Russian Jewish grandmother talking gently to her cows, living a life's dream of self-sufficiency, and teaching him what to pick from the fields. Seed collecting and saving, like plant selection and breeding, has so many beginnings.

Alan Kapuler's work with Seeds of Change began in *1989*, when he gardened a research and production plot for his family business, Peace Seeds, which later evolved into Deep Diversity, the sister catalog to the main Seeds of Change list. His plot occupied two acres of land owned by Hal and Alice Brown in Corvallis, Oregon. Alan's collaboration with Seeds of Change has touched on many areas of vegetable production, especially corn, squash, carrots, and onions, to name a few. He has also collected and grown vast numbers of flowers, including sunflowers, marigolds, zinnias, and cosmos. Alan's research farm has been tended by an ever-expanding stream of assistants, most notably Carl James and Jennifer Peterson, who have been at the heart of the Corvallis team for some time. A large greenhouse was erected on the site in *1991* for the layout of the first kinship garden based on Rolf Dahlgren's original work, modified by Alan and Olaf Brentmar (see Chapter *5*).

Careening through the Gila Wilderness in southwestern New Mexico, the Gila River has been an ancient giver of life to people along its banks for many centuries. In *1987* Gabriel Howearth, one of the three founders of Seeds of Change and a longtime colleague of Alan Kapuler's in Oregon, found a site on the west bank of

"In our work in Latin America as anthropologists," Howard-Yana Shapiro recalls, "we discovered that it took just one generation for all farming knowledge to be lost in a community. One generation! Currently in the United States, we have the smallest number of farmers since the middle of the nineteenth century, and the average age of these farmers is fifty-five years.

"I chose a piece of land in New Mexico that was about as whupped as it could be. But that land is proof that you *can* make the desert bloom, using the practices discussed in this book. In the first year, when we were working on the land, all the local farmers parked their pickups at the edge of the road and stood at the fence looking at what we were doing. The second year, a few of them ventured inside; the third year, some of them brought their video cameras. When I asked them why they were doing that, one of them told me, 'This is how we did it when I was a kid, when we produced a lot of food in this region. And now that we don't anymore, I want to be sure that my grandchildren can see how it's done, so that if by some miracle they decide to be farmers, there will be models for them to follow.'"

the river that was to become the Seeds of Change research farm. In *1989* Richard Pecorraro joined Gabriel to form the core of an amazingly talented group of individuals who made the first quantum leap in the growth of Seeds of Change possible. Armed with a huge collection of seed, put together by Alan Kapuler, the company was able to begin on a large scale the work begun in Oregon. Among those who contributed over the years to the hard-won success at Gila was Emigdio Ballon, who brought with him an expertise that provided the answers to complex agronomic questions. His experience working in the high altitude of the Andes as well as with the dry-land farming techniques of Native Americans proved essential to the continued success of the company.

The first activity at the Gila farm was to set up plant- and seed-growing strategies for a new bioregion. A test plot was set up to understand what would grow best there. The model was to trial as many species and varietal cultivars as possible. Thousands of Native American, Latin American, Middle Eastern, Asian, and European cultivars were trialed, and a second season of information on a larger scale was necessary to truly understand the ecosystem. Peppers, millets, amaranths, potatoes, onions, tomatoes, corn, carrots, beets, melons, cucumbers, squash, beans, numerous medicinal and culinary herbs, and Andean crops such as quinoa and yacon (as well as a myriad of flowers) were all grown out to enable the company to understand what organic seeds could and should be carried.

In *1991* Howard-Yana and Nancy Shapiro purchased the ancestral farm of Maria de la Lopez—Rancho La Paz—on the Rio Grande in northern New Mexico. Maria's family had come from Mexico to the area with the first conquistadors, farming in the floodplain of the Rio Grande, where they settled and stayed for *350* years. Before that time, the land had been farmed by the descendants of the Tewa people of the upper Rio Grande valley for at least three thousand years. When the Shapiros arrived, the land needed work. There was an old apple orchard and a fairly young peach orchard. Howard and Nancy began growing the soil back to a productive state, in the process becoming involved with Seeds of Change. They began to put into practice the different systems of sustainable agriculture that had been written about over the last twenty years—in particular, the systems of Masanobu Fukuoka, Bill Mollison, John Jeavons, Wes Jackson, and others.

From their experience working on the land in Mexico, the use of equipment was kept to a minimum with most of the work accomplished by hand. It was to be a model of efficiency and diversity. Through the collaboration of Alan Kapuler, multiple grow-outs, trials, selections, and breeding agendas could be accomplished with greater rapidity, to the benefit of the company and in an ecosystem distinctly different from that in Corvallis. Quickly the seventeen-acre plot took on the appearance of a paradise. Large border areas were established with multiple plantings. "Rooms" of plants were grown to help isolate many varieties. To enter a "room" of lemon basil in full flower is to be intoxicated with the fragrance and to be bombarded with the buzz of thousands of honeybees moving pollen. Peppers or flowers would be isolated in these "rooms" walled with corn or sorghum or Maximilian sunflowers, so that from above, the space resembled a checkerboard.

In *1992* Stephen Badger joined the agricultural team at Seeds of Change to help expand the network of family farms that produce the majority of the organic seeds sold. He brought a youthful enthusiasm that proved infectious, and Stephen later assumed the role of president of Seeds of Change. Shortly afterward, Steve Peters joined Seeds of Change as agricultural planning associate.

When the Gila research farm closed in *1994*, some of its responsibilities were consolidated at El Guique. Emigdio Ballon moved north to help run the research farming operation and seed cleaning. Rancho La Paz is where all the seeds sold by Seeds of Change are finally cleaned and inspected, using the most basic of equipment. The farming model has been built so that visitors to Rancho La Paz can replicate virtually every aspect of the operation, no matter where they come from. In this sense, Rancho La Paz is in the business of the export of appropriate technology.

Many projects have begun at Rancho La Paz and been transferred to other locations as the exact nature of this complex high desert–Rio Grande valley ecosystem is learned each year. Shade gardens, waffle gardens, kinship gardens, and every kind of garden that can be imagined are planned and executed here. Many of the Seeds of Change varieties are grown next to those of competitor seed companies, so that evaluations can be made. Extensive work on garden vegetables and flowers, perennial plantings, and cover crops such as sorghum, cowpeas, clovers, desert and prairie grasses, vetch, sanfoin, and buckwheat is constantly being evaluated. Then there is the diversity aspect of gardening, involving growing rare species to continue the viability of lines and to enable the company to consider these varieties for larger-scale production. Seeds arrive from all over the world, sent by a wide network of seedspersons helping to save invaluable genetic material.

In *1998* Seeds of Change launched a one-hundred-percent-certified organic food line which is sold throughout the United States and the European Union to complement its knowledge in organic seed production.

Examples of Research Work Conducted by Seeds of Change

At Gila, the trials and selections were legendary for their depth and diversity. The need to grow so much plant material close to other material of similar species gave rise to extensive learning about sequences of planting for varied pollination dates, for example, and patterns of bordering breeding or selecting areas with displays of flowers to entice the bees in their search for pollen. One crop trialed extensively in Gila by Seeds of Change was amaranth, and after years of trials and observation, selections were made for characteristics such as flavor, uniformity, large heads, productivity, resistance to drought and lodging, dye color of the flower heads, ability to hold seed after the frost, cleanability with simple threshing and fanning techniques, and popping ability. Amaranth became a staple food for the crew at Gila, just as Emigdio opened the company's eyes to quinoa, the extraordinary grain of the Indian peoples of the Andes.

The Gila farm was a garden of bounty. The better the farm became at sustainable organic agriculture, the more diverse the bird and beneficial insect populations became. Much research was accomplished on complex species needs when hundreds of peppers from all over the world were trialed. Another summer, two hundred varieties of tomatoes were trialed to determine whether the inventory carried by Seeds of Change was still the best. Corn was grown in every field, with emphasis on native southwestern varieties such as Hopi, Anasazi, Supai, Apache, and Mandan. Classic early heirloom North American corns and Andean corns were also trialed, and an understanding of the different water needs for each variety was painstakingly arrived at. Hundreds of varieties of melons were also trialed annually at Gila, from the huge oblong fruits to the round and the classic oval shape, and with flesh ranging from dark crimson to bright yellow, and everything in between. At harvest time neighbors would be invited to share in the completion of the cycle. Melons were eaten through the day, and peppers and corn would be roasted over an open fire, in celebration of abundance.

In recent years at the research farm in northern New Mexico, the most extensive plant trials have involved fresh and dry beans, tomatoes, eggplants, squash, peppers, onions, garlic, potatoes, celeriac, chicory, carrots, peas, corn, a wide variety of greens, perennial herbs, and literally hundreds of flower trials. Further research is focusing on cover crops and their combination for soil fertility. As always, the tradition of learning quickly about the ecosystem continues. Pertinent questions are constantly asked, such as "Does Fukuoka's system of natural farming really work here?" "How can Bill Mollison's permaculture be applied to this region?" "What lessons can be learned from Alan York's biodynamic style of orchard keeping?" "What is the application under local conditions of building soil by growing compost, as John Jeavons advocates?" "What is the best of each system, and how can it be made real in practice?" For Seeds of Change, it is not enough just to be a research facility for seed production. Various agricultural systems are tested so that real information about sustainable organic agriculture can be shared with the widest possible audience.

IF YOU WOULD LIKE TO DISCUSS THE problems and solutions raised in this book, please visit our website:

www.seedsofchange.com

The Committee for Sustainable Agriculture, sponsor of the annual Ecological Farming Conference, was established in *1982* and incorporated in *1984* as a nonprofit, tax-exempt organization. It is funded by group activities and projects, contributions, sponsorships, foundation grants, and memberships.

The Committee has the following goals and objectives:

🌿 To promote a sustainable system that is ecologically sound, economically viable, and socially just.

🌿 To facilitate, by education and promotional outreach, an increase in the number of growers using sustainable agricultural practices and consumers demanding organically grown food.

🌿 To function as a networking body for individuals, organizations, and projects focused on sustainable agriculture and to elicit concern and active participation in food production by the widest possible age range of people.

🌿 To remain a decentralized organization involving as many people as possible in the process of creating a sustainable agriculture system.

Committee for Sustainable Agriculture
406 Main Street, Suite 313, Watsonville, CA 95076
831-763-2111

Bibliography

Chapters 1-4:

Pattern and Observation; Design; Soil; Water

E. ANDERSON, *Plants, Man, and Life*, University of California Press, 1969.

M. BANG, *Chattanooga Sludge*, Harcourt Brace, 1996.

K. BARSS, *Clean Water*, Chelsea House Publishers, 1992.

G. BELL, *The Permaculture Garden*, Thorsons, 1994.

G. BELL, *The Permaculture Way*, Thorsons, 1992.

J. BENJAMIN, ed., *Great Garden Shortcuts*, Rodale Press, 1996.

W. BERRY, *The Gift of Good Land*, North Point Press, 1981.

F. M. BRADLEY and B. W. ELLIS, *Rodale's All-New Encyclopedia of Organic Gardening*, Rodale Press, 1992.

G. BRENNAN and E. BRENNAN, *The Children's Kitchen Garden*, Ten Speed Press, 1997.

L. BROWN, C. FLAVIN, and S. POSTEL, *Saving the Planet*, W. W. Norton, 1991.

S. CAMPBELL, *Let It Rot! The Gardener's Guide to Composting*, Storey Publishing, 1990.

A. CARR, *Good Neighbors: Companion Planting for Gardeners*, Rodale Press, 1985.

R. CARSON, *Silent Spring*, Houghton Mifflin, 1962.

R. CREASY, *Edible Landscaping*, Sierra Club Books, 1982.

P. DREYER, *A Gardener Touched with Genius: The Life of Luther Burbank*, University of California Press, 1985.

B. W. ELLIS and F. M. BRADLEY, eds., *The Organic Gardener's Handbook of Natural Insect and Disease Control*, Rodale Press, 1996.

D. A. FALK, C. I. MILLAR, and M. OLWELL, eds., *Restoring Diversity: Strategies for Reintroduction of Endangered Plants*, Island Press, 1996.

N. FERGUSON, *Right Plant, Right Place*, Summit Books, 1984.

G. FOWLER and P. MOONEY, *Shattering: Food, Politics, and the Loss of Genetic Diversity*, University of Arizona Press, 1990.

J. FRENCH, *Backyard Self-Sufficiency*, Aird Books, 1992.

M. FUKUOKA, *The Natural Way of Farming: The Theory and Practice of Green Philosophy*, Japan Publications, 1985.

M. FUKUOKA, *The One-Straw Revolution: An Introduction to Natural Farming*, Rodale Press, 1978.

M. FUKUOKA, *The Road Back to Nature: Regaining Paradise Lost*, Japan Publications, 1987.

G. GERSHUNY, *Start with the Soil*, Rodale Press, 1993.

J. GIONO, *The Man Who Planted Trees*, Chelsea Green, 1995.

A. GORE, *Earth in the Balance*, Houghton Mifflin, 1992.

J. GRIBBIN, *Weather Force*, Putnam, 1979.

K. GRIDLEY, ed., *Man of the Trees: Selected Writings of Richard St. Barbe Baker*, Ecology Action, 1989.

HARMONIOUS TECHNOLOGIES, *Backyard Composting*, Harmonious Press, 1992.

J. B. HARRISON, *Growing Food Organically*, Waterwheel Press, 1993.

SIR A. HOWARD, *The Soil and Health*, Schocken Books, 1947.

J. JEAVONS, *How to Grow More Vegetables (Than You Ever Thought Possible on Less Land Than You Can Imagine)*, Ten Speed Press, 1995.

J. JEAVONS and C. COX, *Lazy-Bed Gardening: The Quick and Dirty Guide*, Ten Speed Press, 1993.

C. JOYCE, *Earthly Goods: Medicine-Hunting*, Little, Brown, 1994.

D. JOYCE, *The Complete Guide to Pruning and Training Plants*, Simon and Schuster, 1992.

C. JUMMA, *The Gene Hunters*, Princeton University Press, 1989.

S. R. KELLERT, *The Value of Life: Biological Diversity and Human Society*, Island Press, 1996.

H. H. KOEPF, *What Is Bio-Dynamic Agriculture?*, Bio-Dynamic Literature, 1976.

H. H. KOEPF, B. D. PETTERSSON, and W. SCHAUMANN, *Bio-Dynamic Agriculture*, Anthroposophic Press, 1976.

E. LINACRE, *Climate Data and Resources*, Routledge, 1992.

W. B. LOGAN, *Dirt: The Ecstatic Skin of the Earth*, Riverhead Books, 1995.

L. MARGULIS and K. V. SCHWARTZ, *Five Kingdoms: An Illustrated Guide to the Phyla of Life on Earth*, W. H. Freeman and Co., 1988.

D. L. MARTIN and G. GERSHUNY, eds., *The Rodale Book of Composting*, Rodale Press, 1992.

D. M. MASUMOTO, *Epitaph for a Peach*, HarperCollins, 1995.

S. McCLURE and S. ROTH, *Rodale's Successful Organic Gardening Companion Planting*, Rodale Press, 1994.

E. McLEOD, *Feed the Soil*, self-published, 1982.

B. MOLLISON, *Permaculture: A Designer's Manual*, Tagari Publications, 1988.

B. MOLLISON, *Permaculture: A Practical Guide for a Sustainable Future*, Island Press, 1990.

B. MOLLISON with R. M. SLAY, *Introduction to Permaculture*, Tagari Publications, 1991.

R. MORROW, *Earth User's Guide to Permaculture*, Kangaroo Press, 1994.

G. NABHAN, *The Desert Smells Like Rain*, North Point Press, 1982.

G. NABHAN, *Enduring Seeds: Native American Agriculture and Wild Plant Conservation*, North Point Press, 1989.

D. H. PATENT, *The Vanishing Feast: How Dwindling Genetic Diversity Threatens the World's Food Supply*, Gulliver Green/ Harcourt Brace, 1994.

E. E. PFEIFFER, *Biodynamics: Three Introductory Articles*, Bio-Dynamic Farming and Gardening Association, 1956.

H. L. PHILBRICK and R. GREGG, *Companion Plants*, Devin-Adair, 1966.

J. PHILLIPS, *Plants for Natural Gardens*, Museum of New Mexico Press, 1995.

M. POLLAN, *Second Nature: A Gardener's Education*, Dell, 1991.

P. RAEBURN, *The Last Harvest: The Genetic Gamble That Threatens to Destroy American Agriculture*, Bison Books, 1995.

W. V. REID and K. R. MILLER, *Keeping Options Alive: The Scientific Basis for Conserving Biodiversity*, World Resources Institute, 1989.

L. RIOTTE, *Successful Small Food Gardens*, Garden Way Publishing, 1993.

H. J. ROBERTS, ed., *Intensive Food Production on a Human Scale*, Ecology Action, 1982.

V. SHIVA, *Monocultures of the Mind: Perspectives on Biodiversity and Biotechnology*, Zed Books, 1995.

V. SHIVA, *Staying Alive: Women, Ecology and Development*, Zed Books, 1989.

W. J. SNAPE III, ed., *Biodiversity and the Law*, Island Press, 1996.

J. SOPER, *Bio-Dynamic Gardening*, Bio-Dynamic Agricultural Association, 1983.

S. STEIN, *Noah's Garden: Restoring the Ecology of Our Own Back Yards*, Houghton Mifflin, 1993.

R. STEINER, *Spiritual Beings in the Heavenly Bodies and in the Kingdoms of Nature: A Lecture Cycle*, Anthroposophic Press, 1992.

R. STEINER, *Spiritual Foundations for the Renewal of Agriculture: A Course of Lectures*, Bio-Dynamic Farming and Gardening Association, 1993.

P. S. STEVENS, *Patterns in Nature*, Penguin, 1974.

W. D. STORL, *Culture and Horticulture: A Philosophy of Gardening*, Bio-Dynamic Literature, 1979.

R. STOUT and R. CLEMENCE, *The Ruth Stout No-Work Garden Book*, Rodale Press, 1971.

R. B. SWAIN, *Groundwork: A Gardener's Ecology*, Houghton Mifflin, 1994.

H. D. THOREAU, *Faith in a Seed*, Island Press, 1993.

S. VOGEL, *Life in Moving Fluids: The Physical Biology of Flow*, Willard Grant Press, 1981.

E. O. WILSON, *The Diversity of Life*, Harvard University Press, 1992.

E. O. WILSON, *In Search of Nature*, Island Press, 1996.

E. O. WILSON, ed., *Biodiversity*, National Academy Press, 1988.

P. A. YEOMANS, *Water for Every Farm*, Second Back Row Press, 1981.

Chapter 5:

Kinship Gardening

E. S. AYENSU and R. A. DeFILIPPS, eds., *Endangered and Threatened Plants of the United States*, Smithsonian Institution, 1978.

L. H. BAILEY, E. Z. BAILEY, et al., *Hortus Third: A Concise Dictionary of Plants Cultivated in the United States and Canada*, Macmillan, 1976.

B. J. BARTON, *Gardening by Mail: A Source Book*, Houghton Mifflin, 1997.

O. BRENTMAR and A. KAPULER, *A Coevolutionary Structure for the Plant Kindom*, Peace Seeds/Seeds of Change *(see the resource list on page 221)*, 1988.

A. CHILD, *Fruits in the Solanaceae*, Solanaceae 2:7.

D. S. CORRELL, *The Potato and Its Wild Relatives*, Texas Research Foundation, 1962.

COUNCIL OF EUROPE, *List of Rare, Threatened, and Endemic Plants in Europe*, Nature and Environment Series no. 27, 1983.

A. CRONQUIST, *An Integrated System of Classification of Flowering Plants*, Columbia University, 1981.

R. DAHLGREN and H. T. CLIFFORD, *The Monocotyledons: A Comparative Study*, Academic Press, 1982.

R. DAHLGREN, H. T. CLIFFORD, and P. F. YEO, *The Families of the Monocotyledons*, Springer Verlag, 1985.

J. DUKE, *Handbook of Medicinal Herbs*, CRC Press, 1985.

P. EHRLICH and A. EHRLICH, *Extinction*, Random House, 1981.

S. FOSTER and J. DUKE, *A Field Guide to Medicinal Plants*, Houghton Mifflin, 1990.

J. G. HAWKES, R. N. LESTER, and A. D. SKELDING, eds., *The Biology and Taxonomy of the Solanaceae*, Academic Press, 1979.

U. P. HENDRICK, ed., Sturdevant's *Edible Plants of the World*, Dover Press, 1972.

V. H. HEYWOOD, ed., *The Biology and Chemistry of the Umbelliferae*, Academic Press, 1971.

V. H. HEYWOOD, ed., *Flowering Plants of the World*, Mayflower Books, 1978.

V. H. HEYWOOD and J. B. HARBOURNE, eds., *The Biology and Chemistry of the Compositae*, 2 vols., Academic Press, 1977.

M. HICKEY, *100 Families of Flowering Plants*, Cambridge University Press, 1981.

M. HIROE, *Umbelliferae of the World*, Kyoto University Press, 1979.

A. KAPULER, *Kinship Gardening: A Strategic Layout for Preserving the Plant Kindom*, Seeds of Change *(see the resource list on page 221)*, 1992.

A. KAPULER, *Peace Seeds Research Journals*, vols. 1–7, Seeds of Change *(see the resource list on page 221)*.

A. KAPULER and O. BRENTMAR, *A Gene-Pool Resource Coevolutionary Garden of the Flowering Plants for the Temperate Zone*, Peace Seeds/Seeds of Change *(see the resource list on page 221)*, 1988.

A. KAPULER and C. CROWDER, *The Extinction of Genera*, Seeds of Change *(see the resource list on page 221)*, 1994.

R. M. KING and H. ROBINSON, *The Genera of Eupatorieae (Asteraceae)*, Missouri Botanical Garden, 1987.

H. KOOPOWITZ and H. KAYE, *Plant Extinction: A Global Crisis*, W. H. Freeman and Co., 1983.

D. J. MABBERLY, *The Plant Book*, Cambridge University Press, 1989.

L. MARGULIS and K. V. SCHWARTZ, *Five Kingdoms: An Illustrated Guide to the Phyla of Life on Earth*, W. H. Freeman and Co., 1982.

C. F. MILLSPAUGH, *American Medicinal Herbs*, 1892. Reprint ed. Dover Press, 1974.

L. A. PETERSON, *A Field Guide to Edible Wild Plants*, Houghton Mifflin, 1977.

L. A. PETERSON, T. ROGER, and M. McKINNEY, *A Field Guide to Wildflowers*, Houghton Mifflin, 1968.

G. A. PETRIDES, *A Field Guide to Trees and Shrubs*, Houghton Mifflin, 1972.

J. SILBA, *Encyclopedia Coniferae*, Phytologia Memoirs VIII, Corvallis, OR, 1986.

Source List of Plants and Seeds, Andersen Horticultural Library (available from Minnesota Landscape Arboretum, 3675 Arboretum Drive, Chanhassen, MN 55317).

T. F. STUESSY, *Plant Taxonomy*, Columbia University Press, 1990.

P. M. SYNGE, *The Complete Guide to Bulbs*, Dutton, 1962.

A. TAKHTAJAN, *Floristic Regions of the World*, University of California Press, 1986.

A. TAKHTAJAN, ed., *Rare and Vanishing Plants of the USSR to Be Protected*, Nauka, 1981.

D. M. VAN GILDEREN and J. R. P. VAN HOEY SMITH, *Conifers*, Timber Press, 1986.

M. M. VILMORIN-ANDRIEUX, *The Vegetable Garden*, 1885.

| **Chapters 6 and 7:** | **Chapter 8:** |

Seed Saving and Selection; Plant Breeding

S. ASHWORTH, *Seed to Seed*, Seed Savers Exchange *(see the resource list on page 221)*, 1991.

N. BUBEL, *The New Seed Starter's Handbook*, Rodale Press, 1988.

C. DEPPE, *Breed Your Own Vegetable Varieties*, Little, Brown, 1993.

P. DONELAN, *Growing to Seed*, Ecology Action *(see the resource list on page 221)*, 1986.

M. FANTON and J. FANTON, *The Seed Savers' Handbook* (for Australia and New Zealand), Seed Savers Network (Australia), 1993.

S. McCLURE, ed., *Preserving Summer's Bounty*, Rodale Press, 1995.

M. SMITH, *Backyard Fruits and Berries*, Rodale Press, 1994.

Chapter 8:

Polyculture

M. FUKUOKA, *The Natural Way of Farming: The Theory and Practice of Green Philosophy*, Japan Publications, 1985.

M. FUKUOKA, *The One-Straw Revolution: An Introduction to Natural Farming*, Rodale Press, 1978.

M. FUKUOKA, *The Road Back to Nature: Regaining Paradise Lost*, Japan Publications, 1987.

W. JACKSON, *Altars of Unhewn Stone: Science and the Earth*, North Point Press, 1987.

W. JACKSON, *New Roots for Agriculture*, University of Nebraska Press, 1980.

W. JACKSON, W. BERRY, and B. COLMAN, eds., *Meeting the Expectations of the Land: Essays in Sustainable Agriculture and Stewardship*, North Point Press, 1984.

Resources

Seed Companies

SEEDS OF CHANGE
100% Certified Organic
PO Box 15700
Santa Fe, NM 87506-5700
TEL: (888) 762-7333
(toll free)
FAX: (888) 329-4762
(toll free)
WEBSITE:
www.seedsofchange.com
EMAIL:
gardener@seedsofchange.com

**ABUNDANT LIFE SEED
FOUNDATION**
930 Lawrence Street
Port Townsend, WA 98368
TEL: (360) 385-5660
FAX: (360) 385-7455

BOUNTIFUL GARDENS
18001 Shafer Ranch Road,
Willits, CA 95490-9626
TEL: (707) 459-6410

DEEP DIVERSITY
A Planetary Gene Pool
PO Box 15700
Santa Fe, NM 87506-5700
(Contact by mail only)

ELIXIR FARM BOTANICALS
Medicinal Plant Seeds
Brixey, MO 65618
TEL: (417) 261-2393

GARDEN CITY SEEDS
778 Highway 93N
Hamilton, MT 59840-9448
TEL: (406) 961-4837
FAX: (406) 961-4877

J. L. HUDSON, SEEDSMAN
Star Route 2, Box 337
La Honda, CA 94929
(Contact by mail only)

NATIVE SEEDS/SEARCH
526 North 4th Avenue
Tucson, AZ 85705
TEL: (520) 622-5561
FAX: (520) 622-5591

PRAIRIE MOON NURSERY
Route 3, Box 163
Winona, MN 55987-9515
TEL: (507) 452-1362
FAX: (507) 454-5238

SEED SAVERS EXCHANGE
3094 North Winn Road
Decorah, IA 52101-7776
TEL: (319) 382-5990

SYNERGY SEEDS
PO Box 787
Somes Bar, CA 95568
TEL: (916) 321-3769

Rare Fruit Trees

**EXOTICA RARE FRUIT
NURSERY**
2508 East Vista Way #B
Vista, CA 92084
TEL: (760) 724-9093

**SONOMA ANTIQUE APPLE
NURSERY**
4395 Westside Road
Healdsburg, CA 95448
TEL: (707) 433-6420

**SOUTHMEADOW FRUIT
FARMS**
Box SM
Lakeside, MI 49116
TEL: (616) 469-2865

Interesting Trees and Plants

FOREST FARMS
990 Tetherow Road
Williams, OR 97544-9599
TEL: (541) 846-7269
FAX: (541) 846-6963

GLASSHOUSE WORKS
8950 State Road 144
Stewart, OH 45778-0097
TEL: (740) 662-2142

LOGEE'S GREENHOUSES
141 North Street
Danielson, CT 06239
TEL: (860) 774-8038
FAX: (860) 774-9932

MESA GARDEN
PO Box 72
Belen, NM 87002
TEL: (505) 864-3131
FAX: (505) 864-3124

NORTHERN GROVES
BAMBOO
PO Box 86291
Portland, OR 97286-0291
TEL: (503) 774-6353

OREGON EXOTICS
1065 Messinger Road
Grants Pass, OR 97527
TEL: (541) 846-7578
FAX: (541) 846-9488
WEBSITE:
www.exoticfruit.com

PLANTS OF THE
SOUTHWEST
Agua Frío, Rt. 6, Box 11A
Santa Fe, NM 87501
TEL: (505) 438-8888

RARE CONIFER NURSERY
PO Box 100
Potter Valley, CA 95469
FAX: (707) 462-9536
(Contact by mail or fax only)

Organizations

THE BIODYNAMIC FARMING
AND GARDENING
ASSOCIATION, INC.
Building 1002B
Thoreau Center
The Presidio
PO Box 29135
San Francisco, CA
94129-0135
TEL: (415) 561-7797
FAX: (415) 561-7796
WEBSITE:
www.biodynamics.com
EMAIL:
biodynamics@aol.com

ECOLOGY ACTION
SUSTAINABLE BIOINTENSIVE
MINIFARMING
5798 Ridgewood Road
Willits, CA 95490
TEL: (707) 459-0150
FAX: (707) 459-5409

HENRY DOUBLEDAY
RESEARCH ASSOCIATION
FOR ORGANIC EXCELLENCE
Ryton Organic Gardens
Coventry CV8 3LG UK
TEL: (0120)330-3517
FAX: (0120)363-9229
WEBSITE:
www.hdra.org.uk

THE JOSEPHINE PORTER
INSTITUTE FOR APPLIED
BIODYNAMICS, INC.
Route 1 Box 620
Woolwine, VA 24185
TEL: (540) 930-2463

LAND INSTITUTE
2440 Water Well Road
Salina, KS 67401
TEL: (785) 823-5376
FAX: (785) 823-8728

THE PERMACULTURE
INSTITUTE
PO Box 3702
Pojuaque, NM 87501
(Contact by mail only)

THE SOIL ASSOCIATION
Bristol House
40-56 Victoria Street
Bristol BS1 6BY UK
TEL: (0117) 929-0661
FAX: (0117) 925-2504
EMAIL:
info@soilassociation.org

Other
There are a large number of
societies dedicated to almost
every type of popular plant
or tree. For information and
further sources, contact your
local botanical garden or
agricultural extension agent.
Alternatively, check the
Internet.

The assistance of the following individuals was invaluable for the completion of this book: Ryan Stellabotte, Robin Michaelson, Glen Edelstein, Sol Skolnik, and Toni Burbank, our extraordinary editor, friend, and protagonist, who patiently believed in us and encouraged us to write with grace and intelligence. Thanks to Susan Caldwell for making the book beautiful. Jim Bones and Scott Vlaun for their inspiring photography. Jacqueline Badger Mars and David Badger for their devotion and support of Seeds of Change during our darkest hour. To Russell Hochman, whose great wisdom, and unflappable patience brought Seeds of Change through a most turbulent time, a thousand thanks. To Eddie Stephens, whose enthusiasm and vision helped propel Seeds of Change into an international forum, thank you. John Harrisson, my collaborator, many, many thanks. To my associates at Seeds of Change, who provided invaluable help and support throughout this entire project, thank you. Special thanks to Lester Ketchie, our master seed cleaner. To my beloved colleague Stephen Badger, who never wavered from the belief that this work deserved the effort necessary to do it right, thank you from the bottom of my heart. Finally, to those individuals who are the inspiration for the book, you have moved me intellectually and spiritually.

Howard-Yana Shapiro
Summer Solstice 1999
Rancho La Paz, El Guique, New Mexico

Thanks to Trez Harrisson for her input and counsel during the writing process; Howard and the folks at Seeds of Change; and the dedicated and colorful characters featured in this book, whom it was a pleasure to meet and whose ideas and practices are truly inspiring.

John Harrisson
Kula, Hawaii

MICHAEL ABELMAN:

Insert 2—page 7, bottom right

JIM BONES:

Insert 1—page 2, bottom left; page 3, top right; page 4, top right; page 5, bottom left; page 6, top left; page 7, bottom right; page 8, bottom

Insert 2—page 1 (3); page 2, top left and top right; page 3, top and right; page 6, bottom; page 7, bottom left; page 8, bottom and top right

Insert 3—page 3, top; page 4

Insert 4—page 1 (2); page 6, bottom left; page 8 (4)

ELIXIR FARM:

Insert 1—page 6, top right

Insert 2—page 3, bottom

KUSRA KAPULER:

Insert 1—page 3, top left

THE LAND INSTITUTE:

Insert 2—page 4, top and bottom left

Insert 4—page 4, top left; page 5

HOWARD-YANA SHAPIRO

Insert 1—page 1, bottom left and bottom right; page 2, top; page 3, bottom; page 4, top left; page 5, bottom right; page 6, bottom; page 7, top and bottom left; page 8, top left and top right

Insert 2—page 2, bottom; page 4, bottom right; page 5, top; page 6, top; page 7, top left

Insert 3—page 1 (2); page 2 (4); page 3, bottom; page 5 (4); page 6, top; page 7, bottom; page 8, bottom left;

Insert 4—page 2, bottom ; page 3, top; page 4, top right, bottom left, and bottom right; page 6, top and bottom right; page 7 (4)

CAROLYN ULRICH:

Insert 4—page 2, top

SCOTT VLAUN:

Insert 1—page 1, top; page 2, bottom right; page 5, top

Insert 2—page 5, bottom; page 7, top right

Insert 3—page 6, bottom; page 7, top; page 8, top left and bottom right

Insert 4—page 3, bottom; page 4, middle

ALAN YORK:

Insert 1—page 4, bottom

Insert 2—page 3, middle